STEPHEN A. SM[ITH]

16 ANTON ST.

BUCKIE,

The Hamlyn Junior
ENCYCLOPEDIA
of Nature

The Hamlyn Junior
ENCYCLOPEDIA
of Nature

Leonard Moore

Hamlyn
London·New York·Sydney·Toronto

Acknowledgements
Page 6–7 W. F. Davidson
Page 56–57 Barnabys Picture Library
Page 150–151 Popperfoto

First published 1974
Fourth impression 1978
Published by
THE HAMLYN PUBLISHING GROUP LIMITED
London · New York · Sydney · Toronto
Astronaut House, Hounslow Road, Feltham,
Middlesex, England
ISBN 0 600 39510 3
Printed in Czechoslovakia
51132/2

Contents

Air

The Weather

What are clouds?

Have you ever looked at the clouds in the sky and wondered what they are?

Clouds are either formed by enormous numbers of minute droplets of water, or tiny particles of ice. In order to understand this, breathe on a window pane or a mirror. The glass becomes misty for a little while. If it is winter, the mistiness will last for a long time. There is some water in your breath. You cannot see it because it is in a form called *water vapour* which is invisible. When your breath reaches the glass, it is cooled and the water vapour turns into tiny drops of water that cling to the glass. Although you cannot see each drop, together they form the misty patch. If the glass is very cold, as it is in winter, the water will remain as droplets for a long time. They might even turn into ice. In summer, when the glass is only a little cooler than your breath, the mistiness soon disappears because the water turns back into water vapour.

Water vapour turning into droplets in the air is the way clouds are made. In fact, you can make your own small clouds on a cold day by breathing out into the cold air. You can see your breath because the cold air, instead of the glass, has turned the water vapour into drops that are floating in the air. Clouds are millions of floating drops of water.

How clouds are formed in the sky

Clouds are always changing their shape. They may seem to stay still or appear to move across the sky, making different patterns almost every minute. Within an hour, the shapes of all the clouds in the sky may have changed completely. You know that they are made of millions of tiny water droplets, but how are they formed so high up?

Picture the white, fluffy clouds that are so common on a summer day. The air around us has water vapour in it. This has come from the water of the sea, lakes, rivers and ponds, and also from animals and plants which lose water vapour when they breathe. Now the air can hold only a certain amount of water vapour and this depends on how warm or cold the air is. Warm air can hold much more water vapour than cold air.

Above There are small heap clouds around the mountain. There are layer clouds to the right and people beneath them would think the day very overcast. In other places rain is falling and might continue for some time.

Below As this boy breathes against the cold window pane, the water vapour in his breath cools and becomes tiny droplets of water on the glass. These make a misty patch which will disappear quite quickly. Why?

When the sun rises in the morning, its heat begins to warm up the land fairly quickly, which, in turn, begins to warm the air near it. Warm air is lighter than cold air so the warm air begins to rise. More cold air moves in to take its place but this is warmed in turn so that it, too, rises. Gradually a tower of warm air, with plenty of water vapour in it, moves several kilometres upwards into the sky. This tower of warm air is called a *thermal*. But the air of the thermal cannot continue to keep warm and as it goes higher, the temperature falls. Soon the thermal has cooled so much that the

air cannot hold all the water vapour in it and the vapour turns into enormous numbers of tiny water droplets, just as when you breathed on the cold glass. From the ground those water droplets look like a white, fluffy mass, often with a clear, sharp edge. The cloud stays up in the sky because the droplets are so small and light that they are held up by the rising column of air. The cloud, in fact, is sitting on top of the thermal.

Clouds do not often stay still because strong winds generally blow at these heights. So the clouds move and change shape.

Right As the earth warms in the heat of the sun, the air above it also warms and rises. The arrows show this up-current of air. Clouds formed higher up rest on these up-currents.

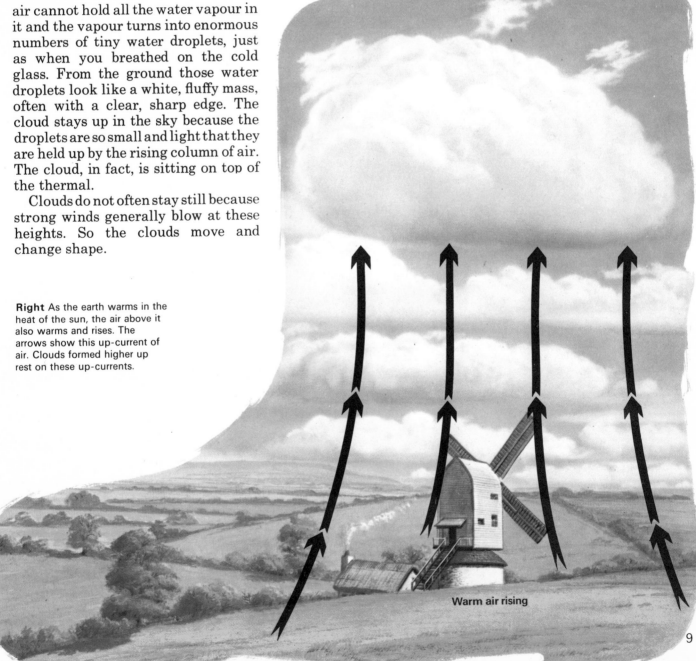

Warm air rising

Cirrus

Cirrostratus

Cirrocumulus

Altocumulus

Altocumulus Castellanus

Altostratus

Types of clouds

If you watch the sky day after day, you will begin to notice that although the cloud shapes are always changing, they seem to fall into distinct types which are easy to recognise. There are clouds that build up into heaps. These clouds are lumpy and sometimes as much as five or six kilometres thick. They are often seen when the weather quickly changes from sunshine to showers, and even better when a thunderstorm is near. These very heavy black storm clouds seem to be so low that they nearly touch the ground, and yet tower up like huge mountains into the sky. Not all heap clouds are so large, and quite often in summer they are just white puffs.

Sometimes in winter, the sky looks grey and it drizzles for hours. On days like this, you will see that instead of being in heaps, the clouds make a layer that covers most of the sky. Layer clouds are not as thick as heap clouds, although this might not be apparent. Now and again, part of the sky will be covered by a layer of very small heap clouds and this is called a 'mackerel sky'.

Apart from heap and layer clouds, there is another type that you can look for. Very high up, wispy clouds may be formed. They are made of ice crystals and are given the pretty name of 'mares' tails' which gives a good idea of their shape.

When you have looked at the clouds and decided whether they are heap, layer or wispy clouds, you should write down what you see every day. If you also write down what the weather is like, you will begin to notice that some kinds of clouds are always seen on rainy days, while others seem to form on warm, sunny days. You may find, after a time, that you are able to forecast what the day's weather will be like by looking at the clouds. Your notebook will help you to do this.

Stratocumulus

Cumulonimbus

Cumulus

Nimbostratus

Stratus

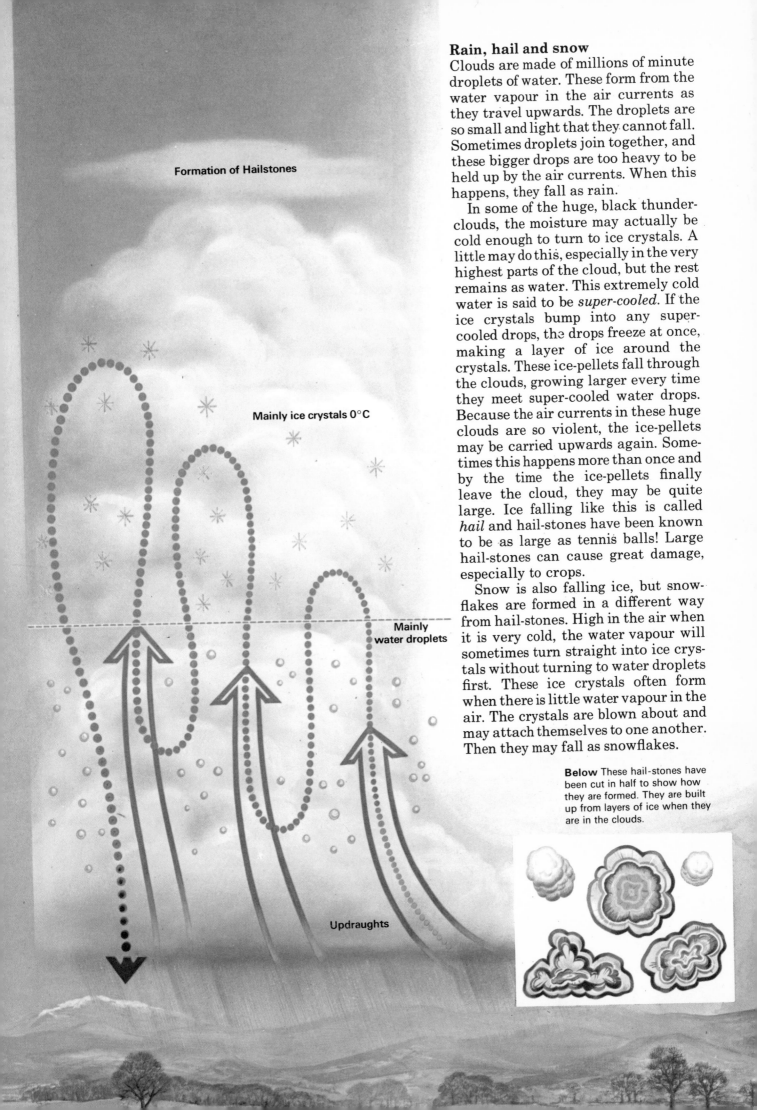

Formation of Hailstones

Mainly ice crystals 0°C

Mainly
water droplets

Updraughts

Rain, hail and snow

Clouds are made of millions of minute droplets of water. These form from the water vapour in the air currents as they travel upwards. The droplets are so small and light that they cannot fall. Sometimes droplets join together, and these bigger drops are too heavy to be held up by the air currents. When this happens, they fall as rain.

In some of the huge, black thunderclouds, the moisture may actually be cold enough to turn to ice crystals. A little may do this, especially in the very highest parts of the cloud, but the rest remains as water. This extremely cold water is said to be *super-cooled*. If the ice crystals bump into any super-cooled drops, the drops freeze at once, making a layer of ice around the crystals. These ice-pellets fall through the clouds, growing larger every time they meet super-cooled water drops. Because the air currents in these huge clouds are so violent, the ice-pellets may be carried upwards again. Sometimes this happens more than once and by the time the ice-pellets finally leave the cloud, they may be quite large. Ice falling like this is called *hail* and hail-stones have been known to be as large as tennis balls! Large hail-stones can cause great damage, especially to crops.

Snow is also falling ice, but snowflakes are formed in a different way from hail-stones. High in the air when it is very cold, the water vapour will sometimes turn straight into ice crystals without turning to water droplets first. These ice crystals often form when there is little water vapour in the air. The crystals are blown about and may attach themselves to one another. Then they may fall as snowflakes.

Below These hail-stones have been cut in half to show how they are formed. They are built up from layers of ice when they are in the clouds.

Young river

Mature river

What happens to the rain

Rain, hail and snow are the means by which water is returned to the earth. If this did not happen then life would not be possible. What becomes of the rain when it has fallen? Some of it falls into the sea and simply becomes a part of it again. In this way it helps to replace the water that is always being taken up into the air as water vapour.

Rain which falls on to the soil of flat areas will sink into it. It will fill the small spaces between the grains of soil to a depth of several metres and this is the water that plants use. Their roots and the tiny hairs on them take up this water and pass it to the stem of the plant. It moves upwards to the leaves where it is used by the plant in its food-making process. The water in the stem and leaves helps to make them stiff, too. You have only to look at a buttercup which has been picked and left for a little while to see how limp it becomes when it can get no water. This underground water makes an enormous water store that never completely dries up. As water is used by plants, or moves into the air as water vapour (both from the surface of the soil and from the leaves of plants), it is replaced by more rain.

Above The arrows show that water is taken from the soil into a plant through its roots.

Rain falls on hills and mountains as well as on flat ground. When this happens, the water will begin to run downhill in little rivulets. These join up and make a small, fast-running stream. Others will join it on its way down until a river is formed. At first, when the ground slopes steeply, the river will flow very quickly and will wear a deep channel for itself. Later, as the ground becomes less steep, the river will make its channel wider but not so deep. It will run a little more slowly, too. When it reaches low ground, it will run very much more slowly and its channel will become full of twists and turns. In the end, the river will reach the sea and pour into it.

Sometimes rivers run over rocks made of limestone. There rivers may plunge down deep holes in the rock and flow under the ground instead of on top. As it flows towards the sea, the water very slowly dissolves the limestone and makes tunnels and caves under the surface.

Above This beautiful cave has pointed *stalactites* hanging from the roof. *Stalagmites* are similar but stand up from the cave floor.

Water condenses into rain

Rain

Water evaporates

Above Water vapour from lakes and sea rises until it reaches colder air. Then it becomes water droplets and forms clouds. Later it falls back to earth again as rain.

Below White light is split up by the prism into the seven colours of the rainbow. Rainbows can be seen near waterfalls because the water droplets of the spray act as prisms.

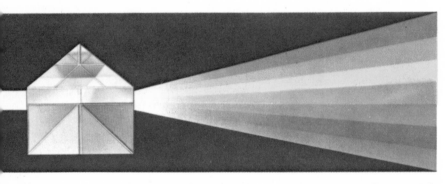

Rainbows

A rainbow is one of the loveliest sights in the sky and is seen when the sun is shining during a shower of rain, or soon after one. Sunlight, like all white light, is really made up of a number of colours mixed together. If it is made to shine through a piece of specially shaped glass called a *prism*, the white light is split up into its colours. There are seven of these colours: red, orange, yellow, green, blue, indigo and violet. You may have noticed these colours around the sloping edge of a mirror, or if the sunlight has been shining through a cut-glass bowl. This is because the mirror edge and the cut-glass have acted as prisms.

Raindrops can sometimes act as prisms, too. When the sun shines through them and the light is split up into the seven colours, we see a rainbow. In a good one, it is possible to see all seven colours, each one blending into the next. Now and again a second rainbow will appear above the first. This second one is much fainter and the colours are reversed. Rainbows are not always the same width and, of course, quite often you can only see part of them. Very few people know that moon rainbows are possible, made by moonlight shining through raindrops. They are always very faint indeed and you will be lucky if you ever see one, but it is worth looking for them.

Snowflakes

Snowflakes are crystals of ice. If you take a magnifying glass out with you when snow has fallen, you might be able to find some flakes which have not been damaged. These have beautiful shapes, usually like flat plates with six sides, or stars with six points.

Years ago, an American boy named Wilson Bentley began to study the shape of snowflakes. Each winter he sat in a shed without any heating in it. As the flakes fell, he caught some and looked at them through his lens. Any perfect ones he photographed. The work was difficult. Only a little warmth, even from his breath, was enough to melt the crystals of snow, but he persevered and his collection of photographs grew. The years went by and the boy became Professor Wilson A. Bentley who probably knew more than anyone about snowflakes and how to photograph them. As he studied, he found that no two crystals are alike and his most famous book has five thousand different snowflake photographs in it. When winter comes, you might enjoy looking at snowflakes and making some drawings of them. It would be difficult to equal Wilson Bentley's photographs, but it would be worthwhile to make a few sketches.

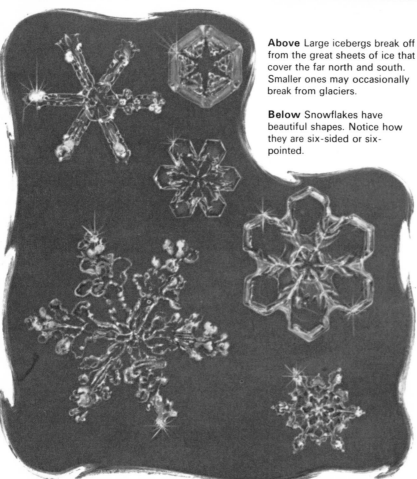

Above Large icebergs break off from the great sheets of ice that cover the far north and south. Smaller ones may occasionally break from glaciers.

Below Snowflakes have beautiful shapes. Notice how they are six-sided or six-pointed.

Glaciers

When snow has fallen, it may melt fairly soon. On the other hand, it may stay for several weeks, even months in some countries, before it disappears. If it falls on high mountains, it may collect in large hollows shaped rather like basins at the top of valleys and never completely melt. Then as more and more snow falls, year after year, the snowflakes left each year get packed closely together. They freeze to one another and turn into solid ice. When the hollow is full of ice, it will begin to fall over the edge and very, very slowly, a river of ice will begin to move down the mountainside into the valley. It may only move a metre or so in a day, but it will travel down to lower ground where it is warmer and the ice will begin to melt. These rivers of ice are called *glaciers* and can be seen in countries that have high mountains and cold winters, such as Switzerland and Alaska. If a glacier reaches the sea before it melts, pieces will break from it and float away. The floating pieces are *icebergs*. Some icebergs are very large indeed.

What is wind?

Watch the washing blowing on the line. It is being blown by the wind. Watch the leaves gently moving on the trees. It is the wind that moves them. Watch the dust being swirled up and hats being whisked off. It is the wind again. We can see what the wind does, but what is wind and why does it sometimes blow as a gentle breeze and at other times as a roaring gale?

Wind is simply air that is moving. Although we cannot see air, it is pressing down upon us all the time. One day it may be pressing down more than another. We do not feel it, but it can be measured by a *barometer*. The amount of air pressing down is called *air pressure*. When air is pressing down heavily, air pressure is high. When it is not pressing down so much, then the pressure is low. Very often it

Below A hurricane is a wind of enormous strength. The damage caused by a hurricane is always serious. Along the coast, waves would be hurled against the sea front, boats would be smashed and even houses destroyed.

is low on a cold, rainy day. But air pressure is never the same over the whole of the earth. In some parts it will be high and in others, low. The air will move from areas of high pressure to areas of low. This is the moving air we think of as wind.

If air pressure is high in one place and much lower in another not very far away, the air will rush quickly and the wind will be strong. If there is little difference between the pressures, the wind will be gentle. Air pressure changes every day and this is why the strength of the wind also changes.

If you want to keep a diary of the weather, the easiest way to record the strength of the wind is to use the *Beaufort Scale*. This was compiled by a sailor, Admiral Beaufort, in the early 1800s. To use it, all you have to do is look at what the wind is doing. Being a sailor, Admiral Beaufort watched what it did to the water, but you can use it on land. He gave each strength of wind a number. If there was no wind at all, he called this 0 and to the strongest wind likely he gave the number 12. Other strengths of wind had numbers in between. This is the Beaufort Scale:

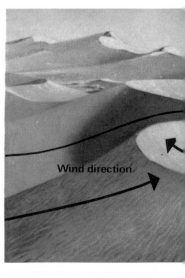

Wind direction

These pictures show the signs to look out for when trying to judge the strength of the wind according to the Beaufort Scale. There is no illustration for strength 0, but this is easy to decide since the air does not move at all.

Number	Signs to look for
0	Smoke goes straight up.
1	Smoke blown about a little.
2	Leaves rustle in the trees.
3	Leaves and small twigs move all the time.
4	Dust and loose paper blown about. Small branches move.
5	Small leafy trees sway.
6	Large branches move. Whistling in telegraph wires.
7	Whole trees move.
8	Twigs broken from trees.
9	Chimney pots and tiles blown off roofs.
10	Trees blown down.
11	Very rare. Vast damage.

Wind 12 is a *hurricane*. In Britain, winds as strong as this hardly ever occur, but in some parts of the world, such as Jamaica and Florida, they are quite common. Hurricanes cause a great deal of damage. The wind is strong enough to blow cars about and even to blow down wooden houses. As it blows from the sea to the land it causes enormous waves to sweep over the coast and these tidal waves cause even more damage.

Winds from strengths 0 to 8 are so common that you will have plenty of chances of using the Beaufort Scale. Winds of force 9 or 10 do not blow so often, but they do happen a few times a year.

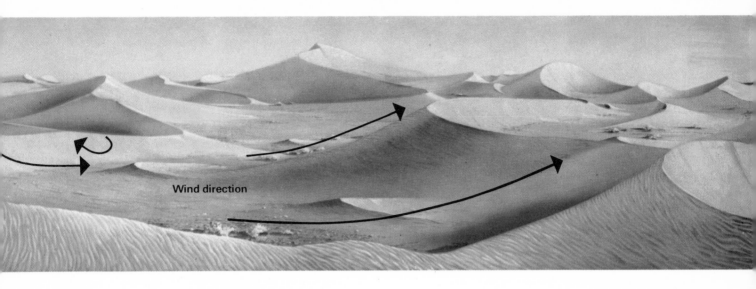

Wind direction

Above Sand dunes are found in hot deserts. The arrows show how the wind blows up the gentle slope carrying sand. Then it swirls about and drops the sand, making a steeper slope on the other side.

Above The wind-vane points into the wind and shows the direction *from* which it blows. The three cups spin round and measure the wind speed which will show on a dial lower down the pole.

Right These rocks have been carved into strange shapes by sand being blown against them by the wind for a very long time. Layers of softer rock are worn away faster than layers of hard rock, and this accounts for the deep grooves in the cliffs.

Winds and deserts

In deserts, the wind may help to alter the shape of the land by blowing the sand into heaps called *dunes*. Deserts are not the only places where dunes can be seen, of course. You may have seen them at the seaside where there is a wide, sandy beach. In the Sahara Desert, in Africa, the dunes are huge; far, far larger than anything you could find in this country. They are often shaped like a half moon and the sand is packed very loosely. Trying to walk up the side of one is very difficult because the sand moves under your feet. One step upwards is usually followed by sliding down again.

Because the sand is so loose, the wind can blow it about easily and the whole position of a dune may slowly shift. For people travelling in the desert, the sand which is always being carried in the wind is very uncomfortable. It grazes their skin and this can be very painful.

If there are any rocks in a part of the desert, these may get worn down by being constantly hit by flying sand. Sometimes they are worn into strange and interesting shapes.

Birds

What is a bird?

There are eight thousand six hundred kinds of birds, varying in size from the tiny humming birds to the largest of all living birds, the ostrich. They are different colours and they live in many different places. They eat different kinds of food and they make different noises. But in spite of all this, birds are a group of animals that are similar in many ways. For example, they all have feathers. They have warm bodies and the feathers help to stop this warmth from being lost. Only birds have feathers so that if you wanted to decide if some unknown creature was a bird or not, you would only need to see if it had feathers.

As well as having warm bodies and feathers, all birds have wings. Most birds use these for flying but there are birds that cannot fly, such as penguins and ostriches, and they may use their wings in other ways. Penguins use their wings for swimming and ostriches use them when they run and sometimes for showing off.

Like any other animal, a bird must eat and every bird has a beak to pick up its food. Because there are many different kinds of food which birds can eat, the shape of the beak varies. In fact, as you will read later on, it is possible to get a very good idea of a bird's food by looking at the shape of its beak.

All birds lay eggs and the baby bird develops and grows inside the egg until it finally grows too big and breaks it open. After it has hatched, the young bird is still rather helpless and has to be looked after by its parents until it is strong enough to look after itself. There are some birds, such as the cuckoo, which do not look after their own young but lay their eggs in other birds' nests. When the eggs hatch, the other birds then look after their 'foster children' as if they were their own.

The long neck of the swan, the odd-shaped beak of the spoonbill and the wonderful display feathers of the peacock— all have a purpose and are important in the bird's life. Notice how the special features of a bird are always there for a purpose.

18

A little about feathers

There are several kinds of feathers that cover a bird's body. Some help the bird to fly, others help to give it shape. Others, called down feathers, help to keep the bird warm.

Try to find a fairly big feather and then look at it. The long, thin, stiff part is called the *shaft* and on either side of the shaft are the flat parts, the *vanes*. These vanes are made up of thousands of separate pieces called *barbs*. The lower part of the shaft has no barbs on it and is often called the *quill*. Years ago, this was the part of a feather that was sharpened and dipped in ink so that it could be used for writing. Quill pens, as they were known, were used for centuries.

A single barb looks quite simple, but under a microscope it is possible to see that there are hundreds of smaller pieces sticking out on either side of it. These are *barbules*. All the barbules have very tiny hooks on them. They are so small that a large wing feather will have millions of these hooks. Their job is to catch on to each other in such a way that the barbs are all fastened together. It is such a useful sort of fastening that if by chance the vane should split because some barbs have come undone, the bird can mend it easily by pulling the feather through its beak a few times.

Plume feathers are much fluffier than flight feathers because the barbs do not hook together. They make a soft layer under the bigger body feathers and help to keep the bird extra warm.

Above Part of an enlarged feather. This shows the barbs and barbules which fasten together to make up the vane.

Below A black-headed gull. Birds need feathers for different purposes and so they vary in shape and size. The largest feathers are found in the wings and tail. The tiny down feathers and the thin filoplumes are the smallest feathers to be found on a bird.

As well as for keeping warm and being important for flying, feathers are also useful for attacting a mate. A male bird may do this by showing off with feathers that are beautiful colours, or that have a special shape. Feathers with certain patterns on them may protect a bird by making it blend with its surroundings so that it cannot be seen. Sometimes, birds can recognise others of the same kind by the colour of their feathers.

Feathers are so important to birds that they look after them very carefully. Birds can often be seen splashing themselves in water. A bird-bath in a garden is a good place to watch this happening. After dipping and splashing several times, they will move away and begin to clean their feathers with their beak and comb them back into place. This is called *preening*. They will also make their feathers waterproof by taking some oil from a gland near their tail and spreading it with their beak.

Although birds look after their plumage carefully, feathers do not last for ever. So each year, adult birds lose their old feathers and grow new ones. This *moulting*, as it is called, may be done fairly quickly in some birds. Others may take half the year, losing only a few feathers at a time and growing new ones before losing a few more. Some kinds of birds moult twice a year if they live in places where their feathers get very worn.

How birds attract a mate

When the time of year comes for birds to lay eggs, they must first find a mate. The male bird tries to attract a female by singing or by looking extra pretty. Many birds have certain movements or 'dances' that they do as well. These are called *courtship displays*.

Male birds make themselves attractive by growing bright plumage in the breeding season. The peacock has some very long feathers just above his main tail feathers. When he wants to display, he can make these stand up like a great big fan. Male pheasants of all kinds have very lovely feathers too, and they strut in front of the females to show them off. Even the male bullfinch grows extra bright feathers on his breast when the breeding season comes.

Some of the most beautiful birds in the world are the male birds of paradise. There are several kinds and they live in parts of Australia and the island of New Guinea where there are thick forests. Not only are the feathers wonderful colours but they are also often strangely shaped. The King of Saxony bird of paradise is a small bird about seventeen centimetres long, but from its head grow two feathers about forty-five centimetres long, which look like pieces of wire with little blue flags attached to them. Some birds of paradise perch on a branch to start a display and slowly tilt forward until they hang upside down so that they show their plumes to better advantage.

Right Male birds of paradise use their magnificent feathers to show off and attract a mate. The females have dull plumage.

Below Most bowerbirds find flowers, shells and coloured berries more useful than feathers when courting. These two colourful bowerbirds are an exception.

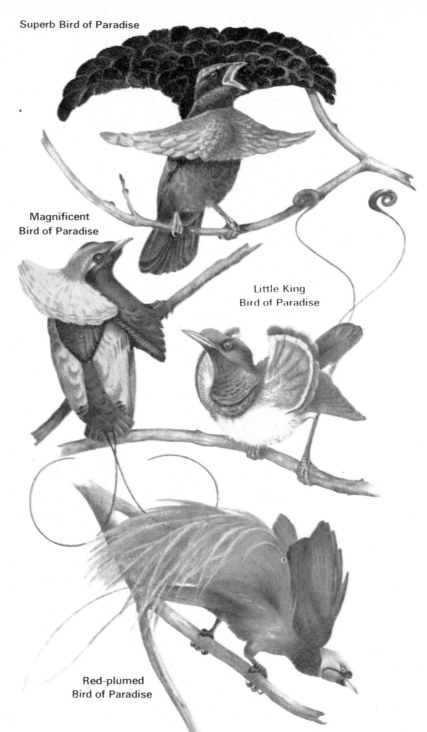

Superb Bird of Paradise

Magnificent Bird of Paradise

Little King Bird of Paradise

Red-plumed Bird of Paradise

Bowerbirds live in New Guinea. Some are brightly coloured, but those that are not display by making a small piece of ground attractive instead. One kind clears a space in the forest about a metre and a half across and covers it with leaves. When the leaves dry, the bird takes them away and brings fresh ones to take their place. Another kind piles up twigs around a small tree and slowly makes a heap shaped like a hut with a pointed roof. It then puts flowers and ferns around the walls and on the ground. When they fade, it picks fresh ones. Often it uses berries and snail shells, too.

Above The nest of the Baya weaver bird. The bird knows how to make this wonderful nest by instinct.

Below Swallows probably built their mud nests on cliff ledges and branches before there were barns and walls available.

Nests

Before laying their eggs, most birds build a nest. This is done so that the eggs can be kept close together and the bird is then able to keep them warm. When the young ones hatch from the eggs, they will be kept together in the same way. In some bird families, it is the female that makes the nest, but more often both birds help each other. They seem to know how to build a nest without being shown but it takes a long time and a great deal of work. Birds build their nests in all kinds of places. Many of them build in trees and hedges, some on the ground. Kingfishers have to dig a tunnel in the river bank and woodpeckers must chip out a nesting hole in a tree trunk. They have only their beaks to use as tools and it takes them several weeks.

If you take an old nest to pieces, it is interesting to see what the bird has used to make it. Each kind of bird has its own special way of nest building, but usually birds that nest in hedges use a lot of grass. Tree-nesting birds such as pigeons and jackdaws are more likely to use twigs. Now and again you can find a nest where the bird has woven-in some pieces of string or even plastic! The shape of the nest is often like a bowl and some kinds of birds line it with mud or soft moss. A few may even use their own down feathers for the lining.

Many birds weave the pieces of grass in a very clever way to make a firm nest, but the most beautiful nests of all are made by weaver birds that live in hot countries such as Africa and India. Their nests are like hollow balls or bottles hanging upside down. Nests this shape make it harder for snakes to steal the eggs.

Mud may be used, not only to line nests, but also to make the walls. Swallows use small pieces of grass and mud to make pellets. They place these one on top of the other to make a very snug, cup-shaped nest fixed to a wall. The ovenbirds that live in South America make their mud nests on top of fence posts or branches of trees. The Spanish Americans call these birds 'the bakers'. Both names are given to these birds because they make a nest something like an old-fashioned Dutch oven. The entrance hole is separated from the nesting part by a mud wall that stretches almost to the back of the nest.

Above Woodpeckers make a nesting hole in the trunk of a tree. The male and female take turns in chipping away the wood with their beaks

Below Ovenbirds make ball-shaped nests fixed to a fence or branch. The eggs are safer than in an open nest.

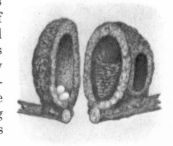

Penguins that live in the far south do not find it easy to make nests because there is very little material for them to use. The Adélie penguins use stones. Some of the birds will walk a long way to collect them, but others are lazy and steal them from the other nests when the owners are not looking. The big Emperor penguins do not even use stones. They have found a way to do without nests. When these penguins leave the water at breeding time, they come on to ice and snow and make for the place where the eggs were laid the year before. Here the females lay their one egg each and at once the males roll them on to their feet with their beak. In this way the eggs will not touch the snow. The males then cover the egg they are looking after with a fold of skin and feathers so that it will be kept warm. Hundreds of male penguins gather together and stand in groups for about two months holding the eggs carefully in place on their feet until the chicks hatch out.

Above Adélie penguins make their nests of stones because there is very little suitable nest-building material in the cold, far south where they live.

Centre Emperor penguin chicks have fluffy feathers. They must moult and grow sleek feathers like the adults before they can swim. Notice the colouring of the penguin's egg.

Below Birds of the coast, like this shag, may build their nests from seaweed. Often many will build close to each other to form a colony.

Eggs

When the nest is made, then the female bird is ready to lay her eggs. There may be only one, as with the Emperor penguin, or there may be more. Many birds lay five or six eggs and a partridge may lay between twelve and eighteen.

Larger birds lay bigger eggs than smaller ones. The tiny goldcrest's egg is just over a centimetre long while the swan's is eleven centimetres. The humming birds lay even smaller eggs than the goldcrest and the largest eggs of all belong to the ostrich.

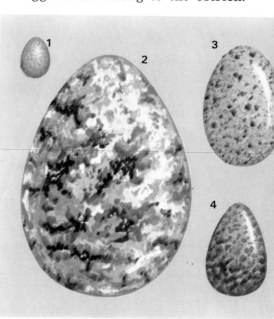

They are between fifteen and twenty centimetres long and weigh just over a kilogram.

Not all eggs are the same shape, some are more pointed than others. Certain sea-birds lay very pointed eggs so that they will not roll off the cliff ledges where the birds lay them. They simply roll round in a circle. On the other hand, owls' eggs are almost ball-shaped.

Colours are different, too. Usually they are either white, brown or blue, but they are not often a plain colour. Usually the eggs have darker spots and markings on them which make them more difficult to see. There are many animals that like to eat eggs if they can find any!

Each kind of bird lays eggs of a similar shape and colour. All song thrushes' eggs are blue with dark spots at the wider end. Moorhens' eggs are a creamy colour with brown blotches on them. Cuckoos, however, do not make nests of their own and lay their eggs in the nests of other birds. Their eggs look very much like the eggs of the bird the cuckoo has chosen to be foster-parents.

Above A cuckoo will remove an egg from a nest and then lay one of its own to replace it.

Below Notice how the sizes of birds' eggs vary. 1 Wren: 2 King Penguin: 3 Sage Grouse: 4 Ruff: 5 Madagascar Bulbul: 6 Brünnich's Guillemot: 7 Macgregor's Bird of Paradise: 8 Broad-billed Humming Bird: 9 Great Tinamou: 10 Black-bellied Plover: 11 Golden Eagle: 12 White-winged Thriller: 13 Sharp-tailed Grouse: 14 Bennett's Cassowary: 15 Boat-tailed Grackle

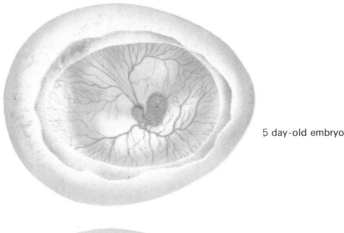

5 day-old embryo

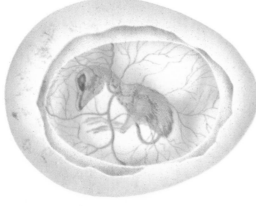

15 day-old embryo

23 day-old embryo

Turkey chick

Inside the egg

Inside the egg the baby bird will live and grow. It starts as a tiny speck, called an *embryo* and begins to develop even before the egg is laid. Once the egg is in the nest, it must be kept warm or else the embryo will die. The parent birds sit on their eggs and use the warmth of their bodies to stop them from getting cold. Usually both the parents share the work of sitting on the eggs and while one is sitting, the other can feed. In some kinds of birds, though, only one parent does the sitting. This is normally the female, but not always.

As the days go by, the embryo within the shell grows larger. It must have food for this and its food supply is the ball of golden yellow yolk which you see when you eat a hen's egg. The embryo lies on the top of the yolk and the food is carried to it through tiny tubes called *blood vessels*. Around the yolk is a thin skin. The yolk and the embryo do not sink to the bottom of the shell because they are floating in a liquid that is often called the white of the egg, although a better name for it is *albumen*. This is like a cushion all around the yolk. The inside of the shell is lined with some more thin skin and at one end is a small pocket of air.

For some time, the embryo does not look much like a bird, but soon a beak begins to grow, the eyes are large and when the wings and legs have developed, then it is clearly a bird. A little longer and the feathers begin to show but only certain birds get all their feathers while they are still in the egg. Others do not get them until they have hatched.

When the young bird has no more room inside the egg and it has used up its food, it breaks open the shell. On the end of its beak is a blunt, hard piece called the *egg tooth*. With this, the bird chips away at the shell from the inside until it makes a hole. It makes the hole bigger and struggles free.

If the bird is a small variety, such as a whitethroat, it will only take about eleven days to grow in the egg. Larger birds take longer. A baby albatross takes as long as eighty days before it hatches.

Left Inside an egg, the young bird grows and develops, feeding on the yolk which is slowly used up.

Looking after the young

Young birds are not ready to look after themselves when they hatch. Some, such as ducklings and chicks, have all their feathers even before they come out of the eggs and they soon learn to feed themselves. Most baby birds, though, have to be fed by their parents, but they have to make certain movements when the adult bird brings the food otherwise they get nothing. The beak of an adult herring gull has a red spot on it and when it brings food to the nest, the young gulls must peck at the red spot before they will be fed. Some young birds seem to have very big mouths and when they feel a movement of the nest made by the parent bird, they open their beaks as wide as they can

Above A young, hungry gull must peck at the red spot on the parent's beak. The parent bird will then bring up food from its crop for the chick to eat.

Right Young herons open their beaks and call whenever the parents come to the nest. In this way they beg for food and are certain to be fed.

Below The open beak and begging movements of a cowbird nestling makes adult foster parents want to feed them, even when the young are not their own. Young cuckoos and cowbirds manage to obtain food in this way.

and stretch their necks upwards. The mouth of a young bird is quite brightly coloured and the sight of this makes the parent want to push food into it.

Not only must the young birds be fed, but they must still be kept warm. The nest must be cleaned out, too. Within a few weeks most young birds are ready to fly and begin to look after themselves, but king penguins look after their young for months.

In America, cowbirds do not have any of the hard work of feeding the young. By laying their eggs in the nests of other birds, the foster-parents look after the young cowbird who pushes out all the other eggs from the nest so that it has all the food for itself.

Food

What do birds eat? Like all other animals they may be meat-eaters or plant-eaters or both. Those that are plant-eaters usually eat seeds, although there are birds that prefer fruit or leaves and some, like the tiny humming birds of America, live on the sweet nectar from flowers.

The meat-eaters may catch insects. There are plenty of these and birds such as swifts and nightjars catch flying insects. The tree creeper will poke its beak into the cracks of the bark on trees to find the very small insects that live there. Woodpeckers work harder and chisel into the bark and rotting wood for insects that are under the surface. Meat may also mean worms and grubs under the ground. It may mean the small creatures of the shallow water, or fish, or mussels on the shore.

There are birds, however, to whom meat means a mouse or even a rabbit. This is the kind of food eaten by birds of prey, such as hawks and eagles. The vultures of Africa and India eat the remains of animals which have been killed by others. Birds which eat 'left-overs' are called *scavengers* and they play a very important part in keeping places clean.

Beaks

A bird that eats nuts needs a very differently shaped beak from a bird which has to rip up meat. So among the birds all beaks do not look alike and it is often possible to get a good idea of what a bird eats from the shape of its beak.

Many seed-eating birds have a short, cone-shaped beak. This is strong enough to break the hard outside coat of the seeds. Hawfinches can crack cherry stones and that certainly needs a strong beak. Of course, not all seeds are this hard and some can be eaten without being broken open. It is interesting to find that an English bullfinch, an American cardinal and an African waxbill all have similar beaks, even though they live in different countries. This is because they all eat the same kind of food—seeds. Brazil nuts are very hard kinds of seeds, but even these can be broken by macaws. Crossbills eat the seeds of pine trees—the pointed ends of the beak are crossed-over so that the bird can get at the seeds in the pine cones more easily.

Great-horned Owl

Kingfisher

Waxwing

Flamingo

Zapata Wren

Humming Bird

Griffon Vulture

Egyptian Vulture

Crossbill

Curlew

Eagle

Pelican

Nightjar

Toucan

Chestnut-sided Shrike

Insect-eaters do not need a strong cracking beak. Instead, they need a longer, thinner one for picking up tiny insects from leaves, or for pushing into cracks in the bark on trees. Numbers of very small insects live in these cracks and birds such as tree creepers spend hours hunting for them. Other birds are better at catching insects as they fly. Fastest of these are the swifts and swallows which fly many miles in a day catching foods.

In Africa, cows are often seen with small birds perching on their backs. These birds are called ox-peckers and they look for small creatures called ticks that live on the skins of cattle. Larger white birds called cattle egrets walk among the cows, waiting to catch any creatures that get disturbed by the cows as they move.

Long, sharp beaks like daggers belong to birds which catch fish. Herons and kingfishers have this type of beak. The heron waits silently, standing in the pond or river until it sees a fish or a frog. Then, as quick as lightning, its head and neck plunge into the water and the fish is caught.

The kingfisher, which is a much smaller bird, sits on a branch over a stream to watch for fish. If it sees one, it dives right in so that its whole body goes under the water.

Vultures and eagles—birds that are meat-eaters—have strong beaks with a hooked end so that they can tear at dead animals. Owls have hooked beaks, for they live on small animals such as mice or lizards.

One of the strangest beaks among the birds belongs to the flamingo. These beautiful birds that are found in many parts of the world, hold their beaks in the water in such a way that they can pump water and mud through them. As they do this, they take from the water the tiny animals and plants that it contains.

A few kinds of birds live on the nectar of flowers. This is a sweet, sugary liquid and a bird needs a long, thin beak to get at it. The American humming birds have this sort of beak, which may be even longer than their body in some cases. They hover close to the flowers while they push their beak right into them to feed.

29

Rhea and chick

Birds that do not fly

Although most birds can fly, there are some that cannot. The largest living bird, the ostrich, is one of these. To make up for not being able to fly, it can run very fast on its strong legs—up to fifty-six kilometres an hour. As it runs, the small wings help it to keep its balance. There are large feathers at the end of its wings called plumes. Sometimes the male birds use these when displaying and years ago they were sold to be used for decorating ladies' hats. Even before that, knights decorated their helmets with them.

The kiwi of New Zealand is another bird that cannot fly and walks about, poking for worms with its long beak.

Penguins have wings that are no use for flying, either. Instead, they use them for swimming. They are wonderful swimmers, cutting through the water for the fish that they eat. Penguins do not have the large feathers that flying birds do. Their bodies are covered with very small feathers and their wings with even smaller, stiffer ones, which make the penguins look very smooth and sleek. There are fifteen different kinds of penguins and all of them have dark grey, almost black feathers covering their back, and white ones over the front of their body. But each kind of penguin has a special pattern of feathers on its head. In this way, any penguin can recognise others of the same kind.

Emu

Ostrich

Kakapo

Ostrich chick

Emperor Penguin

Takahe

Kiwi

Cassowary

30

Feet and Claws

Many birds have four toes on each foot, three pointing forwards and one backwards. It is unusual for birds to have more than four toes, although some have less. Birds with three toes on each foot are fairly common, and ostriches only have two! The arrangement of the toes varies as well. This depends on the bird's habitat.

Birds that live in and around hedges and bushes perch and hop a great deal. Perching birds need feet that will grip the twigs firmly and the 'three toes forward, one toe back' type of foot is best, with the back toe curling right under the twig so that the bird will not fall.

Other birds like woodpeckers, for example, need feet that help them to cling to tree trunks while they lean back as they hammer away with their beaks. The ideal foot for these birds has two toes pointing forwards and two backwards. Parrots do not cling to trees but they have this type of foot so that they can hold their food, perhaps a nut, as they work at it to break the shell.

Birds of prey hold their food with their feet. They have to carry their prey as well as kill it, so their toes are often very rough underneath for gripping the prey, and the claws, or talons, are very strong and curved for killing.

Birds that live by the water have other problems. If they walk in shallow water, probing in mud for food, they need fairly long legs. They also need long toes to prevent them from sinking into the mud. Most waders, as these birds are called, can be spotted by their long legs and large feet. The swimmers need feet for power, so their legs are shorter and their feet often webbed. The skin may lie on each side of the toes as it does in the grebes, or it may fill the space between the toes as in ducks and swans. They have skin between three of their toes, but pelicans and cormorants go even further and have skin between all four toes, which helps to make them very powerful swimmers indeed.

Left A number of birds cannot fly. Most people know of the ostrich, but here are several others that are not so familiar.

Right Look at these different types of feet and see how their shape is adapted to the bird's way of life.

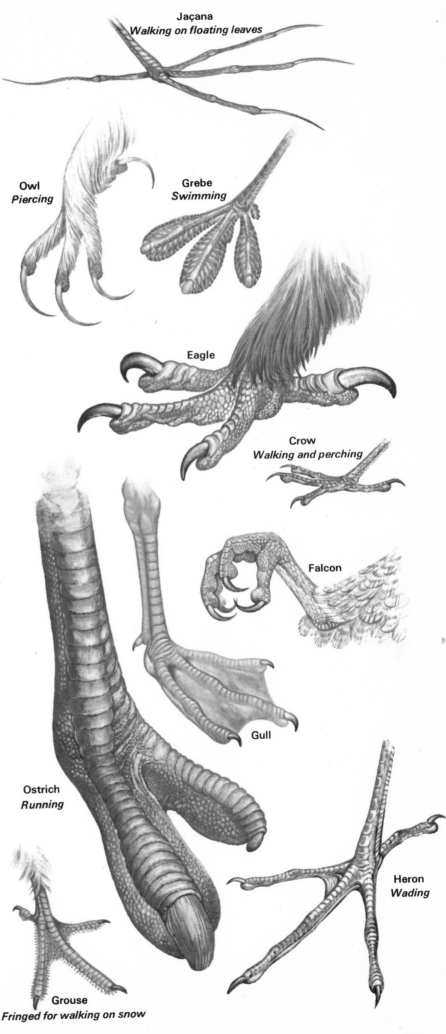

Jaçana
Walking on floating leaves

Owl
Piercing

Grebe
Swimming

Eagle

Crow
Walking and perching

Falcon

Gull

Ostrich
Running

Heron
Wading

Grouse
Fringed for walking on snow

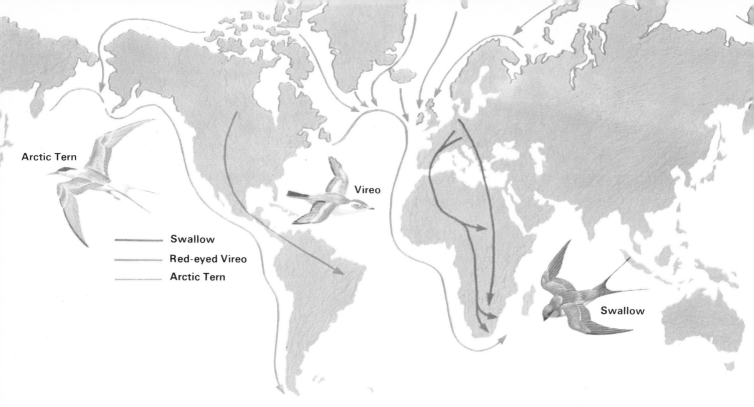

Arctic Tern

Vireo

—— Swallow
—— Red-eyed Vireo
—— Arctic Tern

Swallow

Migration

> The cuckoo comes in April,
> He sings his song in May,
> In the middle of June
> He changes his tune,
> In July he flies away.

This old rhyme tells us that the cuckoo only stays in Britain for a part of the year. You may have noticed how swallows are only here for a few months and then they too leave. Did you know that there are some birds that will spend the winter in a country and then leave as summer comes? Where do all these birds come from?

The cuckoos and swallows that go to Britain have come from Africa. They will breed at the time of the year when there are plenty of insects for the young birds to eat. By the end of the summer and the beginning of autumn, the days are growing shorter and the number of insects is getting smaller, so the birds that are Britain's summer visitors begin to fly back to the warmer countries where there is plenty of food again. This is the time when the winter visitors begin to arrive. Food is becoming scarcer in the bitter cold of Norway and Sweden, but in Britain the winters are warmer and there are plenty of berries and seeds which are perfect food for them.

All over the world birds make these long journeys from one country to another. This is called *migration* and

Above This map shows the routes taken by certain birds when they migrate. The longest flights are made by Arctic terns. Many birds die en route, but many more manage to finish the journey.

Below Some kinds of waterfowl breed in cold northern countries. In winter they fly south where there is more food before the breeding season begins again. Shelduck migrate to certain places when they are ready to moult.

for many birds it is the only way in which food can be found all through the year. Sometimes these journeys are very long indeed and the birds fly huge distances. There may be strong winds and storms and thousands of birds may die on the way, but many more arrive safely. The longest journey is made by the small Arctic terns. These little birds leave their breeding grounds in the far north of Canada at the end of summer and fly to the seas of the Antarctic. They make this journey twice a year which must make them the champion long-distance fliers among the birds! But there are other birds that also make trips of several thousand kilometres.

For many years people were puzzled by these migrations because they could not understand how birds could find their way. Now we are beginning to learn how they are able to do this, although we certainly do not know everything about it. We think that the birds are able to steer by looking at the position of the sun during the day and the stars at night. Sailors can do this too, but they need special instruments for watching the sun and they also need very good clocks. With these, they are able to work out their position but birds are able to do it without instruments. What is more, the young birds are able to do it without being taught because they are born with the knowledge.

Above Crowned cranes migrate northwards from Africa for the summer. When they arrive the courtship dances begin. Males bow and leap in front of the females until they join in, too.

Below By keeping starlings in special cages, Gustav Kramer, a German, discovered that migrating birds use the sun's position to guide them.

Top Sunlight shines into the cage and the starling faces the direction it normally takes when migrating.

Bottom right and left Mirrors are used to change the direction of the sun's rays and the bird faces a new direction. It must keep the same angle between itself and the sun's rays.

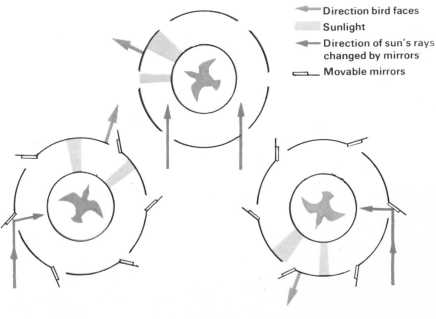

→ **Direction bird faces**

■ **Sunlight**

← **Direction of sun's rays changed by mirrors**

▭ **Movable mirrors**

33

Insects

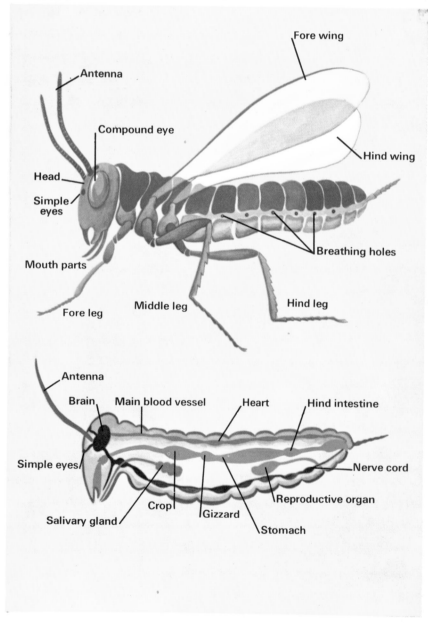

Antenna

Compound eye

Head

Simple eyes

Mouth parts

Fore leg

Middle leg

Fore wing

Hind wing

Breathing holes

Hind leg

Antenna

Brain

Main blood vessel

Heart

Hind intestine

Simple eyes

Salivary gland

Crop

Gizzard

Stomach

Nerve cord

Reproductive organ

What is an insect?

What could be nicer on a warm summer day than to lie in a meadow among the wild flowers and watch the living creatures around you? A grasshopper or two will leap now and again. Flies will buzz around. Bees will move busily from flower to flower. Maybe a large dragonfly will dart towards the nearest pond and butterflies will drift silently through the air.

All these are insects, just a few of the millions that are alive all over the world at this moment. There are probably more insects than there are all other kinds of creatures put together. There are insects in every country, in deserts, in jungles, high up on mountains, in hot places and cold ones. There are insects that eat wood, meat, paper, seeds, in fact almost everything you can think of.

What is an insect? It is an animal that has no bones but it does have a skeleton of tough, hard skin on the outside of its body. Its body is made up of three sections. At the front end is the head. The middle section is the *thorax* and the third section is the *abdomen*. Most insects have wings and they all have three pairs of legs. An insect's body is usually fairly small but the wings may be quite large. Some insects that lived millions of years ago had a wing span of nearly a metre.

Life history—eggs

Almost all insects start their lives as an egg, but insect eggs are very different from those laid by birds. For one thing they are a different size. Insect eggs are tiny and you may well need a magnifying glass to see them. If you grow cabbages in your garden, look on the underside of the leaves during the summer months and you will very likely see clusters of tiny eggs, each about the size of a pin head. These are eggs laid by one of the butterflies with white wings that are so common. Many insects lay their eggs on leaves but usually underneath them so that they are hidden from birds and protected from the rain. Look on leaves of plants in the garden, especially on rose trees, for the yellow or orange eggs that have been laid by ladybirds. Flies' eggs are easy to find. Leave a small piece of meat in the open on any warm day in the summer and very soon it will be found by the big bluebottle flies. If you watch carefully, you may be able to watch them lay their white eggs on the meat. Although these eggs are small too, it is possible to see that their shape is much longer than that of the butterfly eggs on the cabbage. Under a microscope, an insect's egg can be seen to have beautiful patterns of ridges and hollows all over it. These can trap a layer of air against the egg if any water should happen to cover it, perhaps after heavy rain.

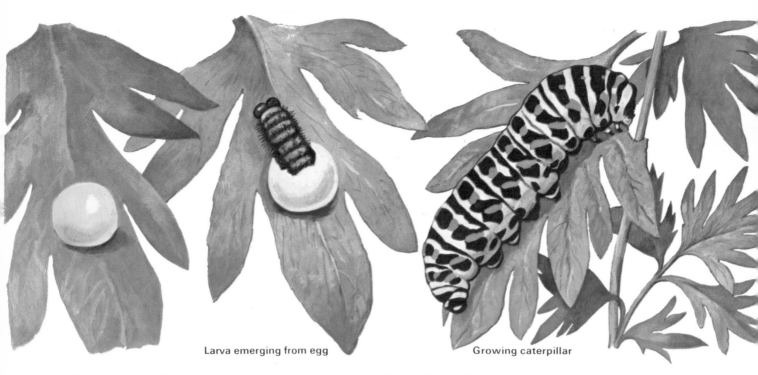

Larva emerging from egg

Growing caterpillar

Life history—larva

The egg is only the first step in the life story of an insect. If you are lucky and are able to watch some butterfly eggs, you will see that out of each egg will crawl a tiny creature that does not look much like a butterfly. It is a *larva*, or perhaps you call it a caterpillar, which is a special name given to the larva of a butterfly or moth. At once it will begin to eat the remains of the egg and then it will begin to eat the leaf it is on, starting at the edge. This is the work that any insect larva does. It must eat and eat and eat, storing up energy for the next step in its life. The parent insect has laid the eggs on a good supply of food so that the larva does not have to search for it.

As the days of eating go by, the caterpillar grows and soon its skin becomes too tight for it, so the old skin splits and out of it crawls the caterpillar with a new skin that can stretch a little more. This will happen several times to the caterpillar as it grows.

The larva that hatches from the fly's egg is not much like a caterpillar. Its body is white and has none of the caterpillar's colours. It has no legs either, but it can wriggle about if it has to and as it grows it, too, will change its skin.

The life story of the beautiful swallowtail butterfly begins with the laying of an egg. Out crawls the tiny caterpillar and from that moment it eats and grows, until at last it spins a silken cord and attaches itself to a plant stem. This is a safety belt to stop it from falling as it loses its caterpillar skin for the last time and becomes a pupa. When ready, the full-grown butterfly struggles out of the pupa skin, dries its wings and flies off.

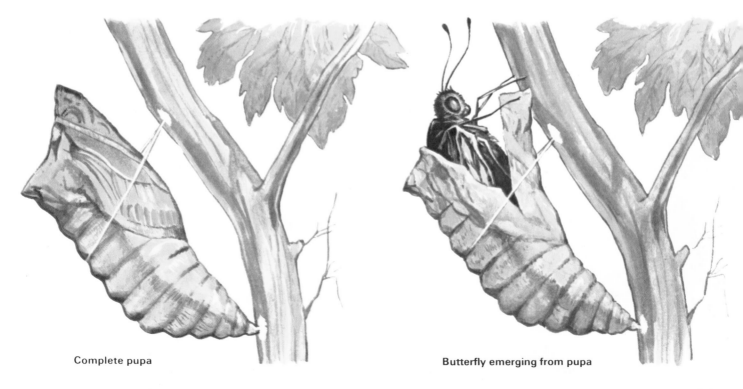

Complete pupa

Butterfly emerging from pupa

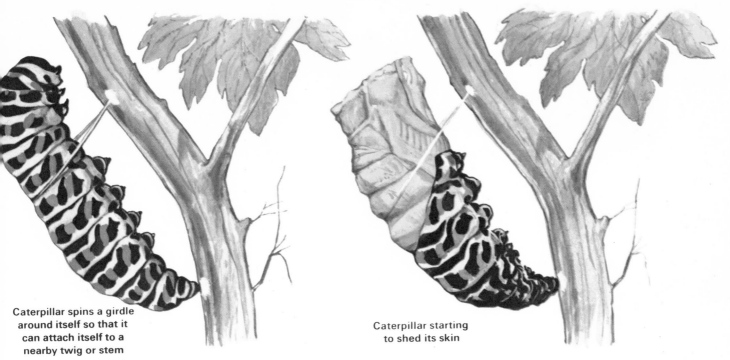

Caterpillar spins a girdle around itself so that it can attach itself to a nearby twig or stem

Caterpillar starting to shed its skin

Life history—pupa

After a while, the larva will have stored up enough energy so that great changes can take place in its body. After the last change of skin, the outside becomes harder and the creature stops eating and begins to rest. It is now called a *pupa*. The outside skin may turn brown and become very tough as it does in the pupa of the fly. Some moths may spin a case of silk, called a *cocoon*, and turn into a pupa inside that. There are many kinds of silk-moths that do this and the cocoons of one variety are very carefully undone and the long, long threads of silk are used for weaving silk material.

Other insects may burrow under the ground and the pupa will then have a small room in the soil.

Within the skin of the pupa, the insect begins to get its adult shape. This needs a great deal of energy which is why the larva had to store it up. Really, the whole of the insect's body has to be re-built. Adult mouthparts have to form, and the wings must be produced. But the time comes when it is finished and the old brown skin of the pupa will open. Out will struggle a newly formed insect. If it is a butterfly or moth, the wings will be crumpled at first and it will be some time before the wings unfold and the insect can fly.

Complete butterfly with crumpled, dampened wings

The final stage – with wings completely dry

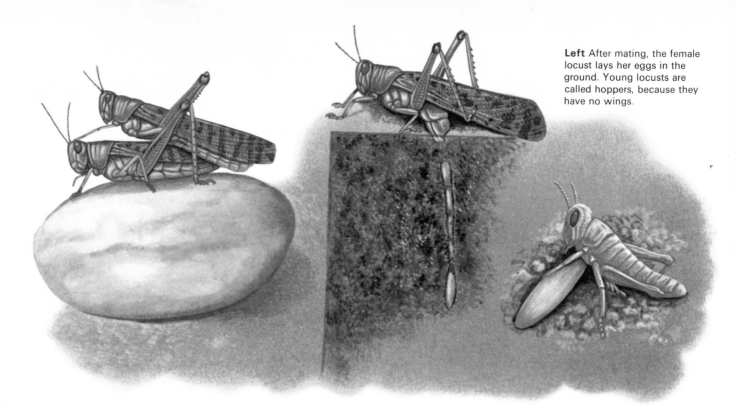

Left After mating, the female locust lays her eggs in the ground. Young locusts are called hoppers, because they have no wings.

The life history of locusts

There are some insects that do not go through all the stages of egg, larva, pupa and adult in their life history. They hatch from the eggs looking very much like the adult although usually much smaller. Locusts are insects of this kind. They are like large grasshoppers that live in hot countries such as Africa and India. At egg-laying time, the female locust bores a hole in the sand with the end of her body. The eggs are laid in the lower part of the hole, mixed with a frothy stuff which will soon harden. After about two weeks, the eggs break open and each tiny larva, called a *nymph*, wriggles to the top of the hole, gets a new skin right away and looks just like a tiny locust, except that it has no wings. It is now often called a hopper, because of the way it moves about. The hopper eats leaves and grows quickly. Every so often it has to change its skin, like the caterpillar, so that it can keep growing. At each change of skin, or *moult*, its wings get a little larger and after the last moult, everything about it is complete.

Stick insects grow in this way, too, and so do dragonflies. The dragonfly nymph lives in ponds and rivers because it is able to breathe under water. When it is ready, it climbs up the stem of a plant that is growing out of the water. When it is above the water, the skin of the nymph splits and out struggles the adult dragonfly.

Below A dragonfly nymph leaves the water by climbing up a stem of a plant. When it is safely out of the water, its skin will split and the adult dragonfly will emerge.

Clouded Yellow

Heliconis amazona

Bright Coerulean

Hypolimnas dexithea

Callitaera pireta

Scarce Copper

Burnet

Peacock

Common Jezebel

Garden Tiger

Painted Lady

Above Wings of butterflies and moths are covered with tiny scales that overlap one another like tiles on the roof of a house.

The variety of insects

A dragonfly, a ladybird, an earwig, and a hawk moth are all insects because they each have the three sections to their body: the head, the thorax and the abdomen. They each have three pairs of legs, too, but in many other ways they are different. The long, thin body of the dragonfly does not look much like the shorter, fatter one of the hawk moth, and where are the wings of the ladybird and earwig? There are thousands of different kinds of insects so scientists put them into groups when they want to study them. There are twenty-two of these groups but we need to look at just a few of them, those that you will see most often.

The group you probably know well already is the one that contains butterflies and moths. These insects have wings that are covered with tiny scales, so small that they look like fine powder on the wings. If you were to look at some of this fine powder under a microscope, you would be able to see the shape of the scales that give some of the colours to the wings of these lovely insects.

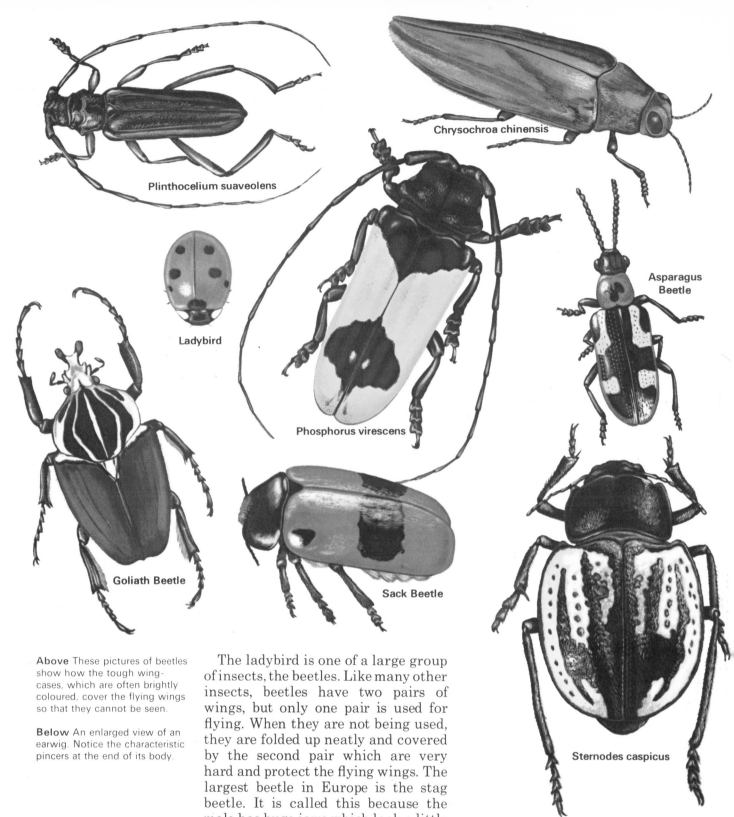

Plinthocelium suaveolens

Chrysochroa chinensis

Ladybird

Asparagus Beetle

Phosphorus virescens

Goliath Beetle

Sack Beetle

Sternodes caspicus

The ladybird is one of a large group of insects, the beetles. Like many other insects, beetles have two pairs of wings, but only one pair is used for flying. When they are not being used, they are folded up neatly and covered by the second pair which are very hard and protect the flying wings. The largest beetle in Europe is the stag beetle. It is called this because the male has huge jaws which look a little like the antlers of a male deer, or stag.

Earwigs make a small group by themselves. They are insects whose front pair of wings have become small, hard flaps and the flying wings have to be folded up very small to be stored away beneath them. Most people can recognise an earwig when they see one because of the pair of forceps or pincers at the end of its body. It used to be believed that earwigs would crawl into the ears of people who were asleep and this is how they got their name.

Grasshoppers have one pair of legs that is much longer than the rest and they are used for jumping. Very much like grasshoppers are the crickets. On a warm, summer day both kinds of insects may be heard making a chirping noise in meadows. Crickets make this noise by rubbing their wings together, but the short-horned grasshoppers rub their wings with part of their hind legs. The hotter the day, the louder they seem to chirp. Cockroaches are put in the same group as grasshoppers, locusts and crickets, but they cannot jump and have flatter bodies. Stick insects are in this group, too.

One of the insects we notice most often is the house fly. The flies make an enormous group that has over eighty thousand different kinds in it. Anywhere on earth where people can live, flies seem to be able to live as well. All flies have only one pair of wings for flying. The second pair has become very small indeed and has become a pair of balancers instead. Some flies look very much like bees or wasps because their bodies are coloured with similar black and yellow patterns. These hover flies can often be seen on flowers or seeming to hang in the air for a few seconds before they dart away.

The real wasps and bees have yellow and black, or yellow and brown markings on them, but they have two pairs of wings. Most people are afraid of these insects because they may sting which can be very painful. The sting is a tiny, pointed tube at the end of the abdomen which can be pushed into the animal being attacked. Poison runs down the tube from a small poison-bag inside the insect and it is this poison which gives us so much pain, but can kill smaller creatures. Ants are related to bees and wasps so they are put in the same group.

Dragonflies can often be seen near water, sometimes flying above it, hunting for other insects which are their food. At other times, they may be resting on a plant beside the water and then it is easier to see the four large wings and huge eyes. Despite the name, dragonflies are not closely related to ordinary flies so they are put in a separate group. Some dragonflies have thin elongated bodies but others have stouter ones. Their eggs are laid in ponds and streams and the nymphs live in the water.

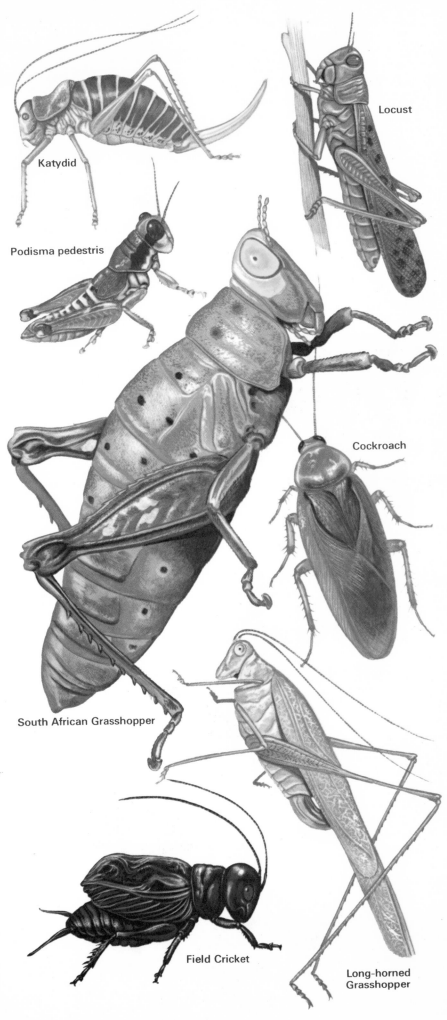

Katydid

Locust

Podisma pedestris

Cockroach

South African Grasshopper

Field Cricket

Long-horned Grasshopper

Bees

Some insects live in groups or colonies. Ants live like this and so do some wasps. Insects that live and work together are called *social insects* and one of the best known social insects is the honey bee. There are many different kinds of bees and some live on their own. Honey bees, though, have been kept by men for hundreds of years for their honey. These insects will live happily in a specially-made wooden box called a hive, so they are sometimes known as hive bees.

In a hive of bees, there are a queen, some drones and thousands of workers. The queen is there to lay eggs and do nothing else. At certain times, she may lay up to fifteen hundred eggs every day! The drones are male bees and they do no work. All the tasks of the hive are done by the workers. They look after the queen and each new larva that hatches out from the eggs that she lays. They make layers of six-sided compartments, or cells, in which the eggs are laid and food stored. They keep the hive cool in summer if it gets too hot by fanning with their wings. They guard the hive so that no robber bees can get in, and they gather food. In summer there is so much for the workers to do that they only live for four or five weeks. The bees that start their lives in the autumn do not have to work so hard and usually live right through the winter.

Go into the garden on a hot summer day and you will be able to watch bees gathering food. They fly from flower to flower collecting nectar, which is sweet and sugary, and pollen. Both nectar and pollen are used for food, but it is the nectar that the bees turn into honey. If you watch carefully you will see that a bee will collect food from flowers of the same kind. Some will be visiting hollyhocks, others going to buttercups. But they will not mix the flowers. The bee sucks the nectar into a special honey stomach, but the pollen is picked up on the hairs of the body as it scrambles into the flower. It is then scraped off into a *pollen basket* on the outside of each back leg. Look hard and you will quite often see bees with their pollen baskets full. They look like yellow lumps on the legs, almost too large for the bee to carry. Bees sting, of course, so do not try to pick one up for a closer look.

Above Bees are kept in wooden hives. The hives are made in sections so that they can be taken apart and the honeycombs gathered. The bees enter at the bottom of the hive.

Above Worker bees are able to cool the hive in hot weather by fanning their wings to make a breeze.

Worker

Queen

Drone

Back in the hive, the food is put into cells, some to be used at once, the rest is stored for the winter when there are no more flowers. To collect all the food that is needed, the bees must know where the right flowers are growing. A few bees act as scouts. They fly around looking for new clumps of flowers. If they find some, they return to the hive and tell the others where the new supply of food can be found. They cannot use sounds for this as we should, but they 'dance' instead. The dances are special movements that the bee makes, sometimes waggling its tail. From these movements, the other bees are able to learn how long it takes to fly from the hive to the flowers and whether they must fly towards the sun or away from it.

When the eggs that the queen has laid in the cells hatch, each larva is fed on special brood-food made by worker bees. If a new queen is wanted, a larva is fed all the time on this brood-food, sometimes called royal jelly. After three days, the others stop having brood-food and are given pollen and honey instead. They will grow into worker bees.

When a new queen comes out of the cell she will fly off one day and mate with some drones that are flying about. The queen then returns to the hive and can start egg-laying. At the end of the summer, any drones that are still in the hive are turned out to die in the cold. They would eat too much and do nothing. In spring, some eggs laid by the queen will become drones.

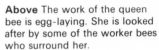

Above The work of the queen bee is egg-laying. She is looked after by some of the worker bees who surround her.

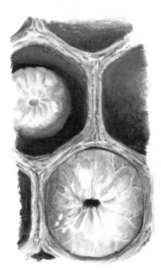

Above The queen bee lays each egg in a separate cell. When it hatches, the larva is fed by the worker bees.

Left A bee that has found food can give directions to the others by 'dances'. A 'round dance' gives the direction of nectar near the hive; a 'tail-wagging dance' if it is further away.

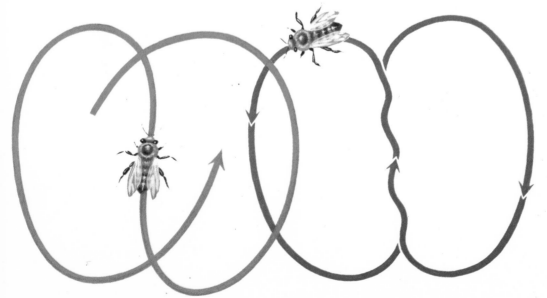

43

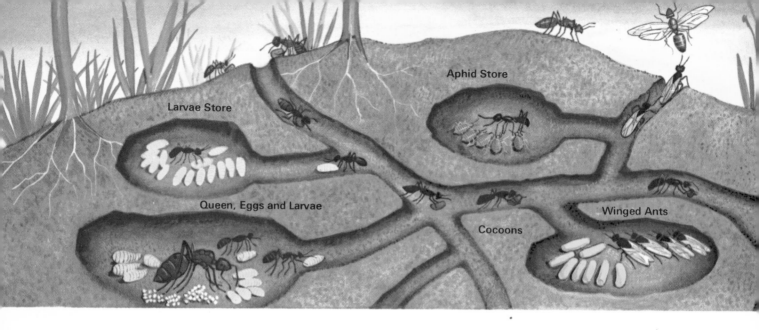

Larvae Store

Aphid Store

Queen, Eggs and Larvae

Cocoons

Winged Ants

Ants and termites

Have you ever lifted a large, flat stone and uncovered an ants' nest? Or perhaps you have been lucky and seen, in a wood, the big mound of pine needles which marks the nest of the wood ants. Ants are always worth watching. Whether they are hurrying down the tunnels of the nest, or struggling over the ground carrying a piece of food, we can watch and learn. Like hive bees, ants are social insects. They live in a group that has a queen, males and workers. There are about six thousand kinds of ants and they are found all over the world. Ants can live for a long time, workers for up to seven years and queens for fifteen. Some kinds of ants are meat-eaters, others feed on seeds and certain kinds are very fond of honey-dew. This is a sweet liquid made by tiny insects called *aphids*, or greenfly. The ants may even keep aphids, rather in the same way that farmers keep cows, and look after them just so that they can collect the honey-dew.

In July and August you can sometimes see swarms of flying ants. They are flying to look for a mate. If a male ant finds a female, they will mate in the air. The female goes to the ground and the first thing she does is break off her wings. Then she goes below ground. She is now a queen and when she is under the ground she makes a small room for herself and begins to lay eggs. She is all alone and goes without food. When the eggs hatch, she looks after the grubs. Each grub becomes a pupa and then a worker ant. Once the workers are ready, they look after the queen and a new colony of ants has been started. The workers must come above ground to look for food but most of their time is spent below ground. They make many tunnels and small rooms where the new grubs are looked after. Wood ants build a great heap of pine needles and sticks, sometimes up to a metre high, over their underground tunnels. This heap also has tunnels in it which join up with the lower ones.

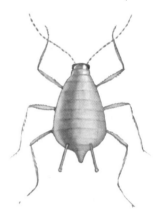

Above Here is an aphid. Ants keep them, either underground or on plants above ground, for the sweet tasting honey-dew they secrete.

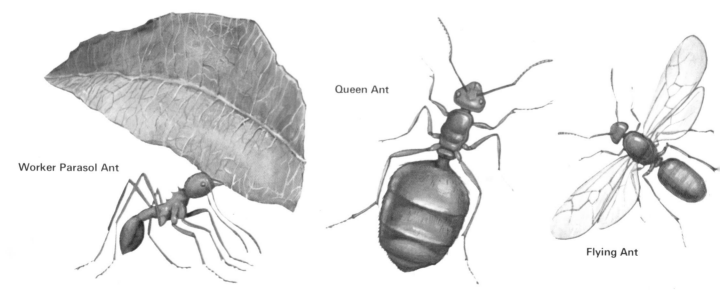

Worker Parasol Ant

Queen Ant

Flying Ant

44

Above An ants' nest is a maze of tunnels and rooms where the work of the colony, such as looking after eggs and larvae, can be carried out.

Food Store

Further Tunnelling

Robber ants are unusual because they will attack the nests of other kinds to capture the pupae in them. They take them back to their own nest and when the new worker ants hatch out from them, they work as slaves in the nest of the robber ants.

Termites look a little like ants, although they are not very closely related to them. They also live in huge groups and build marvellous nests. Termites live in hot countries and in the grasslands of Africa hundreds of termite nests can be seen. They look rather like castles, and are often taller than a man. Each one has been built by termites from tiny grains of soil which they stick together. The really big mounds must have taken a long time to make. Inside there are tunnels and rooms. Some rooms are kept for growing plants. The termites are like farmers and grow these small plants, called fungi, for food. The most important termite is the queen. As well as workers, there are soldier termites. Their job is to protect the nest and fight if necessary.

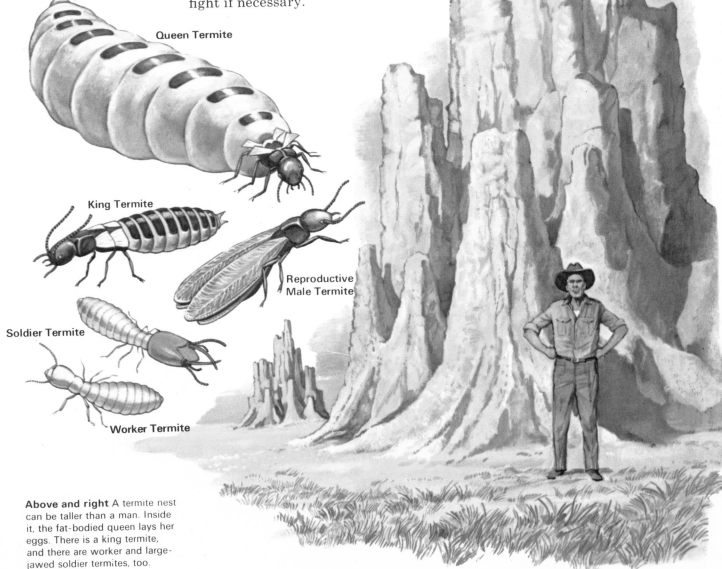

Queen Termite

King Termite

Reproductive Male Termite

Soldier Termite

Worker Termite

Above and right A termite nest can be taller than a man. Inside it, the fat-bodied queen lays her eggs. There is a king termite, and there are worker and large-jawed soldier termites, too.

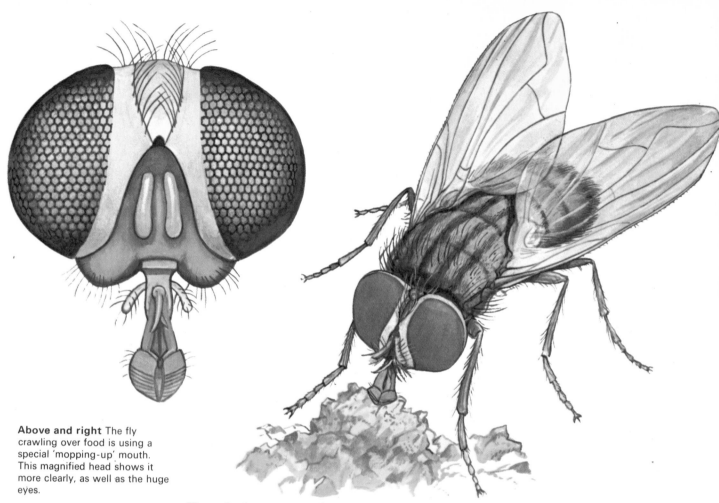

Above and right The fly crawling over food is using a special 'mopping-up' mouth. This magnified head shows it more clearly, as well as the huge eyes.

Above This illustration gives you some idea of how objects appear to an insect.

How do insects see?

Insects see with eyes that are made up of thousands of small lenses. The eye of a house fly has four thousand of these and each large eye of a dragonfly may have nearly thirty thousand! To get some idea of the kind of picture an insect sees, look at a photograph from a newspaper. If you look closely you will see that it is made up of tiny dots and all the dots together build up the picture. When a bee looks at a flower, each of the small lenses sees one small part of it and so the whole eye sees the flower made up of tiny pieces, just as we see a newspaper picture made up from a series of dots.

Although insects can see things that are near, they are not so good at seeing objects that are a long way off. Their eyes are very good, though, at seeing movement. Unless you walk towards an insect very slowly indeed, the insect will notice your movements and be off. Try it in the garden and see how close you can creep up to a butterfly before it flies away.

Not all insects can see the same colours as we do. Bees, for example, and others too, cannot tell the difference between red and black, but unlike man, they are able to see in *ultraviolet* light.

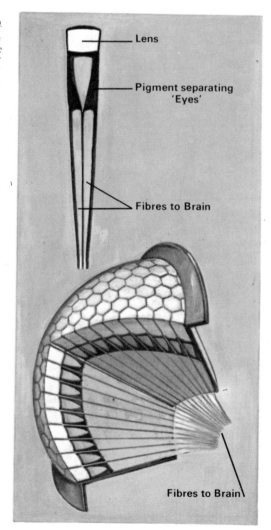

Lens

Pigment separating 'Eyes'

Fibres to Brain

Fibres to Brain

46

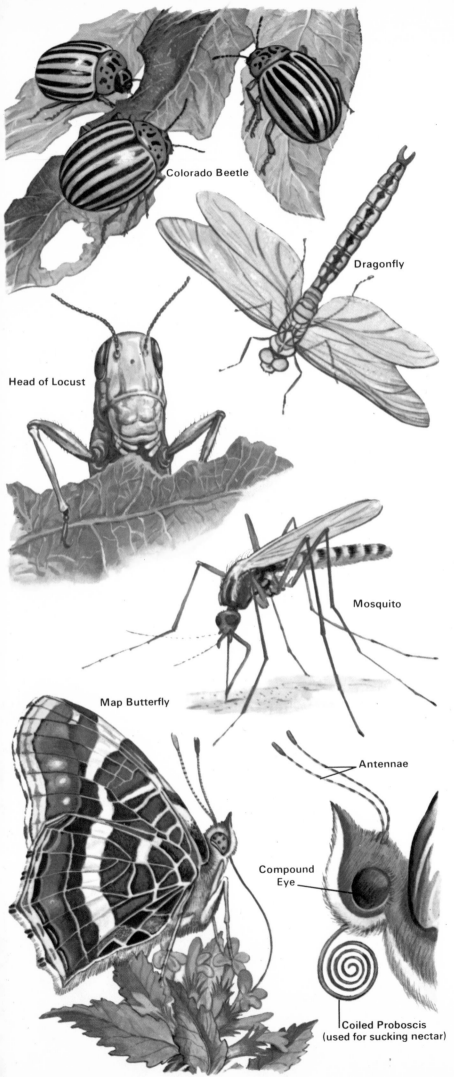

Colorado Beetle

Dragonfly

Head of Locust

Mosquito

Map Butterfly

Antennae

Compound Eye

Coiled Proboscis (used for sucking nectar)

How do insects feed?

Think of anything that is made from an animal or a plant and there will most likely be an animal that feeds on it. There are insects that eat wood, bones, cigarettes, the binding of books and carpets, as well as plant sap and feathers. With so many different foods, it is not surprising to find that not all insects have the same shaped mouthparts. Insects can be thought of as being either chewers or suckers or moppers.

The chewers are the ones that have jaws for biting. They may bite leaves or meat, but the shape of their jaws will be the same. Watch a caterpillar eating a leaf. Its biting jaws move from side to side, not up and down like yours, and other parts help to push the food inside its mouth. There are many other chewers. Ground beetles hunt small creatures that live in the soil and when they catch one it is torn to pieces by the beetle's jaws. Dragonflies hunt when they are flying, but many insects like to eat plants rather than meat. Flowers, seeds, leaves and roots are all food for the plant-eaters.

The suckers are the insects which have a thin tube instead of biting jaws. You will have come across a sucker if you have ever been bitten by a mosquito. When it 'bit' you, it really pushed its tube into your arm or leg so that it could suck up a little blood. When you drink lemonade through a straw, you are feeding in the same way as a mosquito, but the mosquito is not after lemonade! Insects that live on the sap of plants have sucking mouth-parts with a sharp end to the tube so that it can be pushed into the stem of the plant. Butterflies and moths are suckers, too. Their tubes need to be long so that they can stretch inside flowers to reach the sweet nectar. When the tube is not being used, it can be neatly coiled up.

The moppers of the insect world include some of the flies. Watch a house fly walk over a lump of sugar and you will be able to see how it eats. You will see its mouthparts touch the sugar. It looks as though it is using its tongue, because the part which touches the sugar is a soft pad. Under the pad are many small openings that lead into food channels. The fly cannot mop up any food which is solid, so it often has to put a little liquid on the food first to dissolve it. Then it can be sucked into the food channels.

How insects protect themselves

Insects have many enemies. There are plenty of birds that enjoy a meal of insects, and not only birds either. Other insects, spiders, frogs, lizards and insect-eating mammals all need food, too. Insects make good food, so they must try to protect themselves in some way. There are some that have strong jaws and can bite, and others that can run, or fly, or swim quickly, or jump out of reach of their enemies.

But there are others that protect themselves in a different way. Peppered moths are eaten by birds, so to help them avoid being caught, they are very well camouflaged. This means that they are coloured in such a way that they look like their surroundings. When a peppered moth rests on a tree trunk in the country, the markings on its wings and body are so much like the colours and markings on the tree that it is very difficult indeed for any bird to see it. The pine hawk moth is coloured and marked like the trunk of a pine tree, so that it is protected in the same way as the peppered moth. Stick insects of warmer countries go one better than this. Not only are they the same colour as their surroundings, they are the same shape as well. These

insects have long, thin bodies and when there is danger about, they keep still and look just like a twig of the bush where they are feeding.

In the same way, leaf insects have a body shaped like a leaf. The Indian leaf insect is one example. Its wings are a brownish colour and when it rests on a tree with its wings closed, both the colour and the shape make it look like a leaf. There are certain insects, many of them small beetles, that will fall to the ground if there is any danger. They tuck their legs close to their body and manage to look just like seeds or little stones.

Some insects try to make themselves look much more fierce than they really are in the hope that they might frighten the enemy into leaving them alone. Earwigs will act like this. They bend the rear end of their body up over their back and open their pincers in a very threatening way. An insect called a mantid that lives in Africa, has markings on its wings that look like eyes. When it is being attacked, it holds its wings so that it looks as if it is a much bigger animal with eyes wide apart. Quite a number of insects have markings like eyes on their wings. In South America there lives a very strange-looking insect that has a head that looks too big for its body. There is a very good reason for this. Its head has the shape of a reptile's snout and it even looks as though it has the reptile's teeth as well. No wonder any enemy might well be too frightened to attack it.

Above The odd-shaped head makes these rhinoceros beetles look more dangerous than they are.

Right The front of this lantern fly's head is very large. Markings along the side make it resemble a reptile's head. This might make another animal think twice about trying to eat it.

Below These ants are defending themselves by squirting acid from the end of their bodies. To do this, they must push their head and thorax upright and bend their abdomen forward.

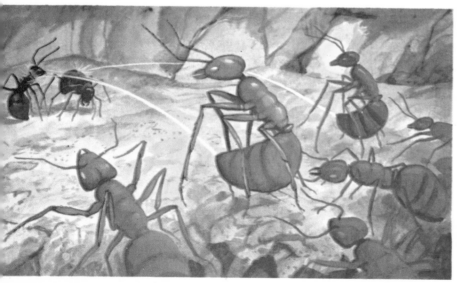

If an insect has a sting, then it really does have a good weapon with which to protect itself. For example, a wasp-sting is a sharp-pointed tube which is hollow. When the wasp attacks, it pushes the sting into the prey and injects poison through the hollow tube. This may cause only pain if the animal being stung is large, like ourselves. If a smaller creature, such as another insect, is stung it may die from the poison. Not all insects sting but some have a very unpleasant smell if they are defending themselves. Some can squirt a jet of poison at their enemies. Red ants can do this very well.

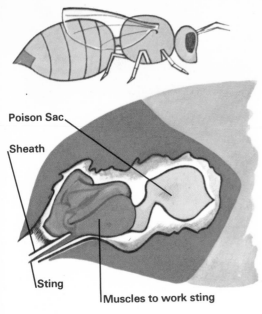

Poison Sac

Sheath

Sting

Muscles to work sting

Diagram of an insect sting

Insects that can sting, or have a nasty taste if they are eaten, or can make a horrid smell, often let it be known. They are usually coloured black and yellow, or black and red. Sometimes the dark colour may be dark brown rather than black. These are warning colours and any bird that is after a meal of insects will not try to eat any with warning colours on it. There are some flies called hover flies, which, as we have said, also are black and yellow. They cannot sting although they look so much like wasps. This kind of protection is called *mimicry*. It means that a harmless insect looks so much like another that has a sting or a nasty taste, that it is left alone by enemies because they cannot tell the difference.

But there is no perfect way for insects to protect themselves. Some will always end up by being eaten.

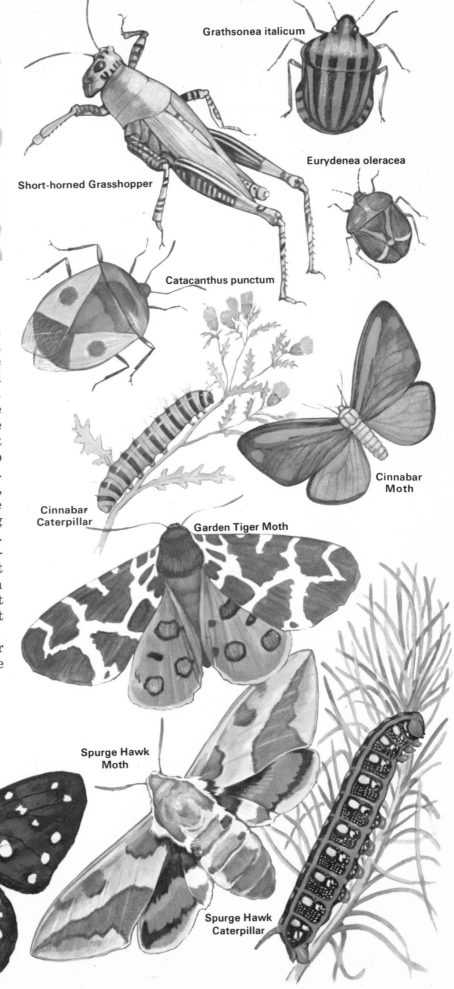

Grathsonea italicum

Short-horned Grasshopper

Eurydenea oleracea

Catacanthus punctum

Cinnabar Moth

Cinnabar Caterpillar

Garden Tiger Moth

Amauris albiniaculator

Spurge Hawk Moth

Spurge Hawk Caterpillar

Serotine Bat

Fish-eating Bat

Mouse-eared Bat

Eastern Pipistrelle Bat

Long-eared Bat

Bats

Bats as mammals

Flitting about in the dusk, just black shapes against the darkening sky, bats seem strange creatures. Although they can fly very well, they are not birds. They are the only mammals that can truly fly. What are mammals? They are animals that feed their young on milk which the mother makes in special parts of her body. If you look at a mammal, a cat or hamster, maybe, you are much more likely to notice

Left Baby bats cling to their mothers' fur, using their wing claws and feet. They are carried by their mother wherever she goes.

that it has a body covered with hair or fur. Hair and fur are really the same thing, but fur is usually the name given to very soft hair. Mammals have warm bodies and the fur coat is to stop the heat from being lost too quickly. You may remember that birds have feathers for the same reason. Perhaps you have a cat that has had kittens and this tells you something else about mammals. The young are born active and not inside an egg. At least, not in most mammals, anyway.

Bats, then, have warm bodies and a coat of hair. Their young are born alive and active and the mother feeds them on milk, or suckles them.

What is so special about bats?

Although a bat may be like any other mammal in many ways, it is very special in one way. It can fly. For this, of course, it needs wings and these are formed from the bat's hands and arms. The fingers are very long and skin is stretched between them. More skin is stretched out behind the arms and is attached to the sides of the body and down along the hind legs. There is even more skin between the hind legs attached to the tail. Only the bat's thumbs are free and have a claw on the end. These are used to help the animal pull itself about after it has landed, perhaps into a good resting place on the wall of a cave. When the wings are stretched out they are large, but they can be folded neatly.

Bats gather together in caves or inside old buildings such as the tow-ers of churches when they want to sleep. Then they hang upside down, clinging to the walls or beams by their back feet. They have become so well adapted for flying that they do not move easily on the ground. Most of the bats that live in Europe are small, often only a few centimetres across the wings. The flying foxes of Java, which are really bats and not foxes at all, have wings that are well over a metre from tip to tip. Some bats can live for twenty years.

There are about 800 different kinds of bats but they can be put into two groups, the insect-eaters and the fruit-eaters. When you watch the little bats darting about in the evening sky, they are catching insects. It must be very hard to find a small insect when flying and when the daylight has almost gone, but bats can do it.

53

How bats find their food

They have a very special way of finding their way about and finding their food, using their ears rather than their eyes. If you throw a rubber ball against a wall, it will bounce back to you. When the wall is close to you the ball comes back quickly, but it will take longer if the wall is further away. When you speak or shout, the sound comes out of your mouth as waves. You cannot see them but they move through the air and if something is in their way, the sound waves act like the rubber ball and bounce back.

In certain places it is possible to hear the sound waves which bounce back and this is called an echo. Bats make use of echoes when they are flying. All the time they are in the air, they are making high-pitched squeaks, much too high for you to hear. The sound waves move in front of them unless there is something in the way. It may be a tree, wall, or an insect. As soon as the sound waves hit, they bounce back towards the bat which can hear them as an echo. If the object is near, the echo reaches the bat quickly, but if it is some way away, the echo takes longer. Just like the ball bouncing back from the wall, in fact. In this way the bat can stop itself from hitting anything that might be dangerous, such as the tree or the wall, but can be led to the smallest insect which it wants to catch. Because sound is so important to an insect-eating bat,

Above Most bats come out to feed in the twilight and they can be seen as black shapes darting about the sky. During the day, they roost in caves or buildings such as church towers.

Below Insect-eating bats find their food by sending out high-pitched sound waves. These will bounce back from anything in the way and the bat will hear an echo.

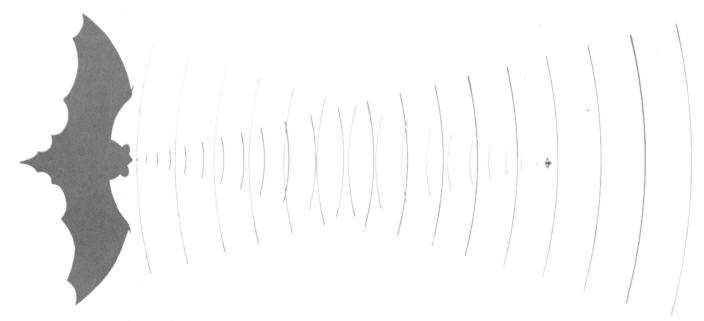

most of them have very large ears and some have odd-looking leaf-shaped pieces of skin on their faces to help direct the sounds that they make.

Fruit-eating bats do not use sound as much as the insect-eaters and so their eyes are larger and their muzzles longer. Their ears are smaller, too, and their face is much more like that of a fox, which is why many of them are called flying foxes. They live in tropical countries where there is plenty of food for them to eat. One or two kinds eat nectar and pollen and these bats have long tongues to reach inside the flowers that bloom at night when these animals come out to feed.

A few kinds of bats catch fish and others live on blood. These are the

Above Fruit-eating bats live in warm countries. Some have a wing span of over one and a half metres.

Below Some bats eat nectar and pollen. They have specially long tongues for this purpose and are found in warm countries.

vampire bats and they have very sharp teeth. When an animal is asleep, the vampire crawls on to it and snips at the skin until a little pool of blood forms. The bat then laps this up with its tongue. These bats can spread a horrible illness called rabies. There are no vampire bats flying around in Europe and you would have to go to Central or South America to see any in their wild state. Most bats, though, are harmless—especially European ones. Many people are rather afraid of them and women sometimes think that bats may get into their hair. This is not true and there is no need to be afraid of bats. They are delightful and interesting little mammals.

Water

Ponds

Life around the pond

A pond is an interesting place. All over the country there are hundreds and hundreds of ponds, large and small. There might be one near your home. If there is, take a walk to it and sit near the edge. There are plants to be seen and perhaps some birds among them. There are interesting noises, too. A soft 'plop' as some little animal dives in and swims away. Exciting rustling sounds among the rushes. Gentle sounds of insects and even gentler sounds of fish coming to the surface. In the water are many kinds of plants and animals. They live in a very different way from those on the land. The animals may swim, or live in the mud. Many of the plants have no leaves or flowers like those you see in fields and gardens. In fact, a pond is a different world, but it is an easy one to explore. All you need are sharp eyes, a net and a jar or two.

When you make your next trip to the pond, use your eyes first. What can you see? Probably some trees with long, narrow leaves. These are willows which often grow by the side of ponds and rivers. Sometimes you can see one

which has had its branches cut off several times. Its trunk has become rather stumpy and grown a lump at the top. The branches may have been used to make baskets or fences. Special willow trees are grown for their wood which is used for making cricket bats.

Around the edge of the pond plenty of plants are growing, but use your eyes again. Do you see how each kind of plant likes a certain place to grow? Some like the ground which is just damp, but others grow right in the water. As you go towards the pond, you will come to the part where the ground is damp and marshy. Here you may see the creamy-white flowers of the meadowsweet. There may be willow herb growing, too, with tall spikes of reddish-purple flowers. In the autumn, the seeds of the willow herb drift away in the wind. Each seed has silky, white hairs which help to keep it in the air. In this way, the seeds may find new places to grow where they will not be choked by too many others. Most of the plants you see will have tall, flattened leaves like large grass leaves. These are the sedges that are always found in damp places.

Ponds are so interesting that some naturalists find they want to study nothing else. From the kingfisher by the water's edge to the pond snails crawling over the stones, there is an amazing variety of creatures to be observed.

As you move closer to the pond and the ground becomes wetter, look for the lovely marsh marigold or kingcup, with large, golden yellow flowers like large, open buttercups. They bloom early in the spring and can be seen long before the willow herb has its flowers in July and August. If you are lucky, you may find yellow iris, or flags, at your pond. The leaves are shaped like swords and some of the yellow petals droop down and move gently in the breeze like little flags. Much shorter than the irises are the plants of forget-me-not and brook-lime, both with lovely tiny blue flowers.

There are plants that like to grow in very wet places and these are often very tall. Perhaps in the swampy parts of your pond the common reed grows. Its flowers are silvery plumes like big paint brushes waving on long stems, taller than you are, perhaps two to three metres high. Or there may be the brown flowers of reedmace. These are like brown, velvet sausages on stems which grow up from the marsh stiff and unbending.

Here are some of the plants you will find growing in the pond and in the marshy ground at the water's edge.

Has the pond any water-lilies? The large green leaves and the yellow flowers float on the surface of the water but the roots are in the mud. The leaf stalks have to grow upwards to the surface. The water-lily is one of the pond plants that likes to grow in the shallow water. The water crowfoot does, too. This is a relative of the buttercup and it has two kinds of leaves. Those that are under the water are very thin and narrow. But those that lie on the surface of the water are flat and circular. The arrowhead is a pond plant that gets its name from the shape of its leaves that grow above the surface of the water. Like the water crowfoot, it also has leaves of a different shape.

Look on the surface of the water. Is there a green layer of tiny floating plants? This is duckweed. Each plant is a small, flat plate, over half a centimetre across. Underneath it, short roots hang down into the water. Duckweed can cover a pond and make it look like dry land. Anyone who tried to walk on it, though, would get a nasty shock!

The Brown rat is often found near rivers in the summer and may be mistaken for the water vole which has a blunter head and smaller ears.

Many birds find ponds good places to live. Some, such as the large herons and swans, need lakes but dabchicks and moorhens can often be seen on quite small ponds.

Mallard

Coot

There are birds and mammals among those plants at the edge of the pond. That soft 'plop' you heard when you first sat by the pond was most likely a water vole. These are often called water rats, but they are not rats at all. Their snout is blunter and their ears are smaller and not easy to see. They are quite large animals. Their body is between sixteen and twenty-three centimetres long and that is without measuring the tail as well. They eat plants and make burrows in the banks of ponds or rivers where they live.

Several kinds of birds live in among the reeds and rushes, now and again swimming out on to the water. Coots with their black feathers and white beak and forehead are easy to spot. The moorhen is smaller and has a red beak and forehead. Coots and moorhens make nests of leaves among the reed beds and lay eggs which are cream-coloured with darker brown markings on them. Another bird you might see is the little grebe, or dabchick. Watch one swimming across the surface of the pond. Suddenly it is there no longer! This little bird swims under water as well as on top and it can dive without a splash.

A much larger bird to look for is the heron. This beautiful bird with a body as large as a chicken, has a long neck and beak. Its legs are long, too, so that

Mute Swan

Black Swan

Moorhen

Coscoroba Swan

Purple
Heron

Heron

Pintail

Pochard

Black-necked
Grebe

Purple Gallinule

Crested Grebe

Weka

Dabchick

it can stand in the water without wetting its feathers. It will stand without moving, looking into the water. Suddenly its long beak will plunge down and come up again holding a fish or a frog to eat. There may be ducks on the pond. During the spring and summer the mallards may have their young ducklings with them. The mallard drake is a handsome bird. He has a glossy green head and a white collar. On each wing is a small patch of purple feathers. The duck is smaller. Her feathers are brown except for purple wing patches. These birds can often be seen up-ending in the water, their tails in the air while their beaks pull at the buds and stems of the water plants.

If the pond is a large one, there may be a swan or two. Swans are the largest birds that live in Britain and they feed mainly on water-weed, but on fish and insects too, if they catch any. A male swan is called a *cob* and a female is called a *pen*, but it is difficult to tell them apart.

It is easy to forget the small creatures, but there will be insects at the pond. Dragonflies are worth looking out for. There are many kinds, all with four wings. Some have long, thin bodies, others are wider. A dragonfly may be ten centimetres across the wings, and with these it can hover or dart swiftly to catch some small insect. Dragonflies perch on the plants by the edge of the pond and can be seen cleaning their huge eyes with their legs. Sometimes a dragonfly may be watched flying above the pond. It will hover and dip the end of its abdomen into the water. This is a female laying eggs. These will hatch in the water and the nymphs will live in the pond. There are smaller dragonflies called damsel flies and they are very common near ponds. So are mosquitoes. There may be many of these buzzing around, perhaps getting ready to lay their eggs on the water where they float like little rafts. Or a mayfly may have just hatched. These graceful insects live only for a day or two, just long enough to mate and lay their eggs.

There are sure to be some insects on the pond, as well as some flying round it. Small insects called pond-skaters can run on the surface without getting their feet wet. Their long legs seem to dent the water, but their bodies are too light for them to sink.

Below This is a food chain. The microscopic plants are eaten by the shrimps, which in turn may be eaten by fish. The chain ends with the heron eating the fish.

Food chains

There are many plants in ponds. Some of them are almost as large as those around the edge. Others are so small they cannot be seen without a microscope. All these plants make their own food, but animals cannot do this, so there are some that eat plants instead. Thousands of pond animals are plant-eaters. But plant-eaters in their turn become food for meat-eating animals. In the pond, tiny plants may be eaten by fresh-water shrimps. A fish, swimming about hunting for food, may eat the shrimps. The heron, which stands so still, sees the fish and in a flash has caught it.

Plants—fresh-water shrimps—fish —heron — these make up a *food chain*. Everything in the pond is part of a food chain and you can find out more about them if you now take your net and begin to find out what is in the water of the pond. Be careful how you use your net. If you stir up the mud too soon it will make your pond-dipping more difficult. Sweep the net near the top of the water first. Later on, push it deeper and push it among the rushes, too. Not until you have found plenty here, will you begin to let your net collect mud from the bottom of the pond. Each time you bring the net out, it is best to turn it inside out into a bowl or jar of water. A small pie-dish is very useful to have

Right A much enlarged view of fresh-water plankton. These tiny plants and animals live in pond water and you will need a microscope to see them.

for this. Anything you want to take home can be put into jars of pond water, but don't put the meat-eaters in the same jar as the plant-eaters! It is better not to keep your pond animals in a jar for too long. Put them into an aquarium so that you can keep them for longer and watch them.

If you have a microscope, look at some pond water and see if you can find any of the very small plants which start the food chains. Some of the prettiest are very small. They are bright green and shaped like curved rods, pointed at both ends. Others are straight rods and some are shaped like stars. Even smaller are plants which have two hairs at one end.

By lashing these, the plant moves through the water. Rolling about in the water, you may see a plant like a tiny ball. This is not just one plant but many living together. You may see certain plants under the microscope as long threads. They look rather like a number of little boxes joined together. Inside each box, or cell, is a green coil. When you collected this plant, there was probably so much that it was like a dark green mat in the water. This plant is named Spirogyra. All these small plants have names but together they are called *algae*, and are very important plants in the life of the pond providing much basic food material.

Larger plants

Not all the plants that grow under the water are small. Canadian pondweed is quite a large plant and so is hornwort. This lives under the water and even flowers under water, too. A curious plant is bladderwort. The leaves are very thin and look like hairs. On many of these are tiny, hollow balls called *bladders*. At the end of each bladder is a trap-door and a few hairs around it. If a very small animal, such as a water flea, touches one of the hairs, the trap-door opens. Water rushes into the bladder, taking the water flea with it. The door closes and after a time, the animal dies. Its soft parts rot and become food for the plant.

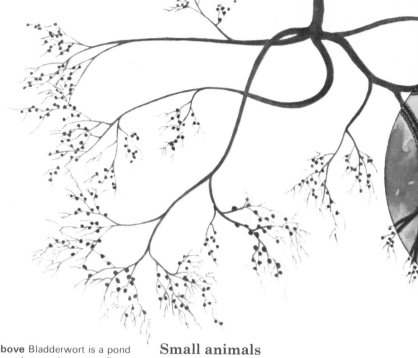

Above Bladderwort is a pond plant that catches water fleas. The inset shows the shape of the bladders that trap Daphnia by carrying them in with a rush of water when the trap-door opens.

Left Daphnia is a water flea that can just be seen by the naked eye. Huge numbers live in ponds.

Below Strange creatures of ponds are 'moss animals'. They are found on water plants. In autumn they form dark brown capsules, called gemmules, which break open in spring to start a new colony.

Small animals

Moving around among the very small plants are the very small animals that eat them. A jar full of pond water will have plenty of these animals in it and they can be seen moving in a jerky way through the water. These are water fleas named Daphnia. They swim with their body upright and they have only one eye. Under a microscope it is possible to look at a live Daphnia and see its legs straining the food from the water. It is even possible to watch its heart beating. During the summer, the female Daphnia lays eggs. They are kept in a space just under her shell called the *brood-pouch*. In a day or two, the young

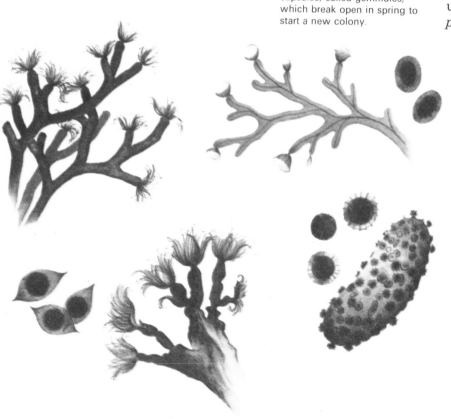

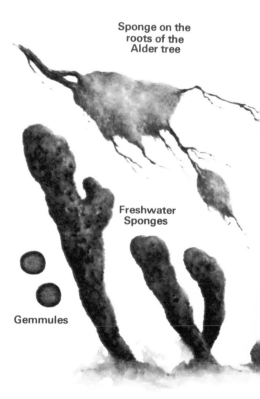

Sponge on the roots of the Alder tree

Freshwater Sponges

Gemmules

water fleas hatch out. As winter comes, the brood-pouch may have very thick walls and the eggs are then in a kind of box which floats in the water. The eggs stay in it until the water becomes warmer again in the spring and then they hatch out.

Another tiny animal has a body shaped like a pear and a tiny black eye in the middle of its head. It is called Cyclops and some of them can be seen with bags of eggs hanging down from each side of their body, near the tail.

Under the microscope, it may be possible to find some animals called rotifers in the water. These tiny creatures used to be called wheel animals. It is easy to see why they were given this name if you can watch one. The body of a rotifer looks as though it has two wheels spinning on it. These are really two rings of hairs which are beating very fast. They make the water move towards the rotifer so that food is brought to it. Although it needs a microscope to see rotifers, they are quite large beside other animals in the pond.

As you watch the life in pond water through your microscope, you may see some animals shaped rather like slippers, moving around. If they bump into something, they move backwards a little way and then move forwards in a new direction. The name of these animals is Paramecium and they are feeding on small water plants.

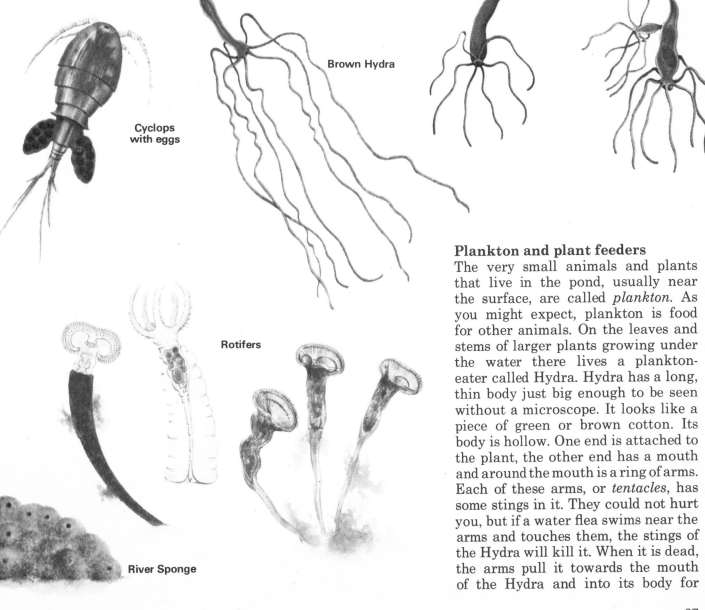

Green Hydra

Common Hydra

Brown Hydra

Cyclops with eggs

Rotifers

River Sponge

Plankton and plant feeders

The very small animals and plants that live in the pond, usually near the surface, are called *plankton*. As you might expect, plankton is food for other animals. On the leaves and stems of larger plants growing under the water there lives a plankton-eater called Hydra. Hydra has a long, thin body just big enough to be seen without a microscope. It looks like a piece of green or brown cotton. Its body is hollow. One end is attached to the plant, the other end has a mouth and around the mouth is a ring of arms. Each of these arms, or *tentacles*, has some stings in it. They could not hurt you, but if a water flea swims near the arms and touches them, the stings of the Hydra will kill it. When it is dead, the arms pull it towards the mouth of the Hydra and into its body for food. Hydra is quite common and we can find it most easily if we bring home some pieces of weed from the pond and let them stay in a bowl of water overnight. Any Hydra on the leaves will be seen in the morning hanging down from them. If you touch the Hydra, or shake the leaf, it will draw itself up into a tiny blob which is almost too small to be seen.

An insect which lays its eggs in the pond is the mosquito. From the egg comes a larva, and this mosquito larva is a plankton-eater. It hangs head down in the water with its tail at the surface. The tail is really a breathing tube so it must come just above the water for the air to pass down it. The head of the larva has two small brushes on it. With these, the larva moves water towards it and strains from it the very small plants and animals of the plankton for food.

When you collect with your pond net, you will be certain to find freshwater shrimps and water lice. These animals have tough, jointed shells on the outside of their body. The shrimps are very difficult to keep in an aquarium for more than a few days, but the water lice are easy. They have a body which is flattened and most of the time they walk on the mud.

Pond snails are plant-eaters. You will certainly find some of them in the pond. One that you will notice is the great pond snail. This has a hard shell, which is coiled, but it grows to a point like an ice-cream cone. The

Freshwater Shrimp

Fish Louse

Water Louse

Freshwater Crayfish

Above Crayfish are occasionally found in streams. Fresh-water shrimps and lice are common in ponds.

Below Life-history of a mosquito.

shell of this animal can be more than four centimetres long. Another kind of pond snail is the ramshorn snail. The shell of this is also coiled but it is a flat coil, not a pointed one. Part of the snail's body always keeps in the shell, but when it is moving, its head comes out and so does its one foot.

Snails move around in the pond eating the algae which grows on stones, wood and plant stems. Sometimes they can be seen upside down, walking along just under the surface of the water. Although they spend all their time in the water, pond snails like these breathe air. On the side of their body is a hole and the snails come to the top of the pond and twist so that the hole goes above the water and air can go in. When they eat, they scrape the algae from the stones. To do this, they have many very small pointed teeth in rows. Instead of these being arranged around the mouth as ours are, they are arranged across the snail's mouth on a movable band. This goes backwards and forwards across the algae and scrapes it into the snail's mouth. When the teeth begin to wear out, new ones grow from the back of the band to take their place. If you set up an aquarium at

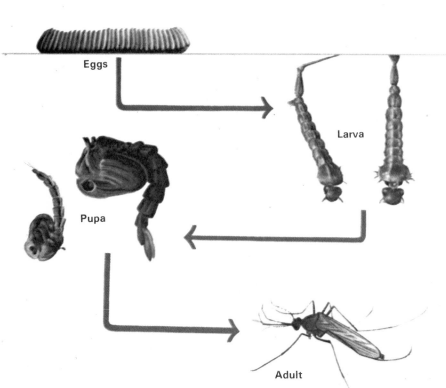

Eggs

Larva

Pupa

Adult

home, it should always have a few pond snails in it. They will help to keep the glass sides of the tank free from algae. As they crawl on the glass, you will be able to see the snail's mouth at work.

When you are bringing up animals from the bottom of the pond with your net, you may find a swan mussel. This is a relative of the pond snails, but instead of having a coiled shell, the mussel has a shell in two parts which fold together like the covers of a book.

Right Fresh-water molluscs such as great pond snails and fresh-water winkles, are easy to keep in an aquarium. Watch how they move and feed.

Below Swan mussels do not move far. They lie half-buried in the mud of ponds, filtering food out of the water. Some kinds of fresh-water mussels may have pearls in them.

The soft parts lie safely between the two parts of the shell. The swan mussel does not move about much. It uses its foot to pull it down into the mud and sand at the bottom. It must not be completely covered by mud, though. One end of the mussel must be out of it. When the mussel is in the right position, it opens its shell a little. Water goes into the mussel's body through a tube called a *siphon*. All the small pieces of food in the water are taken out and used by the mussel. The water that has no food left in it then goes back to the pond again through another siphon. Mussels can grow quite large, perhaps even twelve centimetres long.

Above Pond snails can be found in almost every fresh-water pond. Some have shells only a few millimetres across, but others are much larger. Like land-snails, pond-snails move around on their one foot, feeding or perhaps looking for a place to lay eggs.

Right A mollusc needs a heart, nerves, a foot, and parts for dealing with the food it finds. Its foot may have to come out of the shell when it needs to move, but the other parts are covered by the shell to protect them.

69

Meat-eaters

The small plant feeders such as the water fleas, the fresh-water shrimps and the water lice are hunted by the meat-eaters of the pond. Moving slowly among the weeds or over the mud, the dragonfly larva looks for food. It is about six centimetres long and is a dull colour to blend with its surroundings. Beneath its head are its jaws and these can be pushed forward to catch food a short distance away. The larva, or nymph, of a large dragonfly could live for two years under water, before climbing out and changing into a dragonfly.

Above The large silver water beetle lays its eggs and covers them with a silken bag which floats on the surface. The larva is a hunter. Notice its strong, curved jaws.

Left A number of bugs live in fresh water. Long-legged pond skaters run on the surface. They are able to do so because of the surface tension of the water. Water boatmen and water scorpions hunt below. The water stick-insect and the water measurer have thin bodies.

Water Measurer

Water Boatmen

Pond Skater

Water Scorpion

Saucer Bug

Water Stick Insect

Water Scorpion

The larva of the great diving beetle is a meat-eater, too. Its two curved and pointed jaws are hollow. When some pond animal is caught in them, its soft parts are dissolved and sucked back through the beetle's jaws, leaving the shell to drift to the bottom. The adult beetle is a hunter as well, but swims about after its food. Its body is the perfect shape for moving quickly through the water and is about three centimetres long. It swims by using its back pair of legs which have a fringe of hairs on them. If the beetle stops swimming, it quickly rises to the surface. It must do this often, because although it lives in the water, it breathes air and takes this into its body at the tail end. In the winter, it can sometimes be found in the mud at the bottom of the pond.

Right Whirligig beetles may be found among the pond beetles. This odd name was given to them because of the way they swim in circles at great speed on the surface of the water.

Far right Donacea simplex.

One of the most interesting insects that lives in the pond is the water boatman. Another meat-eater, it moves through the water in a rather jerky way, swimming on its back. The body of the water boatman is shaped very much like a rowing boat. One pair of its legs is much longer than the other two pairs and they have a fringe of hairs on the ends. When the insect is swimming, the two longer legs stick out sideways from its body and it looks like a small boat being rowed along with a pair of oars. This, of course, is how it gets the name of 'water boatman'. Very often the water boatman looks silvery in the water. This is because it is an air-breather. When it rises to the surface, it traps a thin layer of air on the underside of its body and under the wing covers.

It will attack almost any living thing in the pond, even if it is bigger than itself. Be very careful if you handle one, because the sharp-pointed mouthparts can give even your finger a painful jab. There are smaller kinds of water boatmen that do not eat meat, but suck up food from the bottom.

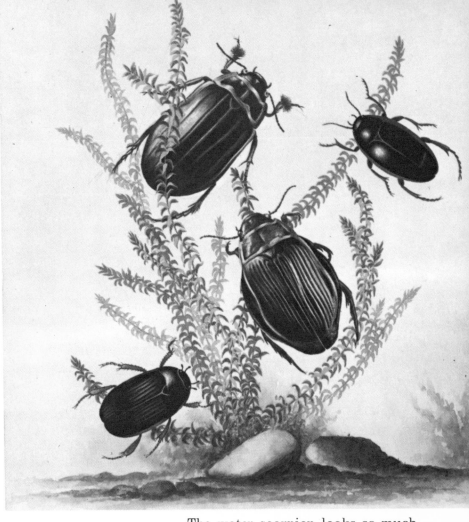

Above Water beetles have a streamlined shape and hairs on their legs to help them swim.

Left Seen edge-on, a water scorpion looks almost as thin as the leaves where it hides.

Below A water spider with its air-bell. It spends the winter inside this silken shelter.

The water scorpion looks so much like a dead leaf that it is very easy to miss seeing it if you catch one with your net. Its two front legs are used for catching small creatures on which it feeds. At the back of its body is a long 'tail'. At least, it looks like a tail, but really it is a thin breathing-tube. Like so many pond insects, the water scorpion is an air-breather. While it is clinging to some weed below the surface, its breathing-tube can be pushed into the air above.

The water spider can often be found in a pond. It looks very much like a spider that can be found on land, but usually looks silvery because of the layer of air trapped by the tiny hairs of its body. Most of the insects of the pond that breathe air must come to the surface quite often. The water spider, though, has an air supply under the water. It makes a web of silk between some water plants which are growing close together. The spider goes to the surface a number of times and collects bubbles of air. It takes these down and lets them go under the web. Soon so much air under the web gives it a bell shape. The spider can live in this air-bell for a long time. When it goes out for food, it usually brings it back to the air-bell to eat it.

Amphibians

Every year, early in the spring, frogs find their way into ponds to lay their eggs. Each egg looks like a small black dot inside a ball of jelly. Hundreds of eggs like these stick together and the frog spawn, as it is called, begins to start the part of its life that will finish with it becoming a full-grown frog.

For some days the egg does not seem to alter. Things are happening to that black dot, but they cannot be seen without a microscope. Then, one day, the dot has a tiny tail. Now each day the dot gets larger, feeding on the yolk inside the egg. The time comes when it wriggles out of the jelly and the small black animal, called a *tadpole*, hangs on to the outside of the jelly. Of course, there will not be just one tadpole, but hundreds of them, all hanging on and hardly moving. A close look at them would show that they have gills growing from the sides of their heads. For a time, the tadpoles eat plants and grow quickly. They lose their gills from the outside and develop some inside their body. The days go by and soon a pair of back legs begin to show. About this time, the tadpoles begin to prefer meat to eat rather than plants.

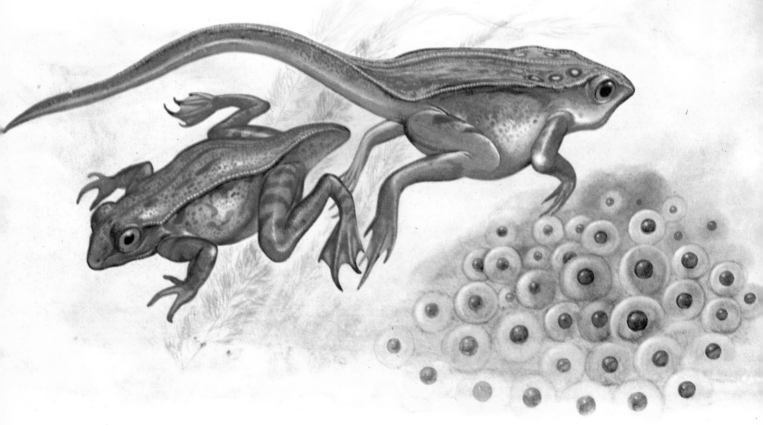

Amphibians are the only animals that start life in water and then leave it later after changes have taken place in their bodies. Notice how a frog tadpole changes its shape. Although you cannot see them, there are internal changes as well.

Front legs appear, and the tadpole's body begins to get the shape of a frog. The only difference is that the tadpole still has a long tail. But this slowly grows shorter and shorter until the tadpole is, without doubt, a small frog. By now, changes have taken place inside its body as well as outside. The small frog has lungs instead of gills for breathing. It can come out of the water now and although it prefers damp places, it can live on land. There is still a lot of growing to be done before it is properly grown up, but after several years it may lay eggs of its own, in the water again.

Animals that lay their eggs in water and can only live in the water at first, then later in their life are able to come out on to the land, are called *amphibians*. Frogs are amphibians, so are toads and newts.

If you look at a frog, you will see that it has a very smooth skin that may be yellow, green, or brown, or a mixture of them all. Its mouth is wide and its eyes large. Its front legs are quite short, but its back legs are long and so are its back feet. When it is on land, it can use these long back legs for jumping, but in the water it uses them for swimming.

Toads are like frogs in many ways but if you put a frog and a toad side by side, you would see two main differences. The first thing you would notice would be that the toad's skin is very different from the frog's. Instead of being very smooth, it is covered with hundreds of tiny bumps, or warts. The hind legs of the toad are not as long as those of the frog, either. So toads on land do not make such large leaps as frogs. They make small hops or just walk along.

Toads must lay their eggs in ponds and streams as frogs do. Instead of the eggs making a big clump in the water, they are laid in a long ribbon which hangs on to the pond plants. A ribbon may be up to four metres long and have seven thousand eggs in it. When they hatch, the tadpoles are very much like those of the frogs' and the same changes take place in their bodies. Of course, if all tadpoles grew up to become adults, there would be huge numbers of frogs and toads. There are not too many of them because tadpoles are eagerly eaten by plenty of the meat-eaters living in the ponds. They may eat each other, too, if they cannot get meat to eat themselves.

Above Toads and frogs look similar but notice the longer back legs and smoother skin of the frog in comparison with the shorter legs and warty skin of the toad.

Below Toads lay their eggs in a long string that looks like a black and white necklace looped around pond plants.

Left In the breeding season, the male toad clings tightly to the female's back to fertilise the eggs as they are laid so that they will develop.

Newts do not look very much like frogs or toads. In fact, they are often mistaken for lizards, but they have smooth skin like frogs. In the same way, their eggs must be laid in the water, too, but the female newt lays her eggs one at a time under the leaves of pond plants. The tadpoles have no legs at first, but soon they look just like very small newts except for the pretty gills on the side of the head. These gills look like small bunches of feathers. In the breeding season, some

Above and left Newt eggs are not found in a mass of jelly. The young newt tadpoles have feathery gills at first, before they develop lungs for breathing.

Left In spring, male newts become very handsome, colourful creatures. Some grow crests down their back.

Below right During the cold months of the year, hibernating newts can be found curled up under stones.

kinds of male newts grow a crest along their back and most of them become orange coloured under their body.

Because amphibians cannot keep their bodies warm if the weather becomes very cold, they usually *hibernate* during the winter. Hibernating means going into a very deep sleep so that very little food is needed. Frogs may bury themselves in the mud at the bottom of a pond. Newts often curl up under big stones.

75

There are amphibians all over the world, of course, and there are many different frogs, toads and newts, although newts are often known as salamanders. In parts of Europe there is a kind of salamander that may grow twenty-three to twenty-five centimetres long. It has a shiny skin and vivid black and yellow colour. Black and yellow colouring is a warning to other animals that the owner is poisonous or unpleasant to eat.

In America, near Mexico City, there lives a very strange kind of salamander. They are black animals like large baby newts with tufts of gills on either side of their head. They never lose their gills and rarely become adult salamanders, although they lay eggs. They stay in the water all the time. These animals are called axolotls.

There are frogs in almost every country and some are very large. In fact, there is one kind that lives in parts of Africa which is so big it can eat full-grown rats. Other kinds are very much smaller and live in trees. These tree frogs have special pads on the ends of their toes so they can cling to the tree trunks and branches. They still need to lay their eggs in water, like all amphibians.

There are some strange toads in other countries. One, called the midwife toad, lays its eggs on land. The male toad then carries the strings of eggs about with him for nearly three weeks. He spends most of the time under a stone and if the weather is very dry, he will come out at night and find some water to swim in, so that the eggs become wet again. When the tadpoles in the eggs are large enough, the male frees himself from the eggs in some pond and the tadpoles hatch out at once.

A very strange toad, called the Surinam toad, fixes its eggs to its back after they have been laid. Each egg slowly sinks down into a little pit in the toad's skin. A lid grows over each one and the tadpoles hatch out and live in these little pits. When they have grown their legs, they come out as tiny toads.

Yellow-spotted Frog

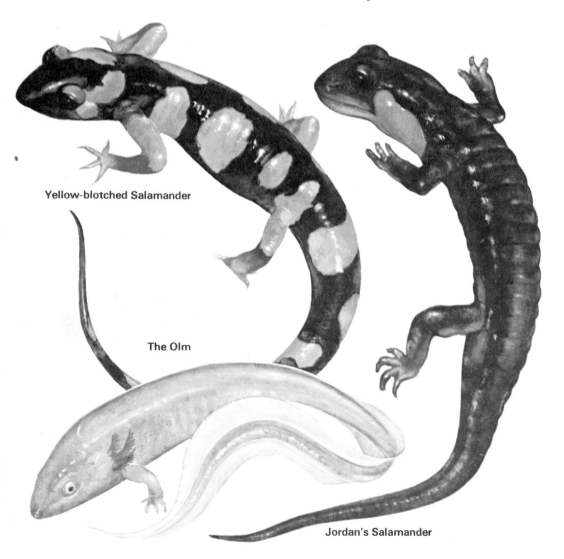

Yellow-blotched Salamander

The Olm

Jordan's Salamander

Leopard Frog

Marsupial Frog

American Green Tree-frog

Golden Mantella

Pickerel Frog

Two-toned Arrow Poison Frog

Freshwater Fish

What is a fish?

Perhaps when you were using your net in a pond, you caught a fish. Maybe it was a minnow or a stickleback. Or have you watched a fisherman sitting by the side of a river or lake with his rod and line, waiting for a fish to nibble at the bait? All the fish that live in ponds and rivers are well adapted for living in the water. They have a perfect shape for moving quickly through it, called a *streamlined* shape. Their tail, moving from side to side, drives them along. The fins that grow from other parts of their body, are used for steering and to help them keep in the right position in the water. Most important of all, fish are able to breathe under water. They do not have to keep coming to the surface for air as so many of the pond and river creatures do. Like the young tadpoles, they breathe by means of gills, so that they can take oxygen from the water. The gills of fish cannot be seen so easily because they are hidden under a tough plate called the *gill-cover*.

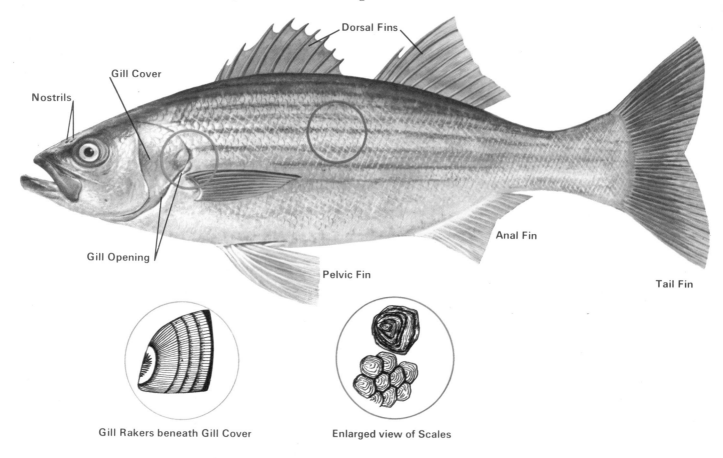

Gill Rakers beneath Gill Cover

Enlarged view of Scales

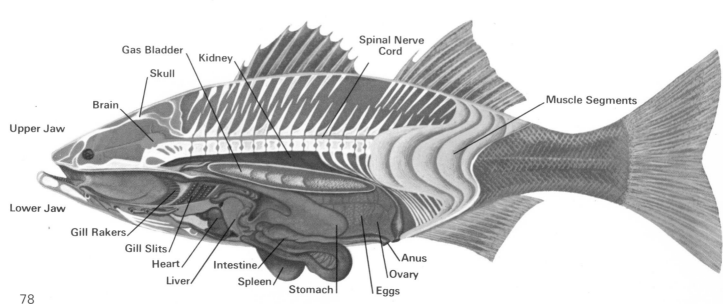

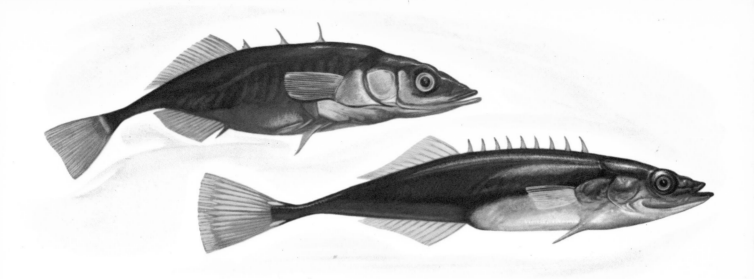

The stickleback

A fish most people have seen is the three-spined stickleback. This fish is small, no more than eight centimetres long, and it is very common in ponds and streams. It gets its name from the three sharp spikes, or spines, which grow up from its back. These can lie flat, but are pushed up for fighting.

Most of the year it is a greenish colour, but when the spring comes, the male stickleback gets a new colour to attract a mate. The upper parts of his body gleam like green and blue metal. Underneath he is a bright red. At this time of the year, country children call him a 'robin' or 'red-throat'.

Now the males are always ready to fight. Often fish are killed in these fights but each of them is trying to claim a part of the stream for himself. When a male has done this, he begins to build a nest.

He first makes a hollow in the bed of the stream. Into this he pokes small pieces of plants which are stuck together with sticky substance. Then he builds the walls and leaves a door in the front.

When the nest is finished, the male leads, or pushes, a female into it to lay her eggs. Several females do this until there are enough eggs in the nest. The females do not stay and the male looks after the eggs and the young as they hatch out. He feeds them on chewed up pieces of food and keeps them in the nest.

After about eight days the nest is taken apart. The young sticklebacks are able to swim away and begin to look after themselves. After all his work, the male stickleback is often so weak that he gets attacked and eaten by larger fish.

Above There are two kinds of stickleback, the three-spined and ten-spined. Sometimes the ten-spined stickleback may only have nine spines!

Below The male stickleback looks after the eggs once the female has laid them in the nest he made at the bottom of the stream.

79

Fish that anglers catch

The angler with his rod and line is not interested in sticklebacks. He is after the larger fish. If he is by the side of a slow-running river, or a lake, he may be trying to catch a tench. This is a heavy-looking fish with a tail that is almost square. It likes to keep close to the bottom, lying hidden among the weeds or poking in the mud for food. The female tench lays huge numbers of eggs among the water-plants, but most of them are eaten before they have even hatched.

In the same kind of water lives the carp. The scales that cover the body of this fish shine like dull gold when

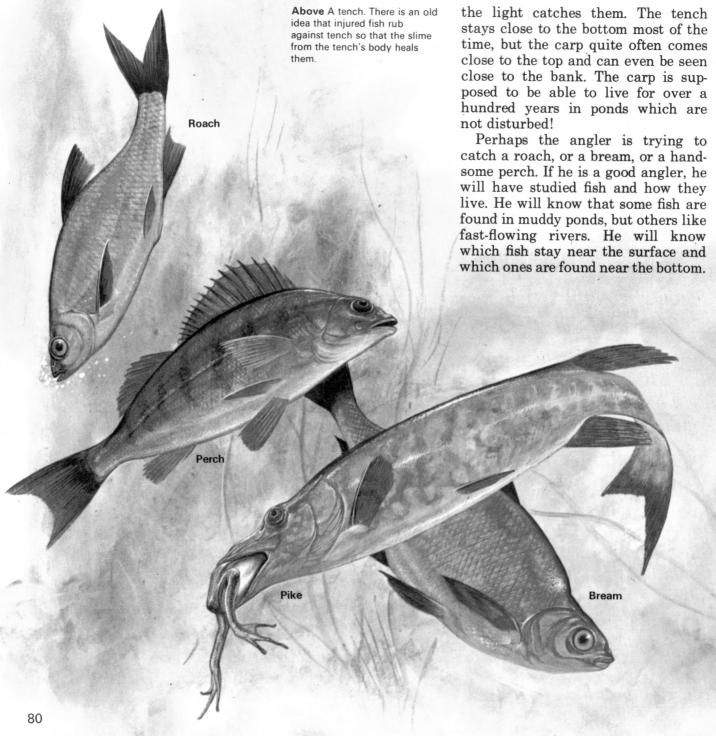

Above A tench. There is an old idea that injured fish rub against tench so that the slime from the tench's body heals them.

the light catches them. The tench stays close to the bottom most of the time, but the carp quite often comes close to the top and can even be seen close to the bank. The carp is supposed to be able to live for over a hundred years in ponds which are not disturbed!

Perhaps the angler is trying to catch a roach, or a bream, or a handsome perch. If he is a good angler, he will have studied fish and how they live. He will know that some fish are found in muddy ponds, but others like fast-flowing rivers. He will know which fish stay near the surface and which ones are found near the bottom.

Roach

Perch

Pike

Bream

He will have found out what different fish eat, so that he can use the right bait. If he is trying to catch a salmon, then he will be standing in a fast-flowing river. Salmon lay their eggs in fresh water and the young slowly make their way towards the sea. They are probably three years old before they get there. When they are very young and small, there is enough food for them in the river, but as they grow larger there is more for them in the sea. But they must go to the shallow waters of the rivers again to breed. In spring and summer, they begin to swim up the fast-running rivers. Sometimes they have to leap

Above When salmon are ready to breed, they swim up fast-running rivers and leap waterfalls to reach the places where the eggs can be laid. The male develops a hooked jaw during the breeding season.

Crucian Carp

up waterfalls. They may not be able to do this at first, but they will try over and over again until they can. When they reach the shallow parts, the eggs are laid in hollows made in the river bed. The journey to the breeding places is so hard that many of the adult salmon die before they get back to the sea again.

The largest fish that the angler may catch will be a pike, which lives in lakes and slow rivers. It grows to be about a metre long and is sometimes called the 'water-wolf'. This is because it is a very fierce fish and may even bite the angler's hand if he catches one and is not careful enough when he takes it off the hook. It hunts other fish to eat, and frogs and water birds as well.

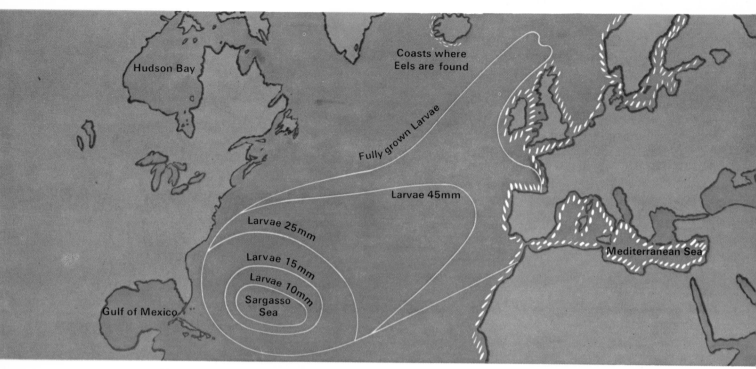

Hudson Bay

Coasts where
Eels are found

Fully grown Larvae

Larvae 45mm

Larvae 25mm

Larvae 15mm

Larvae 10mm

Sargasso
Sea

Gulf of Mexico

Mediterranean Sea

Above This map shows the
journey that European eels make
from their breeding place in the
Sargasso Sea, near America.
The young eels take three years
to complete the journey back to
Europe.

Left Newly-hatched eels are
leaf-shaped. By the time they
have crossed the Atlantic their
bodies have become more eel-
shaped.

Eels

Swimming about in a lake may be
some fish with bodies shaped more
like a snake than a fish. They are
called eels and eels have a very
strange life-history indeed. The eels
that live in our ponds, lakes and
rivers may be ten years old when they
are ready to breed. When this time
comes, they swim down the rivers to
the sea. When they have reached it,
they keep swimming. For five thous-
and kilometres they swim, across the
Atlantic Ocean until they reach the
breeding place near America. When
the adult eels have mated and the eggs
are laid, they are not seen any more.
They most likely die after such a
journey. When the eggs hatch, the
young do not look much like eels and
once people thought they were a
different animal altogether. They are
only just over half a centimetre long,
with flat bodies that look like glass.
Now they must begin the long journey
back to the rivers. It takes them three
years to do this. They grow and by the
time they have reached Europe again,
they are about eight centimetres long.
Their body has lost its flat look and
has become eel-shaped. By this time
they really do look like small eels.
They make their way up the rivers in
huge numbers and they will even
wriggle over land a little way to get to
better water.

Fish to keep in an aquarium

Many people would rather watch living fish than catch them with a rod and line. These people prefer to make an aquarium and very often more than one. It is not very likely that a home aquarium would be large enough to be able to keep a pike in it, or even a carp or perch, so usually small fish from other countries are kept. An aquarium like this may even have a small heater in it to make it suitable for tropical fish. Tropical fish are those that come from hot countries, such as Africa or South America.

Among the cold-water fish, one of the best to keep is the goldfish. This gets its name from the red or golden

Above Ornamental goldfish. Some types of goldfish have very long tails and fins. Another type has the strange shaped head you can see an example of above.

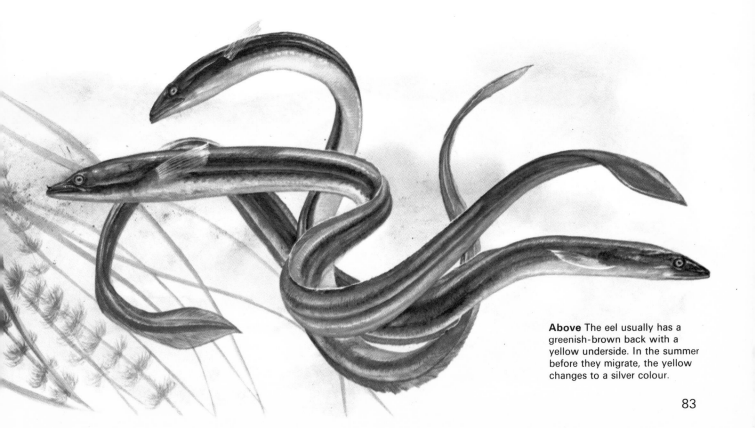

Above The eel usually has a greenish-brown back with a yellow underside. In the summer before they migrate, the yellow changes to a silver colour.

83

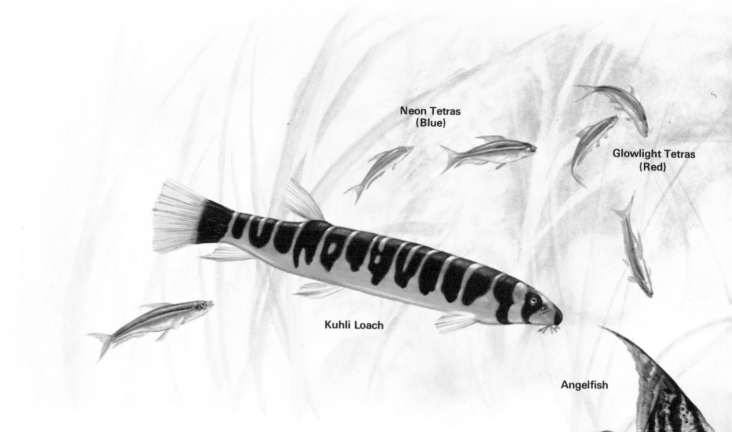

Neon Tetras
(Blue)

Glowlight Tetras
(Red)

Kuhli Loach

Angelfish

colour of its scales. There are now many kinds of goldfish which were bred at first in China and Japan. One kind, the fantail, has twin tails which it holds up like a fan. Several kinds have extra long tails which are very lovely.

But it is in a warm-water aquarium that some of the most interesting fish can be kept. In the ponds and ditches of Thailand, there live fish which are rather dull brown or green. They hide away from the sun among the water plants. If a male fish sees another male, a change comes over them. The fins are spread out and their bodies turn a rich blue or red. Then they will fight, sometimes for several hours. These fighting fish can be kept in an aquarium, but only one male can be kept in each tank, otherwise they will fight until one gives up.

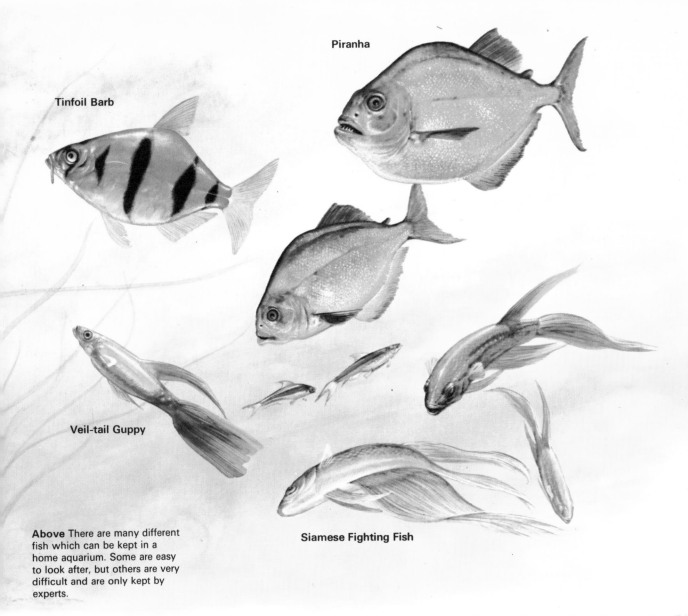

Piranha

Tinfoil Barb

Veil-tail Guppy

Siamese Fighting Fish

Above There are many different fish which can be kept in a home aquarium. Some are easy to look after, but others are very difficult and are only kept by experts.

Below left Siamese fighting fish are kept in aquaria because they are attractive. In Thailand, however, they are kept to fight and money is laid against the outcome of the contests.

Below The body of the glass catfish really is almost as clear as glass. The parts of the body that contain food are in a silvery coloured bag just behind the head.

A very strange fish is the glass catfish. In the wild, it is found in the same country as the fighting fish and also on the islands of Java and Borneo. As you might expect from its name, this fish looks as though it is made of glass and its bones can easily be seen.

The piranha is a very different kind of fish sometimes kept in an aquarium.

Many of these fish live in the River Amazon, in South America. They are meat-eating fish with very sharp teeth. If an animal falls into the water near them, hundreds of them will attack the animal together and quickly eat all the flesh and just leave the bones. In an aquarium, they would eat other fish so they have to be kept in a tank on their own.

A fish that is not often kept, is the archer-fish. It grows up to twenty-three to twenty-five centimetres long, so that a large aquarium is needed if you decide to keep one. It is a very odd fish indeed, because it shoots down insects which are flying above the water. It does this by first taking in a mouthful of water. Then it puts its head above the surface and when it sees an insect it blows out drops of water with enough force to bring the insect down so that it can be eaten. The young fish have to learn how to do this. At first they can only blow drops a few centimetres into the air. The adult fish can fire them a metre or so above the water.

Most people who keep tropical fish like to have fish in their tanks that

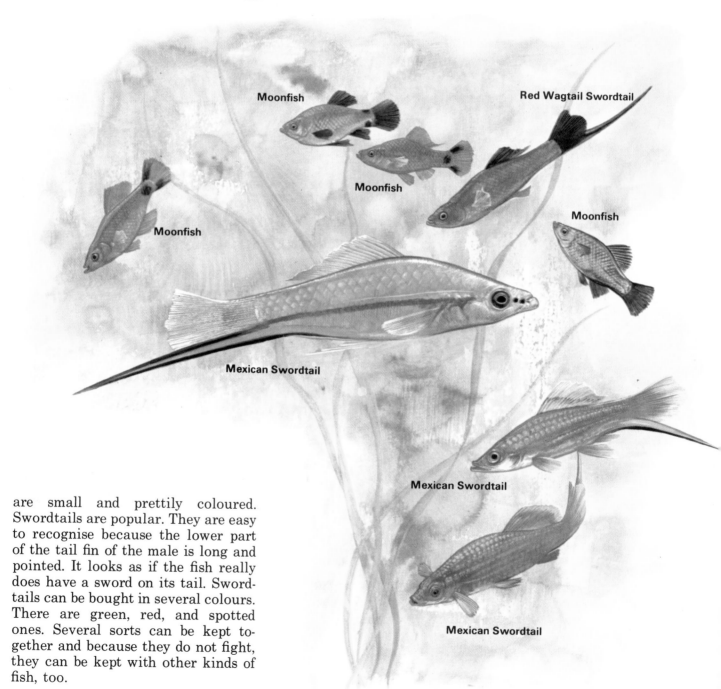

Moonfish

Red Wagtail Swordtail

Moonfish

Moonfish

Moonfish

Mexican Swordtail

Mexican Swordtail

Mexican Swordtail

are small and prettily coloured. Swordtails are popular. They are easy to recognise because the lower part of the tail fin of the male is long and pointed. It looks as if the fish really does have a sword on its tail. Swordtails can be bought in several colours. There are green, red, and spotted ones. Several sorts can be kept together and because they do not fight, they can be kept with other kinds of fish, too.

Another fish that can often be seen in an aquarium is the angelfish. The fins of these fish are large and some are very long so that they trail under the fish as they swim. They have dark stripes on their body which help them to hide more easily among the plants, when they are at home in the rivers of South America where they live.

There are so many different kinds of tropical fish that no aquarium need be the same as another. Of course the fish have to be carefully looked after. They must be fed and the water in the tank kept just warm enough. Sometimes a pair of fish will breed and it is possible to see whether they make a nest. Several kinds of fish make a nest out of bubbles. The male blows bubbles under floating plants. First, the

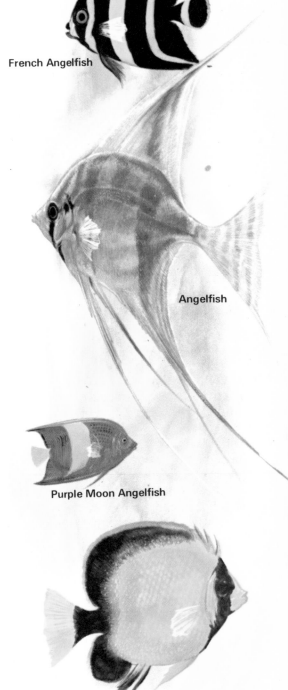

French Angelfish

Angelfish

Purple Moon Angelfish

Chequered Angelfish

Above Archer-fish really can shoot down insects with jets of water, but they have to practise hard when young!

Below right The male betta, a kind of Siamese fighting fish, builds a nest of bubbles which he guards ferociously. He has to keep repairing his nest as many bubbles burst.

Bottom The male tilapia carries the eggs in his mouth. This method of hatching eggs is called mouth-brooding.

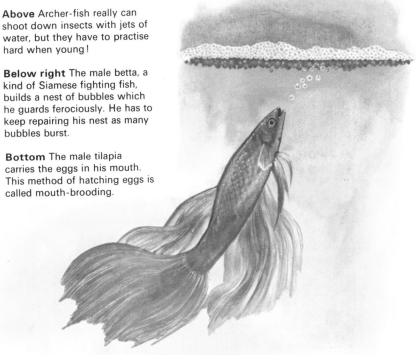

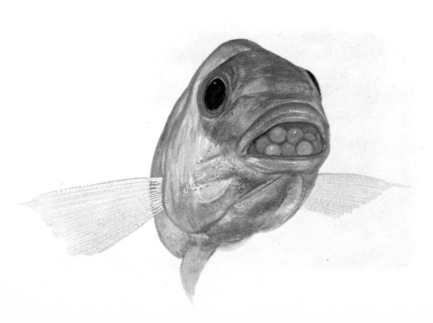

bubbles are large and then smaller ones are made until a big cluster floats around the weed. When the eggs are laid, they float up among the bubbles which do not break up until the eggs begin to hatch. Other kinds scrape a nest in the sand at the bottom. As soon as the eggs are laid, the male picks them up in his mouth. He carries them around like this until they hatch.

Other Freshwater Inhabitants

Crocodiles and alligators

If you were to go to Africa, you would find other animals that you would not expect to find in colder countries, living in rivers. One such creature is the crocodile. To see these animals lying on the river bank, or floating in the water, you would think they were dead. They do not move for hours on end. But they are very much alive. When they need, they can slip into the water and swim silently, using their thick tails to drive them along. These reptiles with their huge jaws and pointed teeth are meat-eaters. They catch fish and frogs, but the larger ones may wait for mammals to come to the water to drink. Perhaps a young antelope will step into the water at the edge of the river and bend its head to drink. The crocodile waiting a little further out will move fast. Its jaws will close around the antelope's leg or head and pull the animal into deeper water to drown it. Then it will eat. Sometimes crocodiles will attack people who go into the water, but not always.

Left Crocodiles lay eggs. Some species make a nest of plants, while others scoop out a hollow in the sand of the shore. The newly-hatched crocodiles are quite small but they continue growing all their lives.

Crocodiles lay eggs. Some let the heat of the sun hatch them, but other kinds make a nest mound. The alligator of America makes one of these. It scoops up mud in its jaws and mixes it with mouthfuls of plants from the marshes. The mound when it is finished may be a metre high and up to two metres across at the bottom. A hollow is made in the centre of it and between twenty and seventy eggs are laid in it. These are covered and the whole mound is smoothed over. The baby alligators make a noise

Above Crocodiles spend much of their time basking on the river bank with their mouths open. However, they do float in the water where they look like submerged logs and are difficult to see.

Below Crocodiles and alligators are very much alike. Crocodiles have a notch on each side of the upper jaw so that when they close their mouths, the fourth tooth of the lower jaw shows.

when they are ready to hatch. When she hears this noise, the mother alligator breaks open the mound so that the young can get out. They are about twenty centimetres long. American alligators have been hunted for their skins. Leather is made from these and used for shoes and bags. So many have been killed that there are now very few of the big ones left.

In India, there is a place where crocodiles are kept for pilgrims to look at when they go to holy places which are nearby. Many of them are supposed to be hundreds of years old, but it is not very likely. Fifty years is old for a crocodile or alligator. Alligators and crocodiles are very much alike. They both have tough, scaly skins. Their nostrils, eyes and ears are on the same level so that when the animal is floating in the water, these parts of its head are above the surface. The difference is really in the teeth. Those of a crocodile are more or less in line. The fourth tooth on each side of the bottom jaw is larger than the others. When it closes its mouth, these two teeth fit into a notch on each side of the upper jaw so that they can be seen.

Alligators have all their top teeth outside their bottom ones and when they close their mouth, the fourth in the bottom jaw fits into a pit in the top one and cannot be seen.

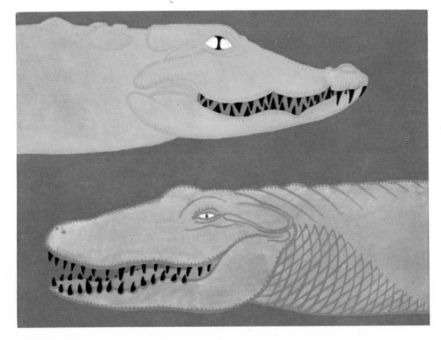

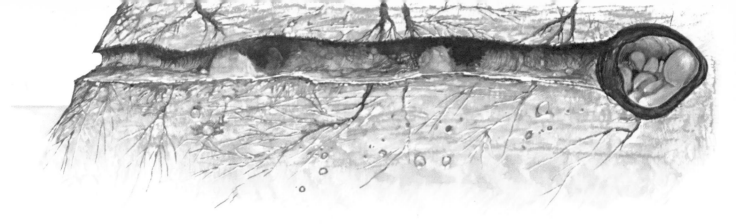

The duck-billed platypus

Australia is the home of many strange animals and one lives in the rivers there. This is the duck-billed platypus. Its body is about forty-six centimetres long and covered with thick, short, brown fur. Its tail is short and flattened. Its jaws are flat and wide so that they look like a duck's beak. Like many water-living animals, its feet are webbed. This means that there is skin between the toes so that the animal can push against the water when swimming. There are five claws on each foot, but the back legs of the males have an extra claw on them. This is the poison-spur. Poison is usually a weapon used by insects and reptiles, but here is a mammal that uses it.

The platypus swims in search of food. It lives on small worms and shellfish from the bottom of the river which it can collect by using its flat 'bill'. The claws on its front legs are used for burrowing. The burrows are made in the river bank. At breeding time, the female platypus makes a special burrow. It may be very long, quite often as much as seven metres. At the end of it, the animal makes a nest of grass and leaves. The entrance is usually blocked for safety and then the female platypus lays two eggs. This is very strange. Mammals normally have living, active young. It is the birds and reptiles that lay eggs. But the platypus is different from other mammals and she lays eggs as well. They are kept warm by her body and when the young hatch from the eggs, they are fed at first on milk. The mother makes this in special parts of her body and it oozes on to the fur underneath her. The little ones suck it from the fur. They are fed like this until they are old enough to eat more solid food.

Above The platypus' burrow may be several metres long. The female makes a special burrow during the breeding season with a nest at the end where she can lay her eggs.

Above The platypus has webbed front feet and the skin extends past the end of the toes. When burrowing, the skin at the end must be folded back so the claws can be used.

Below The baby platypuses are fed on milk made by the mother. The milk oozes on to the fur and the young ones suck the milk from it. Usually the mother has two babies to look after, but sometimes there may be only one.

Beavers

In some parts of northern Europe and Canada there live beavers, which are mammals that not only spend a great deal of time in the water, but also make their own lakes. These large, gnawing animals have always fascinated naturalists because of the way they live and the homes they build. They live in lakes and rivers and may make burrows in the bank with the entrance under the water. Where there is no lake big enough for them, they will make one. A pair of beavers will find a stream, then they will build a dam. Their gnawing teeth are so strong that they are able to gnaw down young trees which they drag to the stream to block it. The spaces between the trees are filled with stones and mud. A dam like this could vary in length from one to a hundred metres. Much of the beavers' time is spent in keeping it repaired. This dam makes the stream overflow its banks and a pond is made. The beaver makes a home, called a *lodge*, in the middle of this pond. The lodge is made of sticks and part of it is under the water. The entrance is under water and when the surface of the pond freezes in winter, the entrance is well below the ice. Plenty of sticks and logs are stored under water so that when the winter snow covers the land, the beavers have food that they can get at. In the summer, most of the day they rest in the lodge. They come out in the late afternoon and evening to feed, work on the dam and play.

Above These beavers are by their lodge. When they carry sticks for the dam or lodge, beavers rest them on their front legs and hold them beneath their chin. The wide, flat tail is used to strike the surface of the water with a loud smack as a signal to the others when danger is present.

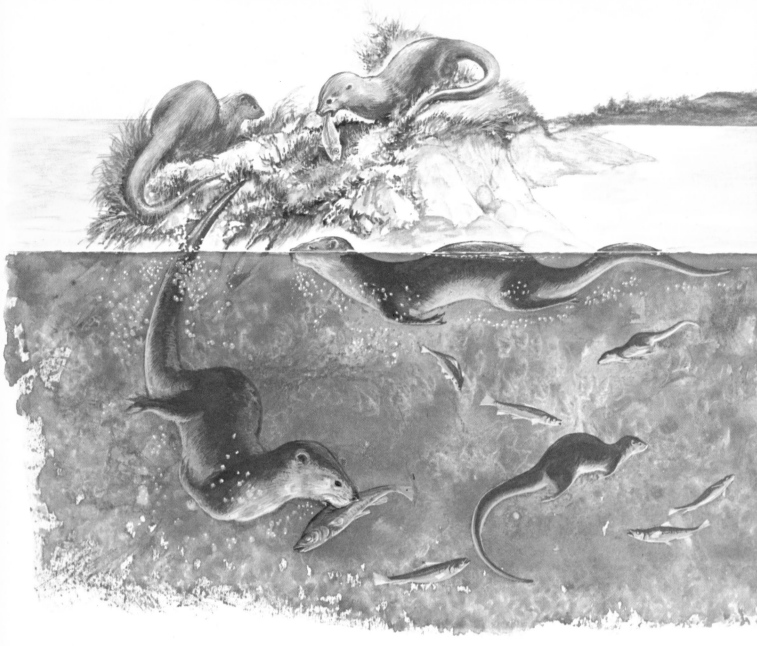

Some more fresh-water mammals

There are plenty of mammals that live in and around rivers and ponds. The water vole makes its burrows in the river bank and swims with hardly a sound. Sometimes when sitting by a river, it is possible to hear a rustling among the rushes and the soft 'plop' of a water vole diving in. These animals are about the size of a rat, and for this reason are called water rats by some people, but this is quite the wrong name for them. They are plant-eating animals mainly, but they do eat some of the smaller fresh-water insects that they can catch.

A much smaller mammal than the water vole is the water shrew. These little mammals have thick fur, even hairs on their tail which is unusual for shrews. Although they swim well, their thick fur soon becomes water-logged. When this happens, the shrew will go to the nearest burrow. The entrance to the burrow is so small that it is quite a tight fit, but this is just what the shrew needs. As it pushes itself into the burrow, the water is squeezed out of its fur and soaked up by the soil. The animal comes out of the other end perfectly dry again. Shrews are unusual animals because some kinds have a poisonous bite. Water shrews have, and they use their poison to help them overcome the struggles of the larger creatures they

Right The water shrew is a mammal that is quite at home in water. It is a fine swimmer but must return to the bank every so often to squeeze the water from its fur.

There are fewer otters now than years ago. This is probably because of the pollution of so many of our rivers. This causes fish to die and so there is less food for the otters.

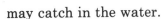

may catch in the water.

Otters are some of the most delightful mammals there are. They are very shy and many people have never seen one in the wild. They are about the size of small dogs, with long bodies and long tails. Their legs are short and they have webbed feet. Their head is rather blunt and their ears are small, so that they are a good shape for swimming. The fur is brown and short. It is made up of two layers. The longer hairs have another layer of very short, thick fur between them. This short coat traps a layer of air in it and stops the water from wetting the skin.

Otters are very playful, even when they are grown up, and often make slides down the river bank so that they can slither down into the water. When the young ones are playing, they will do this over and over again. These shy animals live mostly on fish, but they

will also eat any other animal they can catch in the water and on land, too. They hunt at night and spend the day lying up in a hollow in the river bank, or among the roots of a waterside tree. They can climb well, so they will also go up into a willow tree to sleep. Otters travel a lot and may hunt in a river for only a few days before moving on.

Baby otters are born blind and it is about five weeks before their eyes open. Although otters are very much animals of the water, the young ones have to be taught how to swim. They get used to the water by splashing about where it is shallow, but they will not go into deeper water at first. The mother may have to push them in, or she may tempt them in by showing them some fish. She may even swim with them on her back and then dive under, so that the cubs have to swim to get back to land.

The Seashore

Do you go to the seaside in the summer? If you do, then you know what fun it is to dig in the sand, or explore the rock pools. The seashore is the home of many animals and plants. Twice a day, every day, the water covers the shore and then uncovers it again as the tide comes in and goes out. Have you noticed that on a beach there is usually a line of seaweed left to dry when the tide is out? This is the *strand-line* and is a good place to hunt for things washed up by the sea. There will be pieces of wood and old shoes perhaps, but there will be more interesting things, too. Turn over the weed and underneath the sand may still be wet. Hundreds of little animals jump about. These are sandhoppers. If they stayed in the open too long, they would die. By living under the seaweed, they can keep cool and wet. Replace the seaweed and what else can you find? There seem to be dozens of empty crab shells, pale brown and so easily broken. They are not dead crabs, as you might think. Crabs have a shell on the outside of their body. It protects them well, but it will not stretch. As they grow, their shell becomes too small for them, so they shed the old one and form a new and bigger one. The old one floats away and is washed up on the beach to dry in the sun. If you can find a perfect shell, take it home to start a seashore collection.

Above You may think of the beach as a place to play and sunbathe. However, it is the home of many animals.

Above Crab shells can be found lying among the drying seaweed high up on the beach. They are very easily broken when they are touched.

Left A sandhopper. Turn over the seaweed on the shore and hundreds of tiny sandhoppers will leap about by suddenly straightening their bent bodies.

94

but you will have to be very careful that it does not break up.

Sometimes you can find a 'mermaid's purse' washed up. This is a black, tough case about the size of a flat matchbox, with a curved horn at each of the four corners. They are almost always empty when they are found, but now and again, after a bad storm, one may be washed up which is not empty. Inside will be a young fish, shaped something like a kite. It may look as if it is made of candle-wax, or it may be a greyish colour. This fish is a young skate. Way out to sea, the female skate lays her eggs. Each one is laid inside a tough case to protect it. As it grows, the young fish lives on the

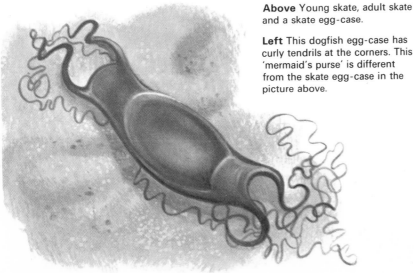

Above Young skate, adult skate and a skate egg-case.

Left This dogfish egg-case has curly tendrils at the corners. This 'mermaid's purse' is different from the skate egg-case in the picture above.

food it has with it. This food is a bag of yolk, very much the same as the yolk inside a bird's egg. Not until this food is all used up, does the young skate come out of the case. The empty case is then washed up on the beach as a mermaid's purse.

Less often, another kind of mermaid's purse is found which is smaller than the skate's. It is not as wide and at the corners are curly pieces. This is an empty egg-case of a dogfish, really a small kind of shark. The curly pieces keep the egg-case attached to weeds or stones. If you can find any egg-cases, they can be added to your collection.

95

Egg-cases of a different shape are those of the whelk. These are found in clusters shaped like a ball. Each case is about the size of a pea and several hundreds may make up a cluster.

Look at any pieces of wood you may find on the shore. One may have many narrow tunnels bored in it. These have been made by a creature called a ship-worm, although it is not really a worm at all. It bores its way into almost any wood that is under the water. In the days of wooden ships, it made holes in the bottom of many of them. Now, it bores into the wood of piers.

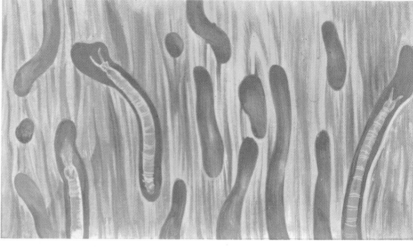

Quite often there are white, oval chalky pieces on the beach. They may be fifteen to twenty centimetres long, but not very thick. It can be a puzzle to think what they are. In fact, they are cuttlefish 'bones'. A cuttlefish is an animal that has no real bones. It is a soft-bodied relation of the octopus. Inside its soft body is a hard, flat shell which cannot be seen from the outside. When a cuttlefish dies, the soft parts of its body rot away, or are eaten by other sea creatures. The flat shell is washed up and called cuttlefish 'bone'. But, you see, 'bone' is not a good word to use for this at all. One can be put in your collection, but after a time, it will begin to crumble.

Above This piece of wood is full of holes made by shipworms. They are molluscs but their bodies are long like that of a worm.

Above Egg-cases of whelks are creamy-white and feel like paper when they are dry.

Above left A cuttlefish. The cuttlefish bone is a hard, flat shell found inside its soft body.

Left A lugworm in its tube. Anglers dig them up for bait when sea-fishing.

Bones of fish are fairly common on the strand-line. You may come across a jaw from a fish, with sharp-pointed teeth still in it. There may be stones with interesting white tubes stuck to them. The twisting tubes were made by a worm to protect its soft body. You know garden worms best, but there are many other kinds living in the sea and on the shore.

If you walk away from the strand-line and go nearer the water, you may walk over a stretch of wet sand. There are some little coils of sand on the surface called *worm-casts* and near to each is a small hollow. The lugworms make these. They burrow into the sand and live in a U-shaped tube. They swallow the sand. Any food in it is used and the sand is passed through the body. It is coiled up at the other end of the burrow as the 'cast'. The hollow is made where the sand is taken into the burrow for eating. Like this, the lugworms can be quite safe when the tide is out.

Most people when they go to the seashore like to collect shells. It is

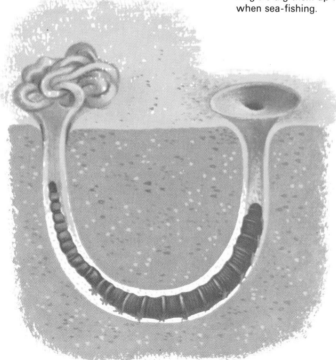

Right Molluscs with shells like these are called *bivalves*. Two of them are showing the tubes used for sucking in and blowing out water when they feed.

Below Here are some of the shells to look for on the sea-shore. Some are more likely to be found where it is sandy, others prefer a rocky coastline.

nearly always possible to find some on almost any beach. There may be the small coiled shells of periwinkles, or the larger coiled ones of whelks. The long, narrow razor-shells are fun to find. They look like the old-fashioned razor your great-grand-father most likely used for shaving, which is how they get the name of razor-shell. Cockles, mussels, limpets and tower shells are other kinds of shells that can be picked up. They all belong to animals called *molluscs*. These are animals that have no bones. They make a hard shell to protect their body. Many of them have a coiled shell like those of garden snails, but in others the coiled shell is much more pointed.

A large part of the mollusc's body lies in these coils, but its head and foot can come out when it wants to move. The shells of sea molluscs are much thicker than those of land or pond snails. Another large group of molluscs have a shell which is in two parts. These are joined in one place to make a hinge so that the two parts of the shell can open and close. These molluscs do not move about as much as the other kind. Like the swan mussel of the ponds, they use their foot for pulling themselves into the mud or sand where they are living.

The rocky shore

If the shore is a rocky one, when the tide goes out pools of water will be left. Some of these rock pools will be quite large, others will be small, but they are all worth exploring. A rock pool is nature's own aquarium in which all manner of plants and animals can stay until the tide comes in again. Walking over the rocks can be tricky work. Many of them are made slippery by seaweed.

Seaweeds are algae, related to those of ponds and rivers. But these algae have changed a little so that they can live in salt water, although not all of them can grow just anywhere on the shore. There may be a stream trickling from the land over the cliffs on its way to the sea. This is fresh water and some may flow into rock pools. In these pools it is possible to find green seaweeds. Some may have fronds which are long, thin tubes. Fronds are the parts of the seaweed plant most easily seen. A green seaweed that is common in rock pools is the sea lettuce. This has very thin, flat fronds with wavy edges.

The seaweeds covering the rocks look brown. Although they do have green colour in the fronds, this cannot be seen very well because the brown colour hides it. These brown seaweeds are called sea-wracks and there are several kinds. Each plant is fixed to the rock by a small, flat piece at the end called the *hold-fast*. They do not have roots as land plants do, but the hold-fast stops the seaweed from being torn from the rocks by the movement of the water. There is a short stalk and then the frond divides into many branches. Each one is covered with a slippery substance which helps it to keep moist when the tide is out. This is why it can be difficult walking over the rocks around the pools. Everyone likes to find the bladder wrack. This weed has small bumps about the size of a pea on the fronds. When these are squeezed hard, they burst with a 'pop'. The bumps are hollow air-bladders. The air in them helps the fronds to float upright when they are covered by the water, swaying gently to and fro in the current.

On those days when the tide goes out a very long way, another kind of brown seaweed can be found. These are the oar weeds. Each plant has a single, tough, flat frond. It is very smooth and may be over a metre long.

Sea lettuce

Bladder wrack

Flat wrack

Oar weed

Toothed wrack

Irish moss

The red seaweeds are the prettiest. These are more likely to be found in the rock pools lower down on the shore. They are not very large and they may be many shades of red. A very well-known one is called Irish moss and may form a thick carpet over flat rocks.

If you want to add a few seaweeds to your seashore collection, it is best to take small ones, as these are easier to manage. Each one must first be washed in tap-water and then put into a dish or bowl of water. The fronds will spread out and then a piece of fairly thick, white paper can be pushed into the water, underneath the plant. Very carefully, the paper can be lifted up and the weed with it. When the water has drained off, the paper and weed can be left to dry. It is best if it can be covered with a piece of muslin, or a piece of old stocking, and some sort of weight placed on it. When it has done this, the seaweed will be stuck to the paper in a good position with the fronds spread out. You must write on the paper where the plant was collected and the date. If you can find out the name of it from a book, you should write this on the paper, too. Instead of writing straight on the paper, you can use a sticky label and stick it on to the mounting paper instead.

Below The skeletons of large sponges are often very delicate and beautiful. The Venus' flower-basket, in the middle of this picture, is among the loveliest. Although the smaller ones may be less spectacular, they are just as interesting.

Sponges

Sponges are animals that are often not noticed on the rocks. There are plenty of them, but not many people know what they are even if they do see them. Look in the cool, shaded places under some of the wet rocks and purse sponges may be found. These flat, white sponges, about two and a half centimetres long, are often attached to pieces of seaweed.

A sponge feeds in a very simple way. The sides of a sponge contain many tiny holes and there is a much larger hole at the end of it. As the sponge hangs in the sea, water goes in through the small holes to the space inside it. Any food in the water is taken out by the sponge and the rest goes out through the large hole.

On the rocks it may be possible to find the breadcrumb sponge. This makes a soft crust on the surface of the rock with many bumps on it. It may be green, or it may be orange. In the cooler seas there are no sponges as large as some that live in the warmer seas. In the Gulf of Mexico, for example, grow the sponges called Neptune's goblets. These may be up to two metres tall. You can sometimes see the skeleton of a sponge called the Venus' flower-basket in museums. Sponges do not have a skeleton of bone as we do, but they may have some hard pieces in their walls to help keep their shape. Venus' flower-basket has a skeleton with the appearance of beautiful glass lace. These sponges are found in deep water near some of the islands in the Pacific Ocean.

100

Above and below

Sea anemones look harmless enough, but to the small creatures of the sea, they may mean death. The tentacles are covered with tiny stinging cells which poison unwary shrimps or other small animals. Anemones attach themselves to rocks and some to shells used by hermit crabs.

Sea anemones

On the rocks near the pools will be blobs of dark red jelly. If you find one of these in a rock pool you will be able to see that when it is under water, the blob of jelly comes to life. Many waving fingers slowly unfold from the top of it, so that the whole thing has the shape of a red flower. These 'fingers' are called *tentacles* and the 'flower' is not a flower at all. It is an animal known as a sea anemone. Watch what happens if a shrimp goes too close to the anemone. If it touches the tentacles, it cannot get away. This is because it has been stung and the poison from the stings kills the shrimp. The tentacles will then take hold of it and pull it to the anemone's mouth. This is a hole in the middle of the ring of tentacles. The red anemone is very common and is known as the beadlet anemone. Not quite so common, but just as lovely, are the dahlia and the snakelocks anemones.

101

Starfish

With luck, there may be a starfish in the rock pool you are exploring. It will probably have five arms, but one may possibly be shorter than the others. Sometimes starfish lose an arm, but they are able to grow a new one. This will take some time to grow, so that at first it will be shorter than the other four. If a starfish is turned over, a groove can be seen running down the centre of each arm. In the groove are many tiny tubes which are the feet of the animal. Where these grooves meet, is a hole which is the mouth. Starfish move slowly over the bottom of the sea after food. They eat molluscs such as mussels. When it finds a mussel, the starfish humps its body over it and grips the two parts of the mussel's

shell with its tube feet. These have little suckers on the end so that they stick to the shell. Now it begins to pull. The mussel tries to keep its shell closed, the starfish wants it open. Very slowly the starfish begins to win. When the halves of the shell are far enough apart, the starfish pushes its stomach in between them and dissolves the meat of the mussel.

The starfish that you find will most likely be a pinkish colour, but in certain parts of the world are some that are bright red or orange, or even bright blue. There are starfish that have more than five arms, too. The spiny sun star may have fifteen arms. The sunflower star from America may even have twenty-four.

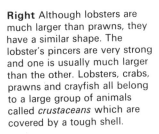

Prawns

Have you ever seen prawns in a fishmonger's shop? They are pink. If you look for one in a rock pool, you will get a surprise. They are not pink. In fact, they do not have much colour at all. This makes them difficult to see in the water. They only turn pink when they are cooked. If you move your hand slowly through the pool, the prawns can be seen darting backwards out of the way. They have five pairs of walking legs. The first two pairs have tiny claws on the end. These legs are used for picking up food.

Behind the walking legs are five pairs of paddles for swimming. In summer, female prawns lay their eggs and carry them in a heap under their body, between their swimming legs. One prawn can carry over two thousand eggs like this. The tail of a prawn can be spread out like a fan. When it wants to move quickly, the prawn flicks its tail round under its body. This pushes the prawns backwards through the water. It only moves like this to get away from danger, which is why they went backwards when you pulled your hand through the water.

Crabs

Hiding under the stones or under the seaweed, there are sure to be crabs. There will be small ones, not much bigger than a finger-nail, and perhaps others as large as a hand. When they are found, they will most likely try to run away, moving sideways on their eight walking legs. But larger ones may stand and hold up their claws ready to nip if they can. It can be a painful nip, too, so be careful if you try to pick up a crab. They eat almost anything, and one way to catch crabs is to tie a piece of string to a bone from a joint of meat. The bone is thrown into the sea and after a little while it is pulled out again by the string. It must be pulled very gently and slowly. When it comes out of the water, there will be several crabs on it. They are eating the pieces of meat that have been left on the bone so you will be able to look at them easily.

These crabs, so common at the seaside, are shore crabs. In some of the rock pools there may be spider crabs. They have very long legs. Perhaps there may be a swimming crab or two. These have flat ends on their last pair of legs which they can use as paddles.

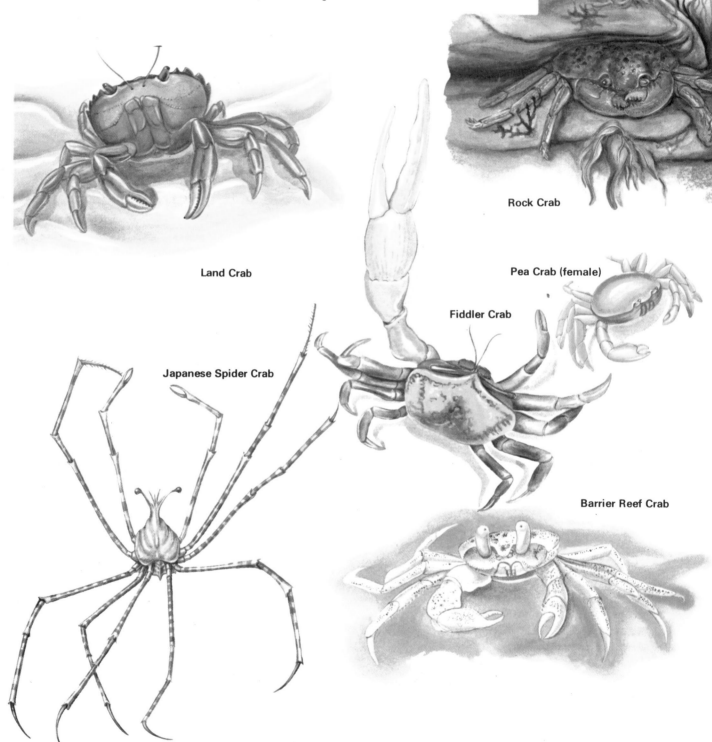

Rock Crab

Land Crab

Pea Crab (female)

Fiddler Crab

Japanese Spider Crab

Barrier Reef Crab

Swimming Crab

It is worth looking for a hermit crab in and around the rock pools. Like the shore crab, it has a shell to protect it, but the shell does not cover all its body. The end of it is softer, and the hermit crab protects this part of its body in another way. It searches for an empty mollusc shell, perhaps that of a whelk. Then it walks backwards into the shell so that only its claws show. When it moves about on the bottom of the pool, its soft parts stay in the shell. Wherever it goes, it carries the shell with it. When it grows too big for the shell, it finds a larger one and changes over from the old to the new. The shells that the hermit crabs carry often have other animals on them. Sometimes a sponge is attached, or a sea anemone.

In deeper water away from the shore, there live larger crabs that can be eaten. In hotter countries there are even bigger crabs. Some of these may spend quite a long while out of the water and are called land crabs. One kind is the coconut crab which is able to climb up trees. It gets its name because its claws are strong enough to open coconut shells. There are spider crabs in some other countries which have legs that are so long that the crab is over a metre across!

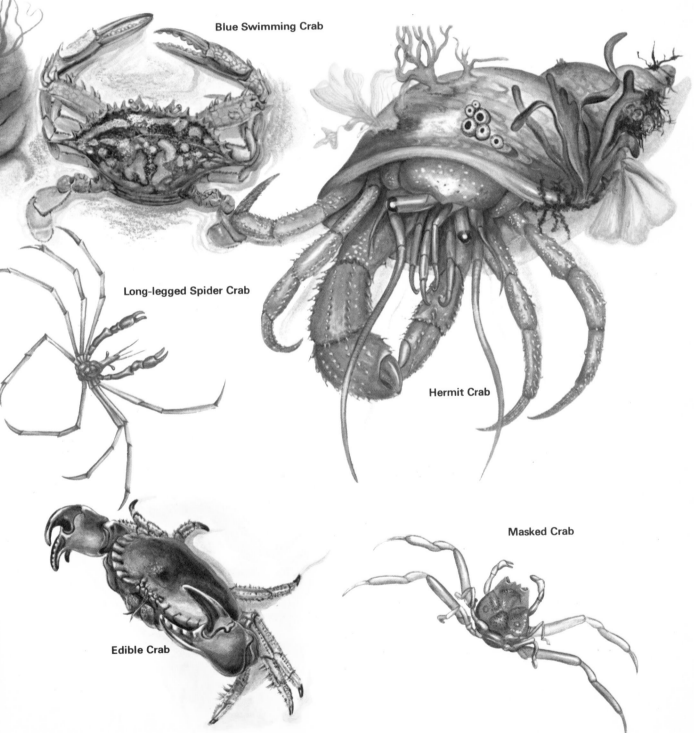

Blue Swimming Crab

Long-legged Spider Crab

Hermit Crab

Masked Crab

Edible Crab

Barnacles

Most of the rocks and pieces of wood on any shore will have barnacles on them. These are little animals whose small, white shells look like little white volcanoes. They are so firmly stuck to the rock that they cannot be pulled off. The hole at the top of the shell is blocked up by four flat pieces of shell. These are like trap-doors and when the barnacle is covered by the tide, they open. The hard shell used to make people think that barnacles were molluscs, but they are not. The young barnacles swim around in the sea when they hatch from the eggs. They do not look very much like barnacles then. As they get older, their shape changes. They sink to the bottom and find the place where they will fix themselves. They stick to the rocks head downwards and grow the shell around them. We know now that barnacles are really relatives of shrimps and crabs.

When the tide comes in and covers the barnacles, then it is feeding time. The tiny places at the top open up and the legs are pushed out. The barnacles move them backwards and forwards, collecting pieces of food from the water. The barnacles kick the food into their mouths! Although they seem very well protected, many of them are eaten. There are some kinds of fish that have jaws strong enough to pull them from the rocks and crunch them so that they can feed on the soft parts inside.

Limpets

Dotted about on the rocks at the seaside are limpets. These interesting molluscs are like flattened cones and they are well adapted for living on the rocks. Limpets have a single foot just as land snails do. When the tide comes in and covers them, the limpets begin to crawl slowly over the rocks. Each limpet moves about to get its food, which is the tiny plants growing on the surface of the rocks. It will not move far, but its strap-like tongue with the rows and rows of rough teeth on it, will scrape away the plants all the time. The limpet has gills, so that it cannot breathe out of the water. When it is nearly time for the tide to go out again, each limpet crawls back to the place from which it started. When it gets to its 'home', it pulls its shell down tightly against the rock. The shell must fit against the rock really well

Above Goose barnacles are so-called because during the Middle Ages it was believed that they actually turned into geese at certain times of the year!

Left Acorn barnacles cover rocks and breakwaters. Any piece of wood that stays in the sea for a long period is sure to gather a few.

Below Limpets are common on rocky shores. The soft body and muscular foot are carefully tucked under the tent-shaped shell. The gills, which the limpet uses for breathing must be always kept moist.

so the rough edge of the shell wears a groove in the rock. Some rocks that have no limpets on them show these grooves, so that it is possible to tell that there have been some there at some time or other.

When the limpet pulls its shell down, it traps a little water under it. There is not very much, but it is enough to keep its gills wet until the tide returns. If you try to knock a limpet from a rock, it clings tighter and tighter. This is exactly what it does when the waves lash against it. The rougher the waves, the tighter it clings.

Cockles

The limpets of the rocky shores feed by grazing on the small plants. When the tide flows back over the sandy shore, the cockles begin to feed again. The cockle, like the mussel and the razor-shell, is a mollusc with two parts to its shell. Using its foot, it pulls itself down into the sand or the mud where it cannot be seen. But how does it feed? Two tubes are pushed up by the cockle just above the top of the sand. Water goes into one of them carrying with it the very tiny algae that live in the sea. Inside the shell, some parts of the cockle strain out the plants from the water and push them to the cockle's mouth. The water then goes back to the sea again through the other tube. In this way, the cockle can feed easily without having to move about very much.

All the molluscs with their shells in two parts feed like this. In some of them the tubes are very long, but in others they are shorter. In many parts of the world, cockles and the molluscs like them, are dug from the sand and mud at low tide. They are cooked and eaten, either just removed from their shells or made into soup. Mussels are eaten also. They do not burrow in the sand, but tie themselves to rocks and breakwaters with fine threads that they make.

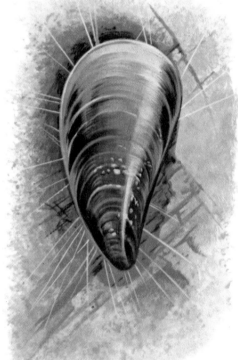

Above Cockles burrow a short distance into the sand. They lie just below the surface because the siphons are short, as you can see in the picture.

Left Mussels do not burrow at all but attach themselves to stones, rocks and breakwaters by tough, fine threads.

Below Five different kinds of cockle are shown here. Some of them are found off European coasts, but others live in warmer seas.

Prickly Cockle

Common Edible Cockle

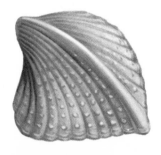

Oblong Cockle

Half-hearted Cockle

107

Heart Cockle

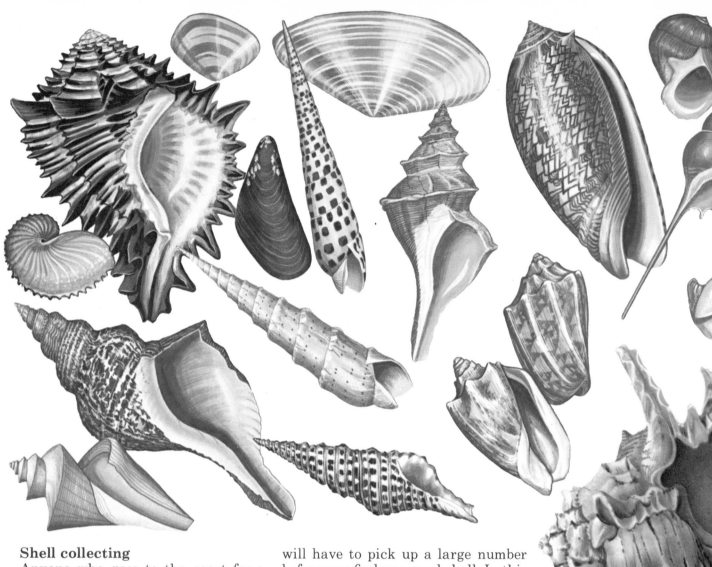

Shell collecting

Anyone who goes to the coast for a holiday picks up shells. Usually they are put in a bag and when the holiday is over, the shells get put in a corner and forgotten, or else thrown away. Next time you go to the seaside, why not start a proper shell collection? Shells are beautiful things as well as being interesting, and once you start collecting, it can easily become a hobby that lasts.

With your collection you will try to show which kinds of molluscs live around the shores of your own country and perhaps those of other countries, too. There are so many different kinds that often collectors keep to a small group. Perhaps one person will be interested in molluscs with two parts to the shell, while another will collect only land snails. But at first you will probably want to collect all kinds.

The shells in your collection should not be broken at all. They should not have rolled about in the sea too long so that they have worn smooth. This means that you must try to find shells that have come from a mollusc that has not been dead for too long. You will have to pick up a large number before you find one good shell. In this way, your collection will not get too big. Each shell should be kept in a small cardboard tray or a matchbox. Small plastic boxes can be bought, but that can soon cost you a lot of money. Shells can be kept in plastic bags and this stops them from getting dusty. They cannot be seen as well as they can in boxes, though. It is very important that each shell has a label with it in the box. You should write on the label neatly the name of the shell, where you found it and the date it was collected.

At first it will not be very easy for you to find the names of your shells and you will have to look in books in your nearest library to help with this. First you must learn to see whether the shell is a single one or a two-part one. The single shells are usually coiled. By the shores of cool seas, they are likely to be periwinkles, whelks, top shells and tower shells. By warmer seas, cowries, conches, olives and auger shells will be found as well. Some, such as the limpets, are not coiled even though they are only single shells.

When you look for two-part shells, you may not always find both parts. The blue-black shells of mussels are often found complete. Sometimes the long razor-shells are, too. Oyster shells with their knobbly surfaces are usually separated and so are cockles and Venus shells and scallops. But this does not really matter.

You may find that after collecting the shells of your own country for a while, you would like to get some from other countries. If you are lucky and go abroad for your holidays, you can collect your own. This is the most enjoyable way of doing it, but it is not always possible, so many people buy foreign shells from shops. In this way it is often possible to get better ones than can be picked up on a beach.

Around the shores of tropical countries molluscs often grow very large. Their shells are large as well, sometimes over thirty centimetres long. The patterns are often very pretty and some have spikes growing out which gives the shells strange and interesting shapes. An interesting family of shells are those of the Murex snails. One, called the dye murex, was used by early Greeks and Romans for colouring cloth. The snail makes a yellowish substance which turns purple when it is boiled. This purple colouring was used to dye the cloth that was worn by very important people such as the emperor in Roman times.

Another group worth finding out about, is the cowries. Many of these are small shells, but the tiger cowry is several centimetres long. The surface of these shells is very smooth and shiny. Years ago, in some parts of the world, cowry shells were used instead of money. Any cowry has a shape rather like an eye and some natives who lived on certain islands in the Pacific Ocean, used to fix them to the front of their boats. They thought the cowries would help the boat to see where it was going!

Some shells are so rare that collectors will pay huge sums of money to obtain one. You will have to be content with those that are easy to collect. In museums you can often see fine collections and also how shells have been used in different parts of the world. By finding out as much as you can about your shells, you will enjoy your collection even more.

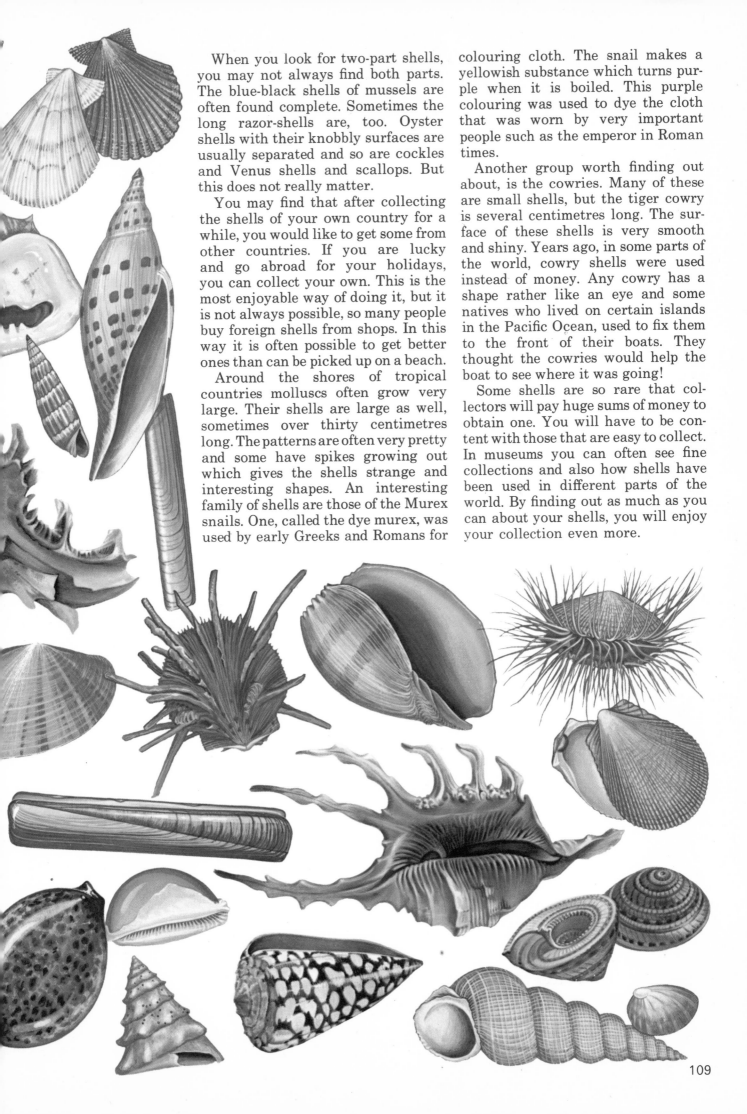

Life In The Upper Layers Of The Sea

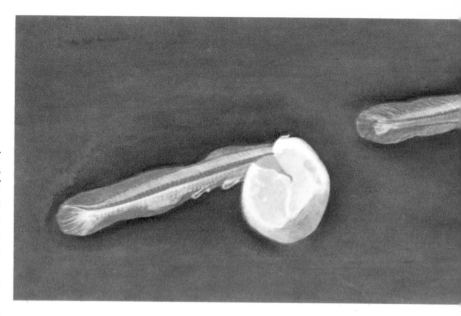

Plankton

The seashore has plenty of living things on it, but the deeper sea looks empty. It is not, of course, and a jar of sea-water has many animals and plants in it. Most of them are so tiny that a microscope is needed to see them. But under a microscope, a new world opens up: the world of the *plankton*. Plankton means the tiny living things that float near the top of the water. There are so many of them that plankton makes the sea like a soup for the larger animals to eat. Most important in the plankton are the plants. Only plants can make their own food. As they need sunlight to help them do this, the plants must live near the top of the sea. If they were too far down, the sunlight would not reach them.

The plants of the seashore are the large seaweeds, but in the open sea the plants are very, very small. The commonest of these are the *diatoms*. They are algae that have only a single cell. They are different from the other algae because they have a case around them which looks like glass. This case has beautiful markings on it. Each kind of diatom has its own kind of markings. When these cases are put under a microscope they look very lovely. Some of the diatoms are joined together into chains.

Not all the plants are diatoms, but most of them have only one cell. Some are shaped like boxes with points at each corner. Others have tiny hairs which lash about in the water to help the plant to move a little. Some of them have points on them also, but many are almost round. A few kinds of algae of the plankton shine with a bluish-green light and a boat splashing through water where they are present, sends up spray which looks like a shower of fireworks. Another kind has white plates around it and these algae are sometimes so thick that the water looks like milk.

It is on these small plants that the animals of the plankton feed. These animals are also very small, although some are large enough to be seen without a microscope. Some of the smallest are the loveliest to look at.

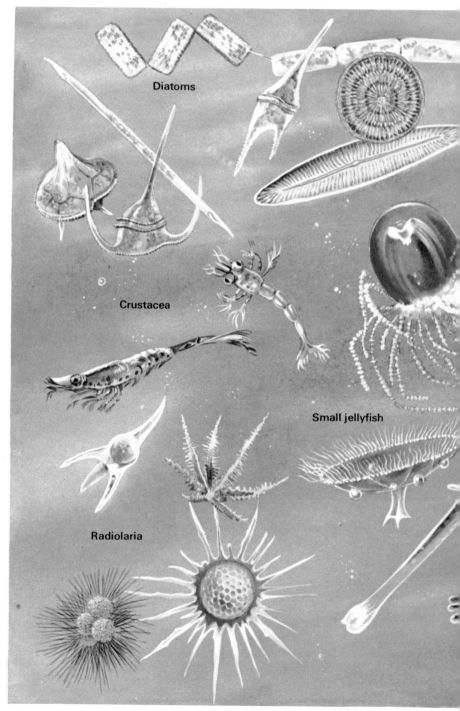

Diatoms

Crustacea

Radiolaria

Small jellyfish

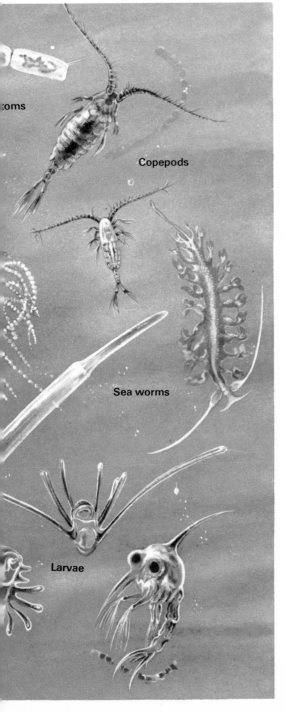

coms

Copepods

Sea worms

Larvae

They are often shaped like a ball with holes all over it, or else like a wheel with a number of long, thin spokes coming out from the centre.

A jar of sea-water will show other animals in the plankton as well as those that have only one cell. There will be animals that look very much like the water fleas of ponds. Many will have the same shape as the sand-hoppers of the beach. Almost certainly, there will be many animals like small shrimps and prawns. Arrow worms, like flat, glass eels with tufts of bristles each side of the head, dash through the water to catch other animals to eat. One may even catch a young fish, for these form part of the plankton. When fish lay their eggs in the sea, thousands of them drift in the upper layers of it, so that when the young fish hatch out, they will be in the middle of their food. In fact, the young of all kinds of animals are found in these layers of the sea and it is often hard to tell what they are.

These *larval forms*, as they are called, often look very different from their parents. To make it even more difficult, they may have two or three different shapes before they become adults. A crab, when it first hatches, does not look at all like a crab. There is a long point growing down from the front of its head and another growing up from the back. As it grows, its shape changes until it looks a little more like a crab, but it still has a tail. Later on, this tail begins to turn under the body so that the larva now looks like an adult crab.

The larval form of molluscs are found in the plankton and so are those of starfish. These are among the

Above Young, developing fish need food. This is supplied by the yolk. The young fish uses up the yolk as it grows.

Below Crabs go through several stages in early life. Each stage brings them nearer to the adult shape.

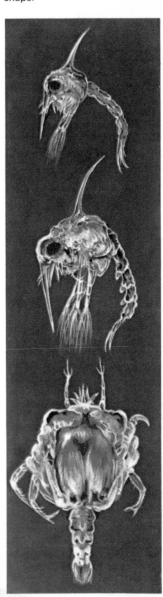

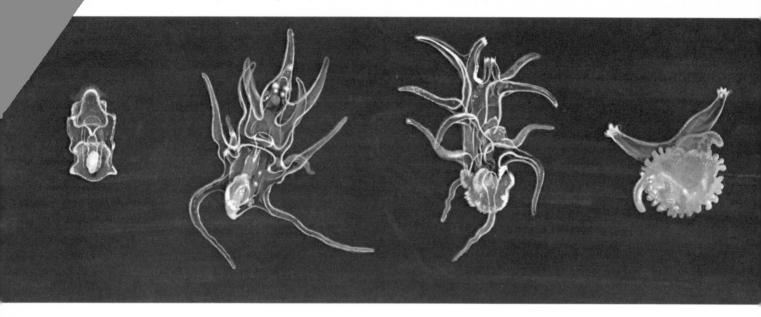

strangest and most beautiful of all the animals of the plankton. They go through several stages in their life and each stage is able to move by bands of tiny beating hairs. It seems odd that an animal which is going to spend most of its life crawling on the sea-floor should start life in the plankton, but only in this way can the larva get plenty of food.

If you have a microscope and live near the seaside, you can find out much more about the plankton for yourself. Scientists who study plankton use a special net made out of silk or nylon. It is shaped like an ice-cream cone with the bottom cut off. Into this hole is tied a glass tube. The net is fixed to a long rope and taken out to sea. It is thrown into the water and towed slowly behind the boat. When it is pulled out, the glass tube is full of plankton. There is no need to go out to sea in a boat to get some. If one of these nets is lowered from the end of a pier, some can be collected. If you do not have a plankton net, then it is worth while using a bottle or a jar and finding out what you can collect in this way.

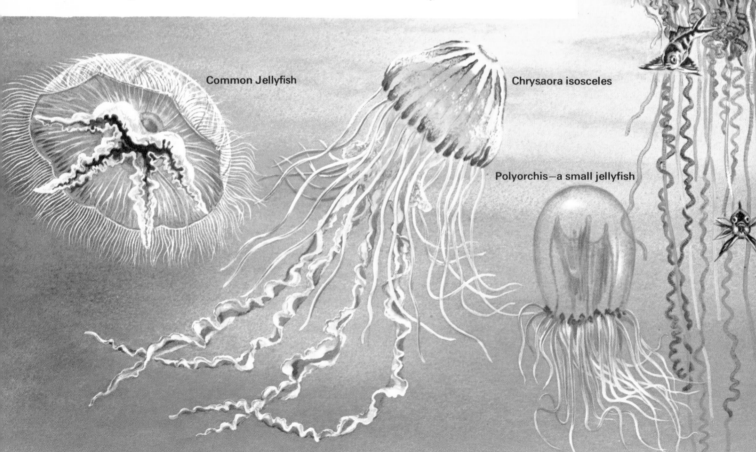

Common Jellyfish

Chrysaora isosceles

Polyorchis—a small jellyfish

Left A starfish larva changes shape as it grows. The parts that look like arms are bands of tiny beating hairs. At first, the starfish is part of the plankton which live near the surface of the sea but much later, it becomes a bottom-feeding animal.

Below right A jellyfish egg usually develops into a creature which is similar to the Hydra found in ponds. In early spring, this creature produces a number of small, star-shaped larvae which grow into large jellyfish.

Jellyfish

Have you ever seen a jellyfish washed up on the beach? It looks a very uninteresting thing. But to see one alive and swimming is very different. Opening and closing like a living umbrella, the jellyfish drifts through the water. Beneath the umbrella are the mouth and the tentacles that sting and kill the animals that the jellyfish eats. There are jellyfish which are large enough to sting people. The sting is painful and can make some people very ill. One relative of jellyfish that comes near Britain now and again is the Portuguese man-of-war, a strange name for a sea animal! Part of it is a bag of gas which floats on top of the water. This float may be thirty centimetres long and is a blue or green colour. The stinging tentacles hang down in a long cluster from under the float. Luckily, these creatures do not get blown to British shores very often. A blue jellyfish that is fairly common around the British coast may be nearly a metre across. But in the Arctic Ocean some monster jellyfish have been found that are as large as two metres across!

These large jellyfish have distant cousins, little jellyfish which look like buttons. They are found in the plankton, moving in just the same way as the large ones and catching their food in the same way, too.

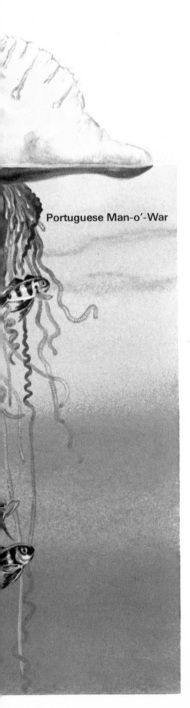

Portuguese Man-o'-War

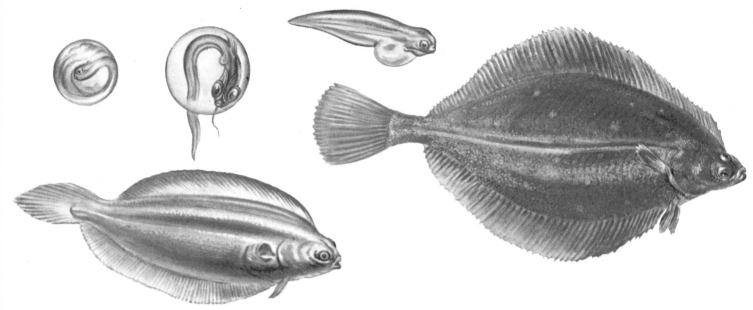

Fish

If you take a walk to a fishmonger's shop, you will see that he sells many kinds of fish for us to eat. Some, like sprats, are small and we need quite a number of them for a meal. Larger ones, like herrings, are sold one or two at a time. The very large cod and hake are so big that the fishmonger cuts them up and only a small piece is needed at a time. Some of the fish are not the shape we always think of as a fish-shape. Instead, they look flattened. These flat-fish, when they were alive, lived near the bottom of the sea. They could rest on the sea-bed and the colour of their skin matched the colour of the sand or mud where they were. In fact, these flat-fish swim on their side. A very strange thing about them is that when they first hatch, they swim like any other fish. Then they begin to tilt over until they swim on their side all the time. As they begin to tilt, the eye on the lower side of the fish's head very slowly moves round to the other side. At the finish, both eyes are on the same side! In this way, when the fish is on the bottom, it is able to use both its eyes to see. Among the many kinds of flat-fish are plaice, sole and halibut.

Above A newly-hatched plaice swims like any other young fish. As it develops, it begins to tilt and the lower eye moves around its head. Now it is a small flat-fish, well-suited to living near the sea bed.

Fish provide us with a great deal of fresh food. All the fish in this picture can be seen during the year in a fishmonger's shop.

Cod

Mackerel

Skate

Sprats

Herring

Hake

Haddock

Turbot

Plaice

115

Food chains

Just as there are food chains in ponds, so there are other food chains in the sea. At the beginning of them all are the plants of the plankton. These in turn feed the animals of the plankton. Together, these animals and plants are food for huge numbers of other sea animals. Many of the fish we eat are plankton feeders and so are the huge blue whales, the largest of all living animals. Dead and dying animals of the upper layers of the sea drift down to the bottom. There they are attacked by starfish and molluscs of all kinds; by crabs and by worms. These in turn become the food for fish that live near the bottom. Cod and haddock eat near the sea bed and feed on these creatures. At the other end of the food chains comes man, always hunting the fish and whales, for food and oils.

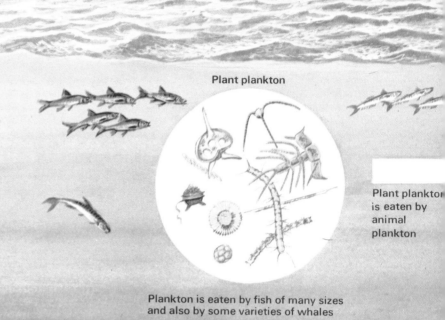

Plant plankton

Plant plankton is eaten by animal plankton

Plankton is eaten by fish of many sizes and also by some varieties of whales

116

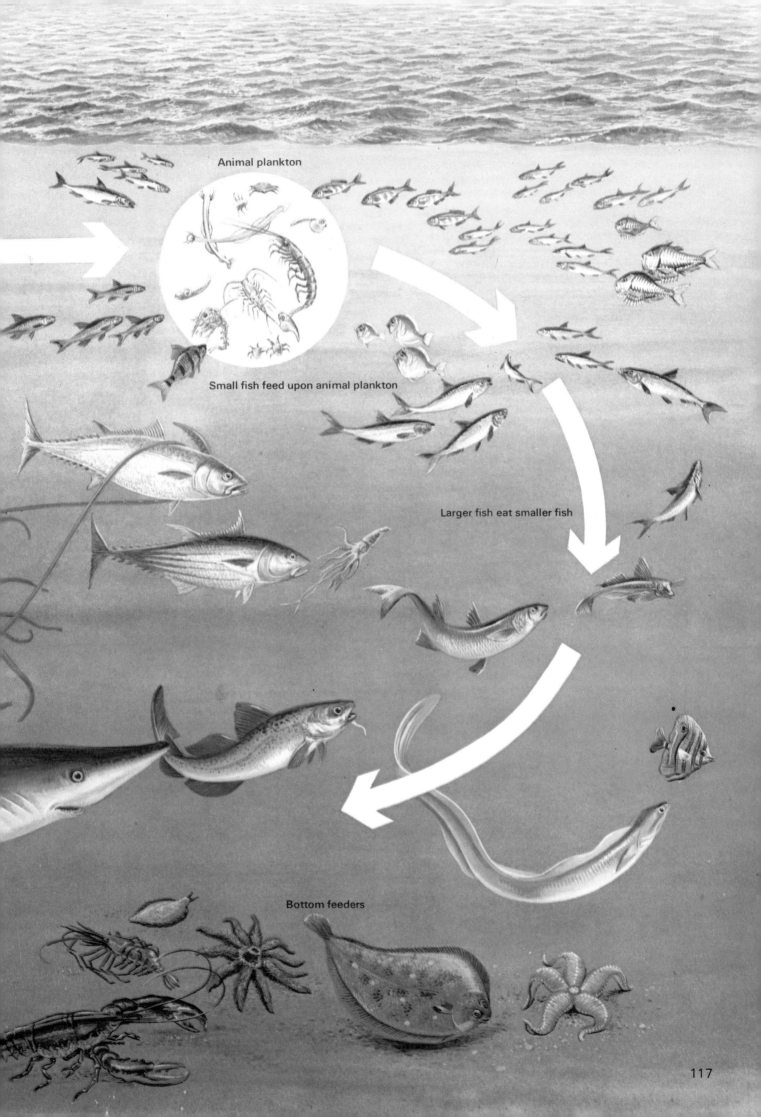

Animal plankton

Small fish feed upon animal plankton

Larger fish eat smaller fish

Bottom feeders

Catching fish

To catch fish for us to eat, fleets of ships have to go to sea, often in very bad weather. The kinds of fish they are looking for are found in deep water. Some parts of the sea are better for fishing than others and these *fishing-grounds* are many miles from our coasts, often in the colder seas. The fishing boats are called *trawlers* or *drifters* depending on which way they are going to catch the fish.

To catch the plankton-feeders such as herring, mackerel and pilchards, a net is used near the surface. It is a very long net that has cork, glass or plastic floats fixed to it. When the net is put into the sea, it hangs like a curtain down into the water, held up by the floats. The net is held to the ship by a rope and when fishing starts, the engines of the ship are stopped and it just drifts. This is the type of fishing that is called *drifting*, so the fishing-boat used is a drifter. The fish that are swimming near the surface to eat the plankton get caught in the mesh of the nets. After drifting for some time, the net is pulled in and the fish shaken from the net into the boat. The net may be put out again in the same place, or the ship may go somewhere else.

Trawling is a very different method of fishing. It is the way to catch those fish like cod, haddock, plaice and skate which live close to the sea-bed. The net used is called the trawl. It is a

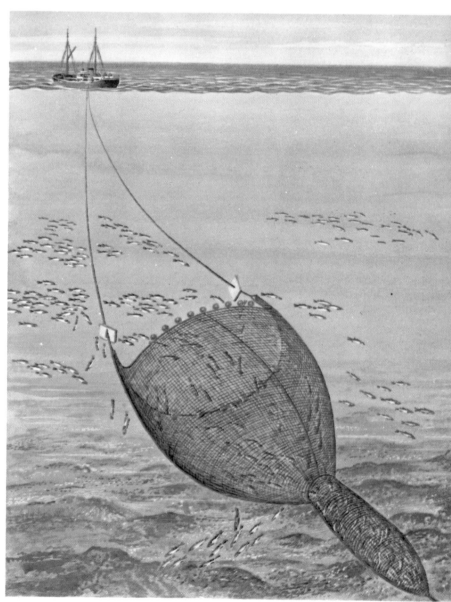

Left Drift-net fishing is designed to catch fish that swim fairly close to the surface. The net can be nearly three kilometres long and huge numbers of fish are caught. Pulling in the nets is a long heavy job and then the fish have to be shaken from the nets to release them.

Right This African fisherman is throwing a circular net from the front of a canoe. He will probably catch only a few fish, but it does not take long to pull in the net, shake out any fish and try again. Nets that are small enough to be thrown by hand are used in many parts of the world.

Left Trawling is the method used to catch fish that live close to the sea bed. There are several different types of trawl but they are all cone-shaped so that the fish are gathered at the narrow end. The mouth of the net is kept open by the water pushing against two boards called 'otter-boards'.

Below In some parts of the world, the Canary Islands for example, the fishermen take their boats out at night carrying large lamps to attract the fish to the water's surface.

large net, shaped like a cone. Very heavy weights have to be put on it so that it will sink to the bottom. The trawl has a very long rope on it. One end is fixed to the front of the net and the other end to the boat, called the trawler. When the net is lowered over the side of the trawler, it goes down to the bottom. The trawler then begins to move and it pulls the net along the sea bed, catching the fish that are feeding or resting there. When it is at last pulled up, full of fish, the end of the net can be opened so that the catch falls into the ship.

Fishing of some kind is done all over the world. Not all the fishing fleets have big, modern ships. In many countries the fishing boats are small, wooden ones. They may have a simple square sail to help them get to the fishing-ground, or the fishermen may row the boat out. In some places, the fishing-boats go out at night with large lamps fixed to them. The lights seem to bring the fish nearer the surface and towards the boats so they can be caught more easily. In parts of Africa, the fishermen may not even have boats. Instead, they wade into the sea and throw their nets out by hand to catch a few fish if they are lucky. It does not matter how they catch fish, fishermen are very important people. Without them, there would be far less food to eat than there is now.

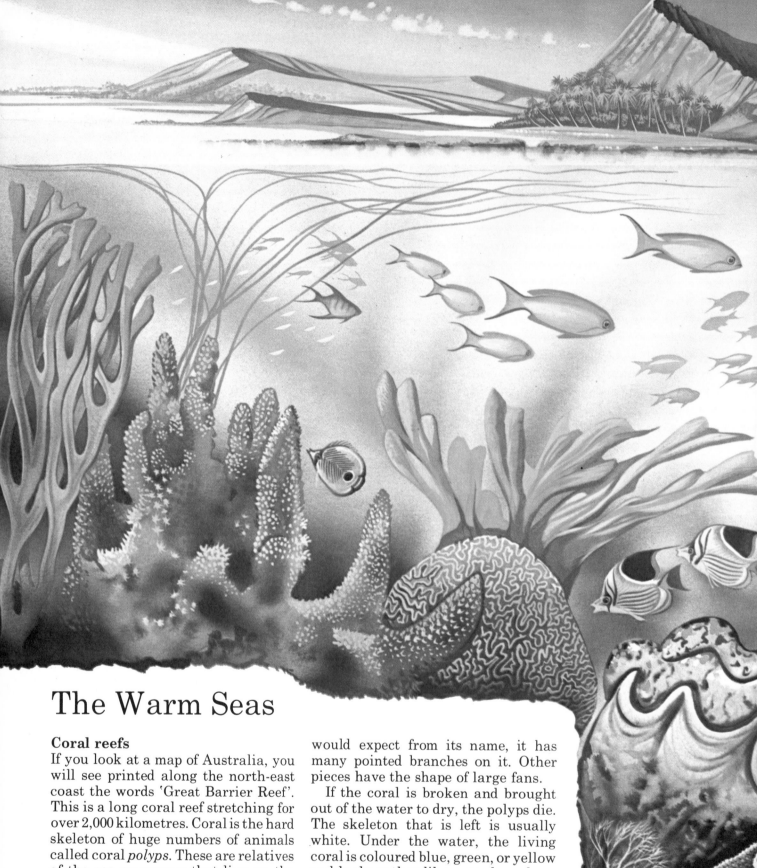

The Warm Seas

Coral reefs

If you look at a map of Australia, you will see printed along the north-east coast the words 'Great Barrier Reef'. This is a long coral reef stretching for over 2,000 kilometres. Coral is the hard skeleton of huge numbers of animals called coral *polyps*. These are relatives of the sea anemones that live on the rocky shores. The coral polyps look like small sea anemones but they make a hard skeleton to support themselves. The skeleton is cup-shaped and the polyp grows in the top of it. When the polyps are very close to one another, the skeletons join together. In this way, large pieces of coral are formed. Some look like the antlers of deer and this is called stag's-horn coral. As you would expect from its name, it has many pointed branches on it. Other pieces have the shape of large fans.

If the coral is broken and brought out of the water to dry, the polyps die. The skeleton that is left is usually white. Under the water, the living coral is coloured blue, green, or yellow and looks rather like a garden where all the flowers are in bloom. When masses of coral grow a little way out from the shore, it is called a *reef*. Coral likes to grow in warm seas so reefs are found only in hot parts of the world. They are dangerous to sailors because the sharp points of the coral are often only a little way under the water, and could easily tear the bottom out of a boat.

Tourists enjoy seeing reefs if they can because the coral is so beautifully coloured and because bright coloured fish swim in and out amongst it, too. There are molluscs as well, and shell collectors may visit reefs when they are uncovered by the tide to see what shells they can find. Now that skin divers can stay under water for quite a long time, people on holiday in countries where there are reefs are able to swim down to explore them.

Giant clams

Some of the molluscs that live on the coral reefs are the giant clams. These have two parts to their shell and they may bore their way right into the coral, or they may stay on top. Which-ever they do, the opening of the shell always lies upwards. The soft part which shows when the shell is open is usually green with perhaps some yellow in it. These clams may be a metre or more across, but they do not catch food by closing their shell and trapping fish. They get food in an unexpected way. The green colour of the soft parts is caused by small algae living in the clam. These tiny plants are able to make food, of course, and the clam is able to feed on this. Swimmers near reefs, or people walking over them at low tide, have to watch for clams. If they put their foot into one it could close its shell up. The person would be trapped and it might be difficult to free him.

The octopus, squid and cuttlefish

The octopus, the squid and the cuttlefish are relatives of snails and clams, but they do not look very much like them. They are molluscs that have no shell on the outside of their body. Perhaps this is because they hunt their food and they can move more quickly without one. Many people shudder at the thought of an octopus but there are many wrong ideas about them. The eight arms that grow from the head of an octopus are used for crawling over the sea-bed and for capturing food. The octopus feeds on a large number of crabs and attacks them from behind so that the crabs cannot use their claws to defend themselves. The arms have suckers along the underside so that the octopus can hold its prey very firmly.

There are many animals that can change colour to help them blend in with their surroundings. The octopus can do this, too. It is able to hide itself between rocks and become very difficult to see. This helps when catching food because crabs will get very near and not see the octopus until it is too late. If it is frightened and wants to move quickly, an octopus jet propels itself along. It takes water into a part of its body and then blows it out again through a short tube. As the water spurts out, it drives the octopus in the opposite direction.

Right Squid are strange-shaped creatures. They have eight thick arms and two long, thin ones.

Baby octopuses and squids are transparent. They have large dark eyes that show clearly in their head.

Below The octopus crawls on the sea bed but it can swim if necessary. It swims by taking in and squirting out jets of water.

The small picture shows enlarged clusters of octopus eggs. There may be as many as 1000 eggs in each cluster which are fastened to rocks.

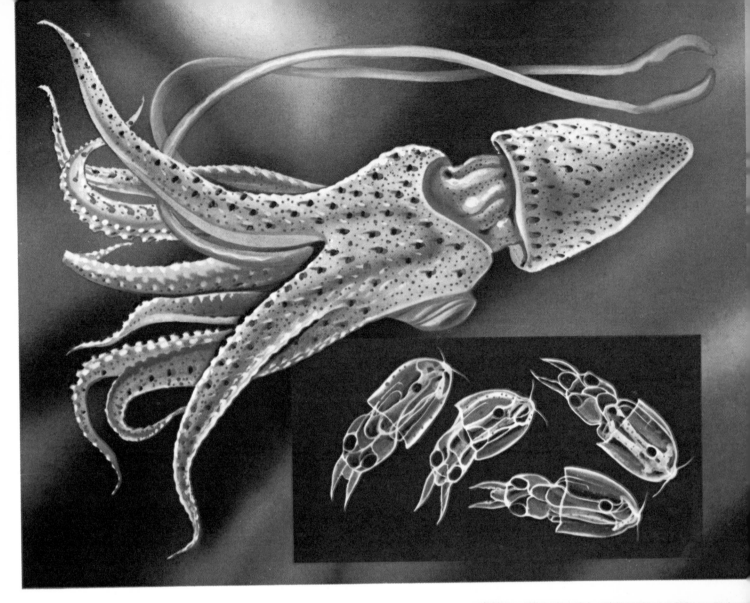

Squids are similar to octopuses but their body is longer. They can move faster and turn more quickly, so they can hunt for fish. They often hunt in packs and catch fish with their arms. Squids have ten arms, and two are longer than the other eight. These are the ones that are used for first taking hold of the food. The other arms are then used for pulling it towards the squid's mouth to be eaten. Some squids are very large. The giant squids that live in colder waters may have arms as long as nine metres and a body four and a half metres long. These giant squids are eaten by some kinds of whales.

The cuttlefish has a flatter body than the squid and octopus. Inside it there is a limy shell which is oval in shape. It is these which are often washed up on the beach.

All these animals are able to make a dark ink. When they are being chased by a larger animal, they squirt the ink into the water. It spreads out like a dark cloud and the attacking animal cannot be sure where its prey is.

Right Cuttlefish have a much flatter body than either the octopus or the squid. Unlike the octopus and the squid, it has a wavy fin around the edge of its body. Cuttlefish bury themselves in sand during the day.

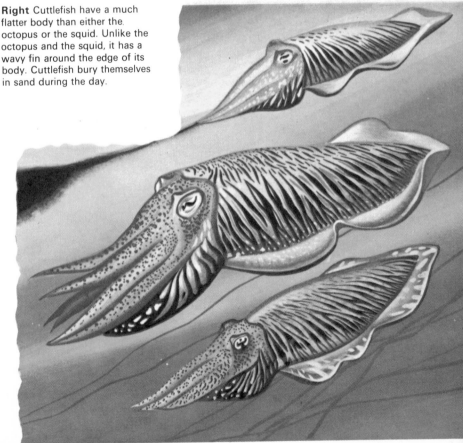

Sharks and rays

Scientists put fish into two groups. There are those that have skeletons made of bone and those whose skeletons are made of hard gristle. In the second group are the sharks and their close relations, the rays.

There are many kinds of sharks. Some of them are meat-eaters and hunters, but others are plankton-feeders. They all have streamlined bodies so that they can swim very fast. On the side of the shark, near the head, are the gill slits. Unlike the bony fish, sharks do not have their gills covered by a bony plate. The shark's skin also is different from that of a cod or a perch. The scales are smaller and pointed. It is often difficult to see them without a lens. Part of each scale is in the skin and part lies on the outside. The mouth of a shark is underneath its head and the meat-eating sharks have a great number of teeth. These often have sharp pointed ends so that if the shark catches a fish, it cannot escape, no matter how slippery it is. Some sharks have teeth with cutting edges so that when the shark bites, its teeth slice through the meat. Flesh-eating sharks eat mainly fish, but they will also eat dead animals and now and again will attack people. They have many sets of teeth so that as they lose some, which they are always doing, there are new ones that can take their place.

The largest of all the sharks, the whale shark is a plankton-feeder only. The strangest looking shark is the hammerhead. From its head pieces grow out sideways. The eyes are at the end of them and this gives the shark a very odd appearance. The saw-fish is a shark, too. The front of its skull may be a metre long, and pointed teeth are fixed on each side. When the saw-fish needs food, it swims through a shoal of fish and slashes from side to side with its saw. Many fish are killed and as they drift in the water, the saw-fish eats them.

Right Sharks do not have a bag of gas or swim bladder to help them stay afloat like bony fish. Instead, they are extremely strong swimmers, and swim all the time to prevent themselves sinking to the bottom.

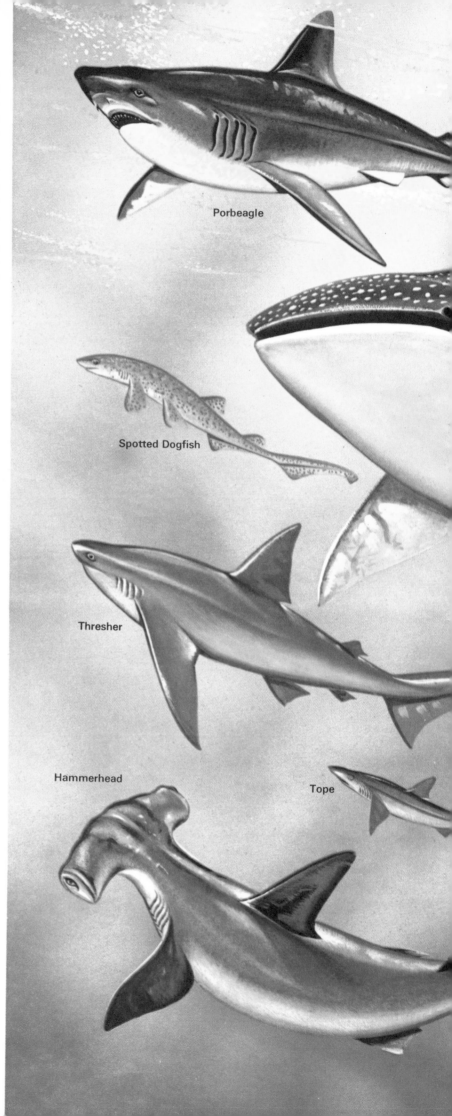

Porbeagle

Spotted Dogfish

Thresher

Hammerhead

Tope

Basking Shark

Whale Shark

Spiny Dogfish

Grey Nurse Shark

125

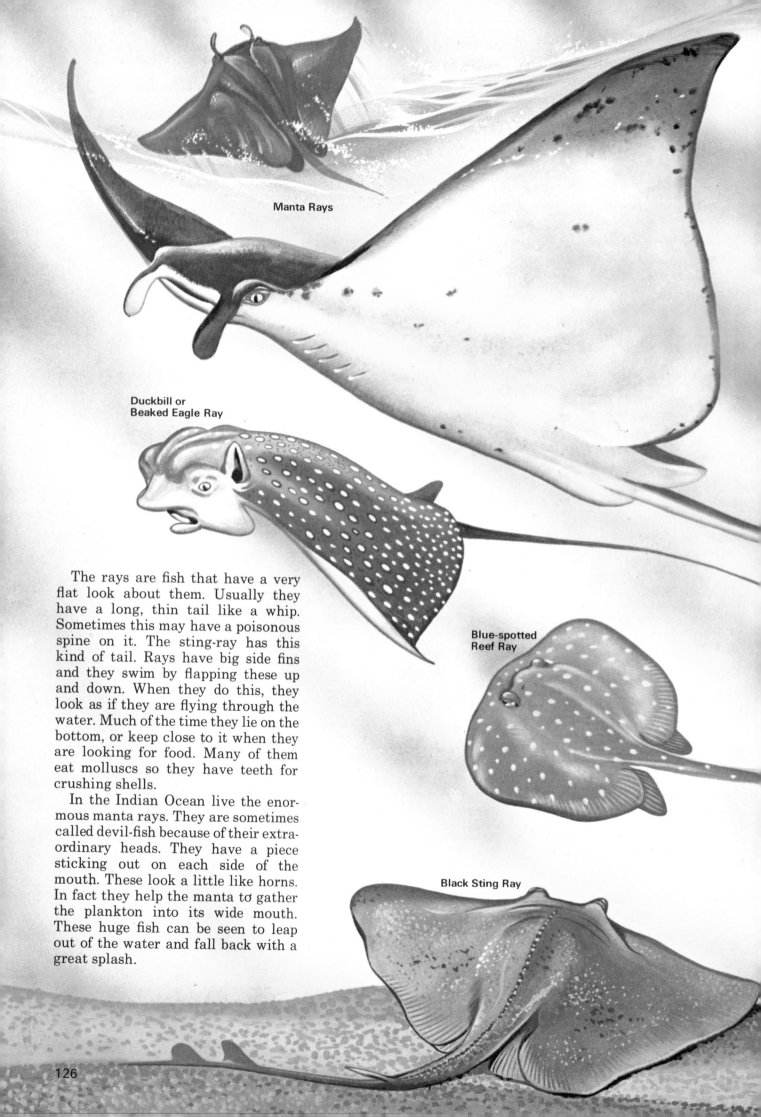

Manta Rays

Duckbill or
Beaked Eagle Ray

Blue-spotted
Reef Ray

Black Sting Ray

The rays are fish that have a very flat look about them. Usually they have a long, thin tail like a whip. Sometimes this may have a poisonous spine on it. The sting-ray has this kind of tail. Rays have big side fins and they swim by flapping these up and down. When they do this, they look as if they are flying through the water. Much of the time they lie on the bottom, or keep close to it when they are looking for food. Many of them eat molluscs so they have teeth for crushing shells.

In the Indian Ocean live the enormous manta rays. They are sometimes called devil-fish because of their extraordinary heads. They have a piece sticking out on each side of the mouth. These look a little like horns. In fact they help the manta to gather the plankton into its wide mouth. These huge fish can be seen to leap out of the water and fall back with a great splash.

Saw-fish

Spotted Eagle
Ray

Skate

Cow-nosed Ray

Lesser Electric Ray

Texas Skate

Sea urchins

Down on the sea bed live the sea urchins. They have the appearance of long-spined hedgehogs, but, of course, they are not related to hedgehogs at all. They belong to the same group of animals as starfish. The pointed spines are attached to a covering of hard plates which make a complete protecting coat for the soft parts of the sea urchin inside it. Rows of tiny holes run down the skeleton and through these go the tube feet of the animal. If you remember, starfish have tube feet as well. The sea urchin uses its tube feet when moving, but also for breathing. On the underside, is the creature's mouth with five strong teeth in it. These are worked by a number of small levers and muscles.

The sea urchins of the warm seas are much more attractive than those around British shores. On the beaches of West Africa can be found dozens of what look like flat, white wheels with spokes half way round them. These are the skeletons of dead wheel-urchins. The sand-dollars of American shores are also flat. When they are alive they sink themselves into the sand. One of the sea urchins most feared by people bathing in warm seas is the hat-pin urchin. The spines of these urchins are black and very thin. They may be up to thirty centimetres long. The urchin can move about by walking on the tips of its spines. What makes them dangerous is that their sharp spines are hollow and may be filled with poison. If anyone treads on a hat-pin urchin, some spines may go into his foot and break off. It can be very painful indeed. Very different from these spines are the ones carried by the slate pencil urchin of the Pacific. This urchin has spines that may be twelve and a half centimetres long and as much as a centimetre thick.

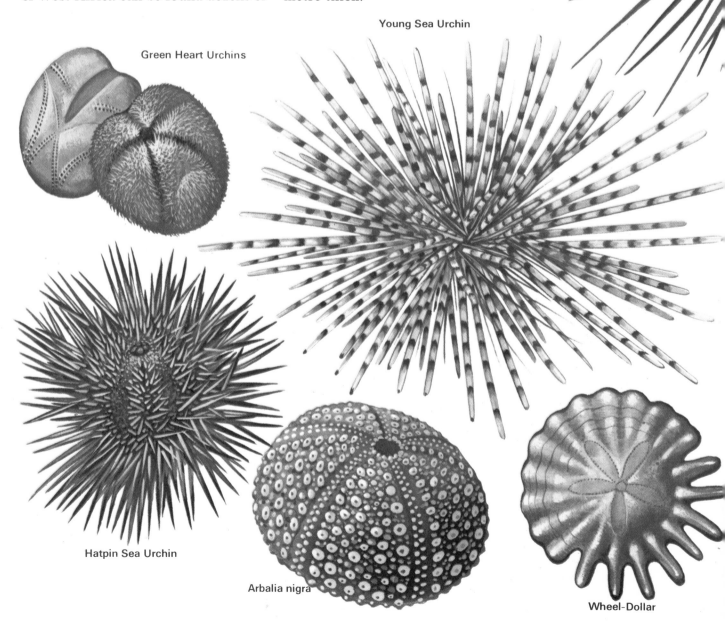

Green Heart Urchins

Young Sea Urchin

Hatpin Sea Urchin

Arbalia nigra

Wheel-Dollar

128

Colobocentratus atratus

The Piper

Echinometra mathaei

Purple-tipped Sea Urchin

Sand-Dollar
(Iron Cross Dollar)

Slate Pencil Urchin

129

Sea snakes

Snakes are usually thought of as being reptiles of the land, or perhaps sometimes going into rivers. They are not often thought of as sea reptiles, but some are. The sea snakes live in the warm Indian and Pacific Oceans. They are most often found around the coasts of India, Malaysia and the islands north of Australia.

Sea snakes have a body which is flattened from side to side and the tail is flattened still more. The snake uses its tail to drive it along. Most sea snakes have a poisonous bite and they kill fish, especially eels, very quickly. Many kinds have living young but some lay eggs on coral reefs. Those that have living young are so well fitted for a life in the sea that they are almost helpless if they are brought out onto the land.

Sea snakes are found only in warm seas, some living around coral reefs. They are much more flattened from side to side than land snakes and are beautiful swimmers. They are sometimes caught in fishermen's nets by accident. Now and again, hundreds of them may lie on the surface of the water, basking in the sun.

Left The only time most of the sea turtles come onto land is to lay their eggs. Slowly, and with great difficulty, the females drag themselves up the beach. When they reach a suitable spot above the strand-line, they make a nest-hollow in the sand.

Below The eggs are laid one at a time into the nest hole. More than a hundred eggs may be laid. Then the female covers them in by pushing sand with her hind feet. The eggs are considered a great delicacy and are collected by people living nearby.

Turtles

You will find turtles gliding through the waters of the warm seas. These reptiles, with their heavy shells and scaly skins, are much like the tortoises you see in the pet shops. They are sea animals, though, and so their body shows ways in which they are adapted to life in the water. Most of them are large, much larger than their cousins of the land. Some are over two metres long and weigh perhaps 500 kilograms, although many are smaller. The turtle's body is rather flattened, so that its head cannot be pulled back into the shell in the same way that the land tortoise can pull its head back. Its feet and legs are flippers for swimming instead of feet for walking.

Every female turtle must come out of the sea to lay her eggs. On a moonlight night, when the tide is high, they

Left Some eggs remain undisturbed and once the baby turtles have hatched, their main task is to get to the sea. Many are killed and eaten by birds before they ever reach the water, but some will survive and become adults.

131

The sea turtles are reptiles. Their bodies have become flattened and their legs have become paddles. They are able to swim easily and gracefully through warm seas where they usually live. Sometimes one or two may be carried by strong currents into colder seas. The leatherback turtle, sometimes called the luth, is the largest of the sea turtles and may be nearly two metres long. The loggerhead may be only half that length and the hawksbill is the smallest of them all. The green turtle is in danger of dying out.

Hawksbill Turtle

Loggerhead Turtle

Green Turtle

come out of the water. Very slowly, they drag themselves up the beaches. When they are swimming, the water helps to support them, but on the land their body is very heavy.

Their legs are not much good for walking so the turtles have to heave themselves over the sand a metre at a time. When each female has dragged herself far enough, she begins to scrape a hollow in the sand. Then she digs much harder and makes a hole about forty centimetres deep. Into this hole she lays her eggs. There can be a hundred or more.

When all the eggs are laid, the turtle covers them over with sand, pushing it with her back feet. Then it is time to make her way back to sea. Very slowly she moves again, leaving deep tracks down the beach. Several weeks later the young turtles hatch out of the eggs. They, too, must go to the sea. Some get there, but many are eaten by birds before they get anywhere near it.

Turtle eggs are eaten by man. Huge numbers are collected but some eggs have to be left so that the turtles will not die out.

The leatherback turtle is the largest in the world but the green turtle and the hawksbill are better known. The green turtle is a plant-eater. It was hunted for its flesh, which was used to make turtle soup. This happens less now than it did years ago.

The hawksbill had a shell that is covered with brown, shiny plates. These overlap each other like the tiles on a house. At one time the plates used to be taken off the dead turtles and used as tortoiseshell.

132

Atlantic 'Ridley' Turtle

Underside of Turtle

Leatherback Turtle

Life In The Very Deep Sea

It is much more difficult to find out about the animals that live in the depths of the sea, than it is to explore rock pools. For this we need a ship and large nets. The nets will have to be let down to great depths, perhaps over two kilometres down. When a net like this has been towed through the water for several hours and the time comes to pull it up, there is great excitement on the ship. There is so much to be learnt about the animals of the deep, that quite often some that have never been seen before will be pulled up in the net.

There are sure to be prawns and creatures of that type. Many will have part of their body red and part completely colourless. Others will be bright red all over. There will be little jellyfish, too, yellow or deep red, like deep-sea flowers. Perhaps the net will have caught some of the deep-water worms. They, too, may be red. It is surprising how many of these animals that live deep in the oceans are coloured red. They only look red when they have been brought up to the light. Where they live, the water is so deep that the sunlight cannot reach them at all and living things appear black.

The net will have brought up some fish as well. What strange fish they are, those that live in this dark world one kilometre or more down. Hatchet

Fish of the very deep sea appear to have very strange shapes. Sometimes they seem to be all mouth! This is because food at these depths is very scarce, and a fish must be able to eat anything that comes along whatever the size.

The large fish at the bottom of the picture is a coelacanth. Coelacanths are a very interesting fish because it was thought that they had died out millions of years ago. Scientists all over the world were very excited when a live coelacanth was caught off the South African coast in 1938. Since then a few more have been caught, but it has not been possible to keep them alive because of pressure changes in the water.

fish look like silver coins with a tail stuck on them. They are not much thicker than coins either. Many of the fish are black but they have lights along their sides. These are special spots along their bodies which shine with a whitish light. When the fish swim, they must look rather like ships with lights shining through the portholes. A few men have been able to see these fish. They have been inside a strong metal ball called a bathysphere which has been lowered from a ship. A bathysphere has windows and powerful lights to shine through the darkness.

There are many fish in the ocean depths that look so strange that it is hard to believe that they really exist. The gulpers have an enormous mouth but a very long, thin body, so that they seem to be nothing more than a swimming mouth! There are angler fish of many kinds. Each has its own 'fishing rod' and 'bait'. They have a stiff, thin rod growing from their head or back. The end of it can light up. This attracts other fish which come closer to see what it is. By the time they are close enough to see, they are close enough to be snapped up by the angler fish. As well as having the 'rod' on their head, some have a shining piece hanging down under their bottom jaw. This looks a little like a white beard and helps to attract other fish.

Mammals That Live In The Sea

Sea otters and seals

Fish are well equipped for living in water. They have the right shape, they can breathe under the water and they can lay their eggs there. Mammals that live in the sea have had to change their way of life a great deal. They have had to find a better way of getting about than walking and running. They have had to change the shape of their body in some cases. And what have they done about breathing and having their young? There are several groups of mammals that live in the sea and they have not all changed in the same way.

The sea otters live in the North Pacific Ocean, but not too far from the coasts. These mammals are very much like the fresh-water otters, but they are larger. They have hind feet which are large and webbed. The sea otters feed on molluscs and they will sometimes break the shell in a strange way. Diving to the bottom, an otter will bring up a stone in its front paws. On the surface, the animal will float on its back and put the stone on its body. Then it will break the mollusc shells by banging them on the stone! Sea otters may sleep floating on their back with a piece of thick seaweed wrapped around them so that they do not drift. In most ways, the sea otters are very much like land mammals. They have not changed very much for life in the sea.

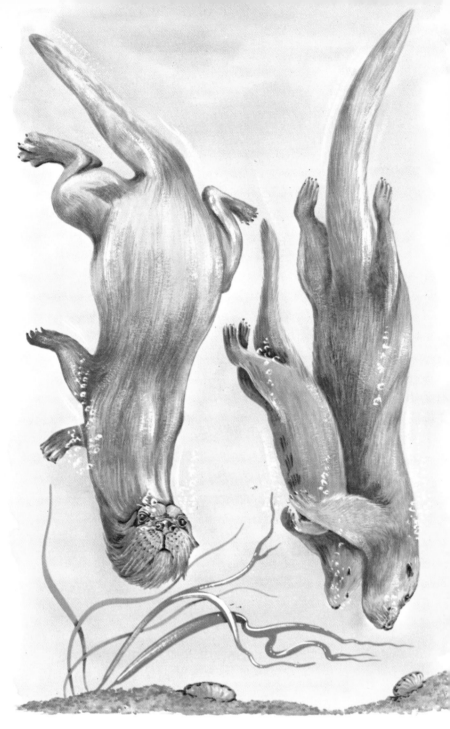

Above right Sea otters are much larger than common otters and their fur is very thick. At one time they were hunted for their fur and were in danger of dying out.

Right Sea otters live fairly close to the shore and at times float lazily on their back, perhaps asleep, anchored by a large piece of seaweed.

This is not the case with seals. Their bodies have changed a great deal. There are three groups of seals. There are the true seals, the sea-lions and the walruses. True seals are quite common in many seas of the world and there are many around the shores of Britain. Grey seals live on rocky coasts for example, around parts of Wales. Where there are no rocks, such as on the Norfolk coast, the smaller common seals are the ones that are seen. Grey and common seals have quite a good streamlined shape and their fur is short so that they can move easily through the water. Their legs are very different from those of a land mammal. The front legs are mostly under the skin of the body but the feet stick out. The toes are long with skin between them and the whole foot has become a flipper. When the seal comes out of the water, it can use its flippers to hump itself along. When it is in the sea, though, it is the back feet that are used for swimming and the front feet are tucked close to its sides. The hind feet point backwards and cannot be moved round. Under the water a seal swims gracefully, turning and twisting easily to catch fish. When it is swimming like this, it cannot breathe, so every now and again it must come up for air. Most seals will stay under for five or six minutes, but they can stay longer if they need to.

Below Some species of fur seals live in the south, and others in the northern parts of the world. In spring, the males make their way to the few breeding places and when they have dragged themselves out of the water each one tries to claim a piece of beach for himself. Fights often break out and the noise of their roaring is very loud. The females come later and each male gathers as many females for himself as he can. Baby fur seals stay with their mothers for about four months.

Grey Seal

Ross Seal

Elephant Seal

Harp Seal

Bearded Seal

Hooded Seal

Ribbon Seal

Weddell Seal

Fur Seal

Leopard Seal

Ringed Seal

Monk Seal

139

When it is time for young seals to be born, the mothers must come out of the water. They struggle on to the beach or the rocks and then the babies are born. At first, a baby grey seal has a thick, white coat. Its skin has wrinkles in it as if it were several sizes too big. Like all mammals, the mother seal feeds her baby on milk. It is very creamy milk and the baby seal grows quickly. Soon the wrinkles in its skin have gone and its body is fat and tubby.

After about two weeks, the mother seal leaves the baby and goes back to the sea leaving the young one. Its coat changes colour, the white fur falling out a little at a time and grey fur growing instead. For a time the baby seal lives on its fat, but soon it goes to the water to learn to catch fish for itself. It quickly learns how to fish so that by the time most of its fat is used up, it can look after itself. The adult seals come out of the water again several months later to moult. Then they lose their old fur and grow new. Except when they have their young and change their fur, seals spend most of their time in the sea.

Above Harp seals live among the drifting ice in the Arctic but move further south in the winter. Thousands of them come together when it is time to have their pups.

Left Leopard seals in the Antarctic waters feed on fish and sea-birds. Penguins are very much afraid of them and try to dash for safety if one appears.

Right A male elephant seal may be over six metres long. Its nose is large and can be blown out like a small trunk.

Far right A sea-lion. It is also known as an eared seal.

Sea-lions are well-known because they are often seen in the circus, balancing a ball on their nose and performing other tricks. These sea-lions are from California, in America. The sea-lions get their name because the big males often have a mane of hair on their neck in the same way as male lions do. Sea-lions have ears which can be seen on the outside of their head, so they are sometimes known as eared seals. Their front feet are flippers and they are used for swimming. The sea-lions really row themselves along. The back feet can be turned to point forward. This is useful when a sea-lion comes on land because they can be used for walking.

Seals and sea-lions are mainly fish-eaters. The big leopard seals that live in the cold seas of the far south also eat sea-birds such as penguins. Walruses, though, are mollusc-eaters. They are heavy animals that live in the cold waters around the Arctic shores. They do not have much hair, but like the other kinds of seals they have plenty of fat under their skin to help keep them warm. The two long tusks that grow down from their

mouth are really two extra-long teeth. Sometimes walruses will use their tusks when fighting and many of them have large scars on their bodies. They may be used as ice-picks when the animals come out of the water on to the ice! Probably they are most often used for stirring the mud at the bottom of the sea when the walrus is searching for clams to eat. A walrus also has a great many stiff hairs growing around its mouth. These hairs are sensitive and are used as feelers when the walrus cannot see in the muddy water. It also pushes clams into its mouth with them. The walrus cracks the clam shell with its strong teeth and the soft parts are sucked out. The shell is dropped to the bottom. When Eskimos hunted walrus, they would often take the stomach out of the dead animal to eat the clams inside it.

Below Dugongs are about two and a half metres long. They are plant-eaters so they keep near the coast where there is plenty of food. The males may have tusks up to twenty-five centimetres long.

Seals are better adapted to a life in the water than sea otters, but they come on to land from time to time. The manatees and dugongs have gone one step further. They stay in the water all the time. These animals look a little like walruses without tusks but they have no hind flippers at all. Instead, they have a wide, flattened tail. The manatees live in warm waters around parts of North and South America, and in Africa. They do not live far out to sea and may go into large rivers for water plants to eat.

Dugongs are very much like manatees to look at. They are found in the Indian Ocean and the warm waters of the Far East, feeding on seaweed. The males do sometimes have tusks. Years ago, there used to be animals called sea cows that lived in the North Pacific. They were like manatees and dugongs in many ways, but were bigger. Some were nearly eight metres long. They were discovered by a man named Steller, in the 1700s, but as soon as they were discovered man began to hunt them. Only thirty years after they had first been found, sea cows were practically wiped out. Today they are extinct.

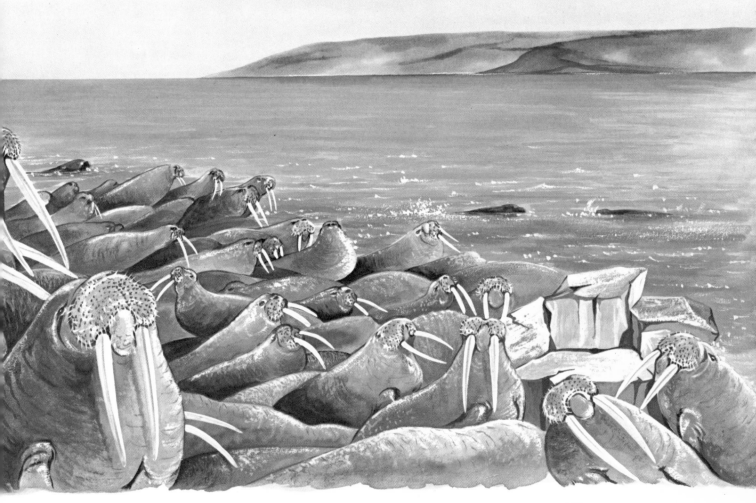

Above Young walruses have yellowish-brown hair on their body, but by the time they reach maturity they have lost it. A full-grown male walrus is a heavy animal. It may be over three metres long and weigh over a tonne. The tusks can be as long as sixty-eight centimetres.

Right Baby manatees are born under water, but the mother quickly lifts the little one above the surface. For a while it stays on her back, but slowly she sinks. After about two hours she is completely under the water and the baby is able to swim with her.

Whales

Whales spend all their time in water and their bodies have changed more than those of any other sea mammals. All mammals have warm bodies, and to stop them from losing heat most of them have a coat of fur or hair. A fur coat would be of little use to a whale. It would very quickly become water-logged, and this would soon make the whale cold instead of keeping it warm. So whales have a thick layer of fat, called *blubber*, under their skin instead of fur. This keeps them just as warm.

Whales have a streamlined shape which is nearly as good as that of a fish. To drive itself along, a whale moves its tail up and down. A fish moves it from side to side. To help it keep steady in the water, a whale has a fin on its back. For steering, it has a flipper on each side of its body. These flippers are really the whale's front legs and if you could see the bones under the skin, you would see that they are like the bones in your hand and arm. Whales do not look as if they have any back legs, but hidden inside their body are small bones which are all that remain of them. Most mammals use their back legs to push them when they are running. A whale uses its tail instead, so it does not need back legs.

If a mammal is going to live in the water and spend a great deal of time swimming a long way down, it is going to be difficult for it to breathe. Whales must come to the surface from time to time and when they dive they have to hold their breath. A large whale can hold its breath for up to three-quarters of an hour. When it comes to the surface again, it breathes through its nostrils which are on top of its head. It also blows out of them a cloud of oily foam. This is called the *spout*. Many people think that the spout is a fountain of water, but it is not.

There is very little light under water and whales cannot see very far. So they use sound to help them find their way about, rather as bats do. They send out waves of sound and these bounce back from anything that is in the way. If a whale hears an echo, it knows that something is ahead of it. Different objects have different echoes. The echo from a shoal of fish will not sound the same as the echo from a large rock. The whales have a good memory for sounds and so they

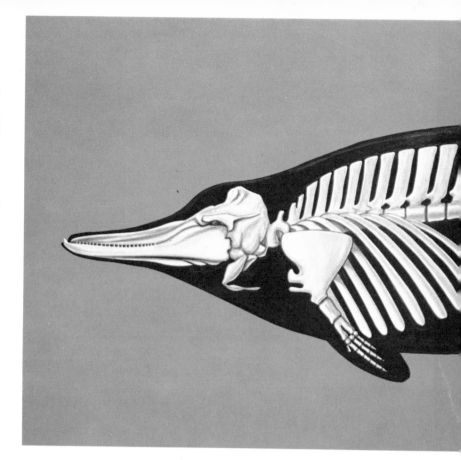

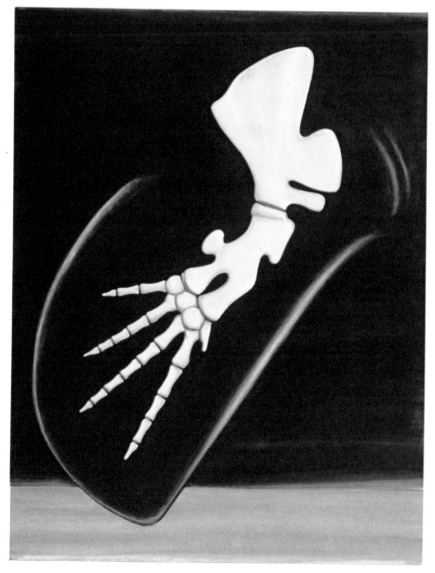

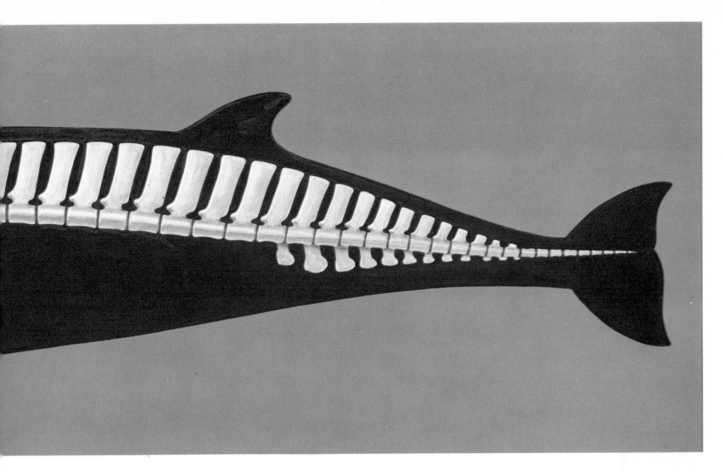

Above A whale's skeleton is much like that of any mammal. There are a few differences because whales are adapted for a life in the sea.

Left The bones of a sperm whale's flipper are similar to the bones of your arm and hand, but larger, of course.

Below The atlantic right whale has baleen plates for straining krill from the water. Sperm whales have teeth, shaped like the one in the picture.

build up a 'sound picture' of their surroundings. This is very important, not only for finding their way about, but also for searching for food.

What do whales eat? There are many different kinds of whales. Some of them have teeth, but others do not. They have 'brushes' inside their mouth. The proper name for these brushes is *baleen plates*. They hang down from the upper jaw of the whales and work as strainers. The huge blue whales are baleen whales and they feed on tiny, shrimp-like animals called *krill*. Where the blue whales feed, in the cold waters of the South

Atlantic, there are enormous shoals of krill. When a whale finds some, it opens its mouth and the krill goes in. But because it is under the sea, water goes in too. So the whale has to sort out the krill from the water. It does this in a very simple way. When its mouth is full, the water goes between the plates of baleen and out between the whale's lips to the sea again. But the shrimps get caught up on the 'brushes'. When all the water has gone, the whale can lick the shrimps off and swallow them. A blue whale's stomach can hold more than a tonne of food.

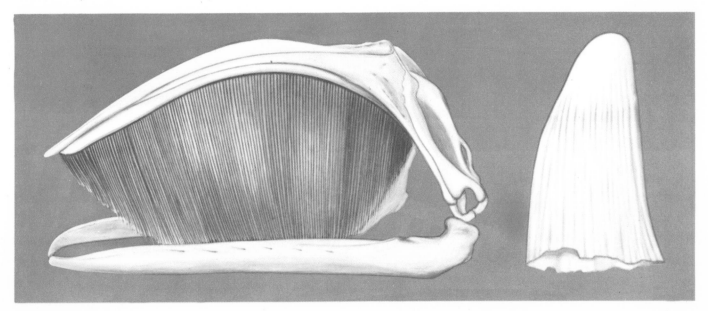

Narwhal (toothed)

Sperm Whale (toothed)

Humpback Whale (baleen)

Beaked Whale (toothed)

White Whale (toothed)

Blue Whale (baleen)

Black Right Whale (baleen)

Killer Whale (toothed)

Bottle-nosed Whale (toothed)

The whales that have teeth eat fish, but the large sperm whales eat squids. Many of the old whales have scars on them from fights they have had with giant squids. The beaks and suckers of these animals have been used to defend themselves and have left their mark on the whale's skin. Killer whales are toothed whales and they will eat penguins and other warm-blooded animals. It is said that they will even attack blue whales. Packs of the killer whales will swim by the side of one and bite at its lips and flippers. They tear it and the big blue whale bleeds so much that it dies.

Then the killer whales eat the soft parts, especially the lips and tongue.

Dolphins and porpoises are whales, too, although they do not grow very large. Those that are kept in large aquariums are usually bottle-nosed dolphins. They are very quick to learn. One trick is to make them leap out of the water to go over a high bar. To be able to jump so high, the dolphins have to swim very fast indeed before they leap and they can be seen swimming round and round the pool to get up speed. When they are at sea, dolphins and porpoises swim in groups, often leaping out of the water.

Above A modern whaling fleet has one large factory ship and a number of smaller, fast boats for catching and killing whales. The dead whales often have air pumped into them to make them float until the factory ship can pull them aboard and process them for their oil and meat. Some kinds of whales are in danger of becoming extinct because too many are being killed by the whaling fleets.

When baby whales are born, the first breath they take must not be under water, or they would drown. As soon as one is born, its mother and other females as well, will nudge it quickly to the surface. Then when it does take its first breath, its head is in the air.

Animals the size of blue whales can live in water because the water helps to support their great weight. They have been known to grow as long as thirty metres and weigh up to 130 tonnes. There are no whales this size any more, because the very large ones have all been killed. Each year, ships go down to the Antarctic to hunt whales for their oil and meat. Too many have been killed and now it is possible that some kinds, including the blue whale, may die out.

Some museums have models of whales. If you can go to the Natural History Museum in London, you will be able to see a life-size model of a blue whale which is twenty-eight metres long. There are models of dolphins and porpoises, too.

Below Porpoises and dolphins look very similar, the main difference being the more pointed head of the dolphin.

Common Dolphin

Common Porpoise

Spotted Dolphin

Bottle-nosed Dolphin

Dall's Porpoise

Amazon Dolphin

Susu or Ganges river Dolphin

Land

In The Soil

Woodlice

Beneath our feet is the world of the soil. It is a dark world and a damp one, too. You can explore it so easily, because it lies just outside your door. But before finding out about life under the soil, there are plenty of interesting animals to see on the surface. They are small animals that do not like light very much and so they hide under stones and logs. To find some, you need to walk into your garden and lift up a large stone or piece of rock and turn it over. There are sure to be some woodlice under it. These little animals, about a centimetre long, are rather oval in shape and slightly flattened. Like many small animals, they would dry up very quickly if they remained in the open air. This is why they keep in dark, shady places because it is usually damper there. A

Above Millipedes and mites, spiders and slugs—millions of small animals live on or under the earth.

Below Among the roots and surrounded by grains of soil live the burrowers, mice and moles, and the lovers of darkness, the worms, ants and wire-worms.

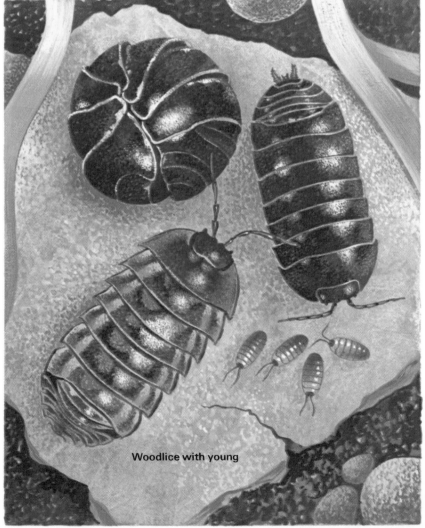

Woodlice with young

country name for woodlice is sow-bugs. They have a very tough shell over them which is made in sections so that it can bend. Some kinds of woodlice have a shell that can bend so much that they can roll up into a ball.

Woodlice are relatives of crabs and shrimps but they took to living on land rather than in the water. If you watch them, you will notice that they have many legs. You may even see one with eggs underneath it. Instead of laying her eggs on the ground, the female woodlouse carries them under her body in a pouch until the young woodlice hatch out. It would be interesting to find out how many different kinds of woodlice there are in your garden. Some are dark grey, almost black, but others are more brown. There are small ones that are very nearly white and if you use your eyes, you will find others. They eat plant food and so it is worth looking in any pieces of rotten wood and in the heap of garden rubbish at the bottom of the garden.

Always remember though, that if you turn over stones or wood, put them back again exactly as they were when you have finished looking at the woodlice.

153

Ants

Sooner or later you are going to find ants when you are turning over stones. If you do uncover part of a nest you will see the ants rushing about. You will see the white ants' eggs. Each one is really a pupa in a case and the ants will struggle to carry them to safety. But much can be learnt about ants by watching them, without having to disturb them. You have read about these insects before, so that you know that many of the ants in a nest are workers. These are the ones you can see almost anywhere in the garden. One interesting study you can make is to try to find out whether they like some kinds of food more than others. If you find a nest, place some pieces of food in little heaps around it, about a metre away. Try some meat of any

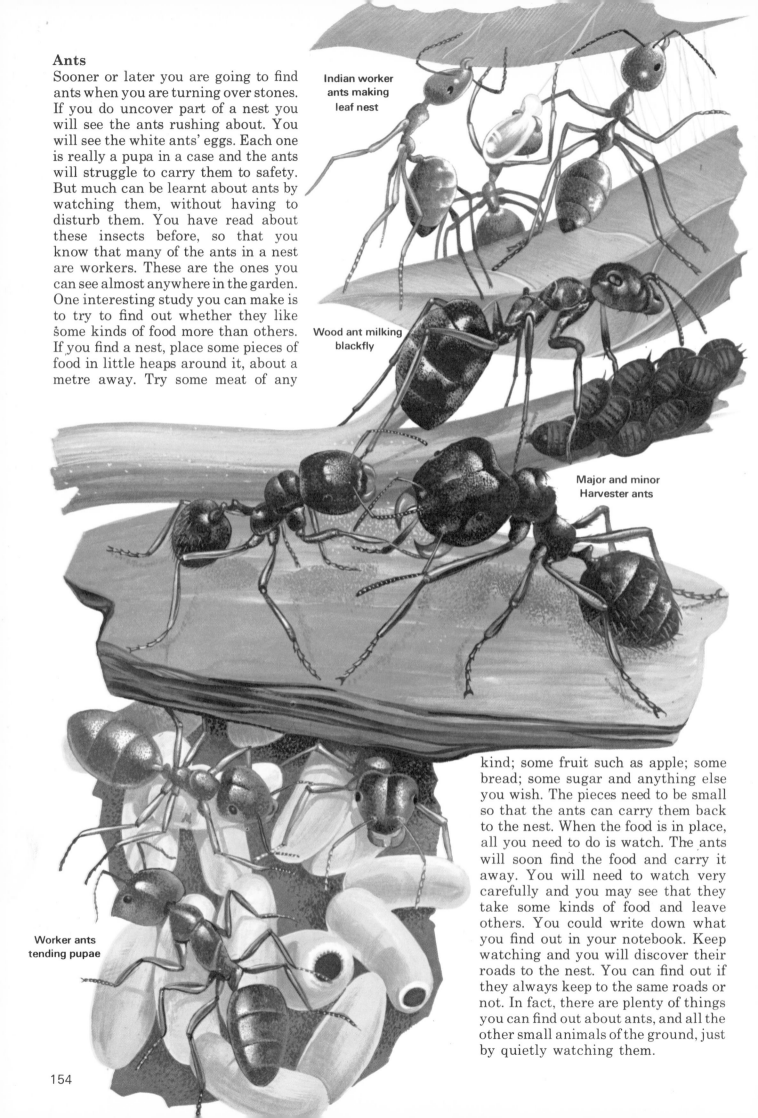

Indian worker ants making leaf nest

Wood ant milking blackfly

Major and minor Harvester ants

Worker ants tending pupae

kind; some fruit such as apple; some bread; some sugar and anything else you wish. The pieces need to be small so that the ants can carry them back to the nest. When the food is in place, all you need to do is watch. The ants will soon find the food and carry it away. You will need to watch very carefully and you may see that they take some kinds of food and leave others. You could write down what you find out in your notebook. Keep watching and you will discover their roads to the nest. You can find out if they always keep to the same roads or not. In fact, there are plenty of things you can find out about ants, and all the other small animals of the ground, just by quietly watching them.

154

Centipedes and millipedes

In the dark places beneath the stones and logs and in amongst the garden rubbish, live the centipedes. The word *centipede* means 'a hundred feet' but, in fact, one of the commonest kinds has only fifteen pairs. Other kinds may have many more. The body of a centipede is long and flattened, with a tough, jointed skin. The animal can twist and turn easily and slip into any crack it likes. All centipedes are meat-eaters and they glide about searching for small insects or worms to eat. When one is found, the centipede kills it by biting and sometimes squirting poison into it. The centipedes in Britain are only four centimetres long. In the West Indies, there are centipedes up to thirty centimetres long. These are large enough to catch lizards and mice, although most of the time they catch large insects.

Millipedes are plant-eaters. They also have many pairs of legs, but their bodies are not flattened like the centipedes. Their name means 'a thousand feet' but that is a long way from being true. A millipede with two hundred legs would be a long one. When they are found, they will often curl up like a clock spring until they think it is safe enough to move again. One kind of millipede has a short body and it can curl up in a tight ball. This kind is called a pill-bug. When a millipede is ready to lay eggs, she makes a nest under the ground. The nest is a hollow ball, smooth inside but rough on the outside. It is made by sticking tiny pieces of earth together. A hole is left in the top and the milli-pede lays her eggs through this. Then she closes up the hole with more soil and the eggs are left to hatch. They do this in about twelve days.

At first the young millipedes are small and have only three pairs of legs, but as their body grows, more legs grow too.

Above Not often seen because they prefer to live in dark places, centipedes are hunters of small soil animals, their long bodies slipping easily between the stones and plants.

Below There are over 6000 species of millipedes. Millipedes lay eggs and some may live as long as seven years.

155

Mites

When trees in a wood lose their leaves in the autumn, they fall to the ground. As the years go by, the carpet of dead leaves grows thicker and this *leaf litter*, as it is called, is the home of many small animals. Among these, are the mites. They are so small that without a magnifying glass, it is hard to see them. But they are there. Thousands and thousands of them, scurrying about on their eight legs. Some eat the eggs of greenflies, others hunt for the small threadworms in the soil. A few live on the bodies of animals. Some of these burrow into the skin and lay eggs there. Others stay on the outside but push their mouthparts into the animal to feed on blood. There are mites that live in the buds of plants. The buds then swell and may even begin to grow in an odd way. These large buds and strange growths on plants are called *galls*. Not all galls are caused by mites, but many are.

Spiders

Mites look very much like tiny spiders. This is not surprising for they are related. But although mites are often too small to be easily seen, spiders are bigger. Some of the spiders from the tropics are even large enough to cover a saucer. In Britain, the spider everyone knows best is the garden spider. Even if the spider itself is not seen, the web it makes cannot be missed. Try to find one in the garden and look at it closely. It is made of fine silk which the spider makes in her body. When she starts web-making, she first squeezes out some silk and lets it drift in the air. When it catches on a leaf or twig, she pulls it tight and then makes it stronger with more silk.

Above Sometimes mites cling to beetles and are carried around by them. You can see them on this long-bodied weevil. The small picture shows an enlarged picture of a mite.

Above The bud on this plant has grown so large because there is a mite living in it. The mite is shown many times larger than life size.

Right A trap-door spider makes a tunnel in the ground and lines it with a silk tube. Here, it waits for its prey, hidden by the trap-door. When it hears an unsuspecting animal nearby, it springs from its hiding-place to catch it. The far picture shows a trap-door spider catching a millipede.

Below Diagram to show a cross-section of a spider.

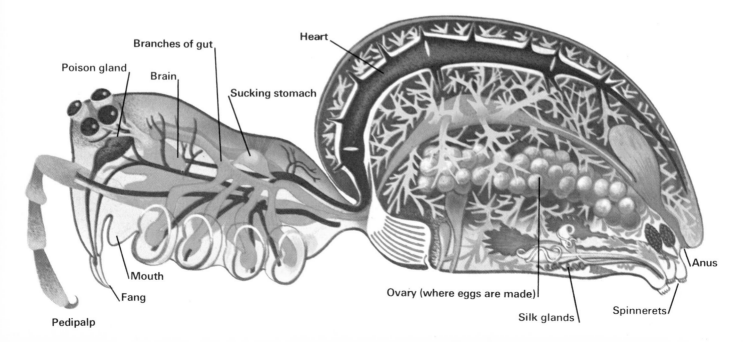

Poison gland

Brain

Branches of gut

Heart

Sucking stomach

Mouth

Fang

Pedipalp

Ovary (where eggs are made)

Silk glands

Spinnerets

Anus

Next she makes a silk frame and then inside it, the threads that run out from the middle of the web just like the spokes of a wheel. After that comes the work of making the threads that go round and round. The first few are near the centre to strengthen it. The spider then moves outwards and puts down a spiral of silk with wide spaces in it. After that she begins to work towards the middle again to make the spiral of sticky silk that will trap the insects she wants for food. A web like this will take a spider about half an hour to make and she will make a new one each day. When a fly touches the web, it sticks to it. As it struggles to free itself, the movements are felt by the spider which is hiding beneath a leaf at the edge of the web. It runs to the trapped fly and because its feet are a little oily, it does not stick to its own web. Quickly it bites the fly and then begins to wrap it in silk. The spider may then take the fly to the middle of the web to eat it, or may take it back to the hiding place.

A selection of Garden Spiders

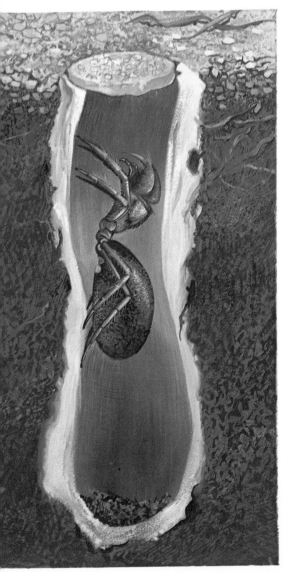

157

A very old name for a spider was 'attercop' which means 'poison head'. When a spider bites, poison goes through its jaws into its victim and kills it. In this country there are very few spiders with jaws strong enough to bite through our skin. Some spiders from other countries can. One of these is the black widow spider which lives in warm countries. It is not very large and has a black body with a red spot on it. This spider has been known to bite people and they have died from the poison. Some of the very large bird-eating spiders do sometimes manage to catch humming birds, but most of the time they feed on worms, mice or large insects. These spiders come to Britain now and again in bunches of bananas. They may give a fright when they crawl out of the bunch!

There are many kinds of spiders that make webs, but they do not all make the same shaped ones as the garden spider. Some make a web like a sheet and the tube spider spins a silk tunnel among plants, or in a crack of a wall. The spider waits in the tunnel until an insect is seen. Then it rushes out to catch it.

Bird-eating Spider

There are spiders that do not make webs at all. In a garden on a warm summer day, it is often possible to see many grey wolf spiders out hunting. They catch their prey by running and pouncing. The little crab spiders do not need to do so much running. They sit quietly in the middle of flowers, usually the white or yellow ones. Their colour matches the flower and makes them difficult to see. They wait with legs stretched out for an insect to come near. Quickly it is held and bitten, and the insect becomes another meal for the spider.

Spiders lay eggs and the female covers them with silk after she has laid each batch. The eggs may be on a leaf or on a stone. They can be found under fallen logs or hanging from silk threads. A number of spiders carry the bag of eggs around with them, attached to their body. When the young spider hatches from the egg, it cannot feed or spin. It has no hairs on its body and no colour either. In a day or two, it sheds its skin and then it becomes a small, but perfect, spider. It may stay for a while in the silk case, but the time comes when it cuts its way out, along with all the other young spiders. They do not run away, but may climb on

Above Most spiders lay their eggs onto silk and then cover them with more silk. The giant or weaving spider then stands guard over its eggs.

Above Crab spiders are hunters that do not make snares. They are called crab spiders because they can move sideways like a crab.

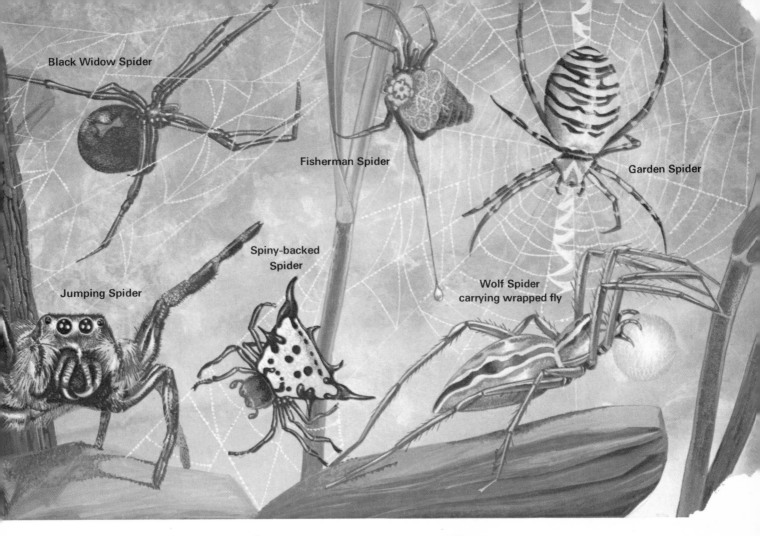

Black Widow Spider

Fisherman Spider

Garden Spider

Spiny-backed Spider

Jumping Spider

Wolf Spider carrying wrapped fly

their mother's back or stay together in a ball. But they cannot keep together for much longer and they start to catch food for themselves. Certain kinds of young spiders may climb to the top of plants and spin some silk threads which are blown upwards by the wind with the baby spiders still on the end. In this way, they float through the air a long way before coming to the ground again. Many of these drifting spiders are eaten by birds while they are in the air. Some come down into water and others cannot find food and die. But there are still plenty of spiders about. In a single meadow, there will be several million of them!

How can you tell that a spider is not an insect? In the first place, spiders have four pairs of legs instead of three pairs as an insect does. The spider's body is not divided into three parts like that of an insect. If you look carefully, you will see that there are only two parts to its body. Spiders do not have any antennae either. On the spider's head, you may be able to see eight eyes, but some kinds have only six. So you should be able to tell whether a small creature is a spider or not fairly easily.

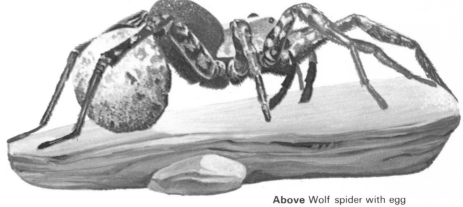

Above Wolf spider with egg mass.

Below A female wolf spider carrying her young on her back.

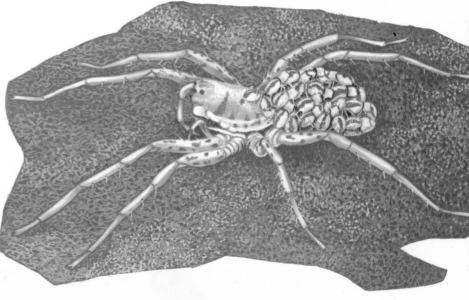

Scorpions

If you lived in Egypt or some other hot country, you would see another relative of spiders, the scorpions. These animals do not look very much like spiders, but they have four pairs of walking legs like them. The end half of their body is very thin, which makes it look like a jointed tail. At the end is a poisonous sting. The scorpion has a pair of claws growing from its head end and these are used for holding and tearing the food that it catches. The claws are like those of a crab. Because of their poisonous sting, scorpions are not liked and, in fact, most people are rather afraid of them. They are shy animals and do most of their food collecting at night. During the day, they hide under rocks and fallen trees. They eat spiders and insects, holding them in their claws and tearing or crushing them. If the insect is very large, then the scorpion may use its sting.

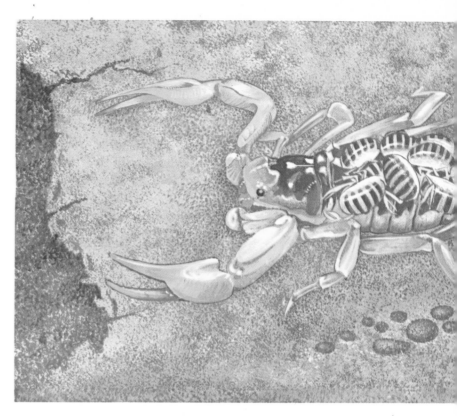

Scorpions are different sizes and colours. Those that live in the deserts are a sandy colour. Those of the jungles are much darker. Some of them are almost black. Small kinds may be only five to seven centimetres long, but the larger kinds are up to twenty-five centimetres long. They do not normally attack people, but they will attack other scorpions. The females do not lay eggs. One or two are born at a time as tiny, active scorpions. After several weeks there is a large number. They cling to their mother's back and ride on her for many days, although they could really look after themselves.

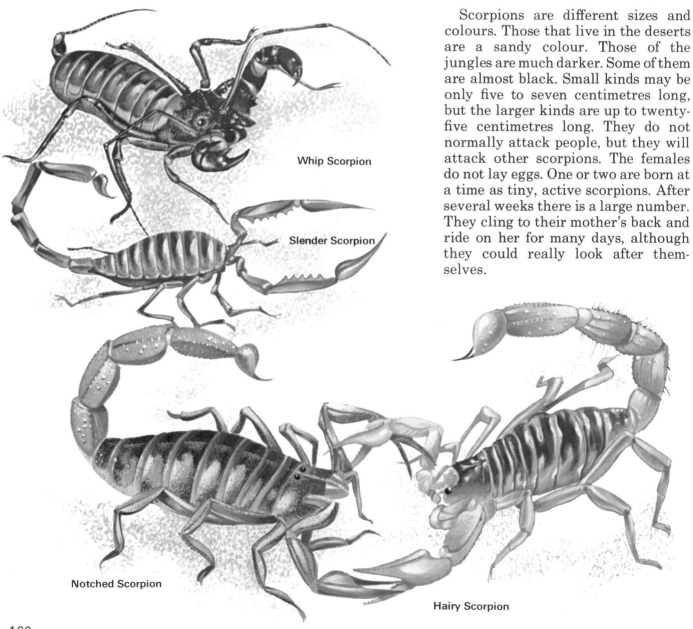

Whip Scorpion

Slender Scorpion

Notched Scorpion

Hairy Scorpion

160

Slugs and snails

Have you ever been for a walk and stopped to look at some silvery trails on the stonework. They are like bands of silver, about half a centimetre wide. If you follow one, it will lead you to a crack in the wall, or to a joint between two stones, and what will you find? A snail with its body tight inside its shell. There are snails that live in ponds and rivers. There are many that live in the sea. There are land snails, too, all of them belonging to the group of animals called molluscs. The single, coiled shell protects much of the snail's body which is coiled inside it. When the snail moves, its head and foot come out of the shell and slime comes from a hole at the side of its body. The slime covers the snail's foot and it is this slime that dries to leave the silvery trail. Snails eat by rubbing off small pieces of food with a tongue that has rows and rows of tiny plates on it, shaped like pointed teeth. Most of the kind of snails that you are likely to find are plant-eaters.

Slugs are very much like snails except that their shells are not big, coiled ones. Instead, they are small, flat ones that lie under the skin. Other than this, there is very little difference. Slugs move and eat just as snails do. All gardeners dislike slugs because they like to eat the shoots of young plants.

It would be interesting to find out the different kinds of snails in your area. You do not really need to know many names as long as you can see the different shape and colour of the shell that each kind has. You might like to make a collection of the different shells, but use empty ones that you find. Where are snails found? How do you start looking for them?

First, it is useful to remember that snails like damp places. A good day

Above For a while, baby scorpions cling to their mother's back and are carried by her, protected by her tail with its deadly sting.

Right Roman snails go through a courtship 'dance' before mating and push a tiny chalky dart into each other's body. The eggs are laid in the ground.

Below Slugs lay their eggs beneath logs and in places where it is moist and shady so that the eggs will not dry out.

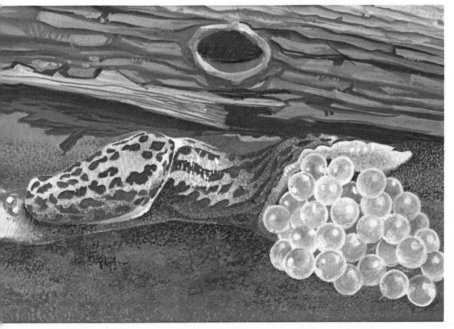

for snail hunting is when there has been some rain, or early in the morning when there is dew on the ground. This is when you will probably see the snails out in your garden. The first sort you find will most likely be the common snail. It has a fairly large shell, often two and a half centimetres high. It is a fawn colour with many patches of dark brown on it. Like the limpet of the seashore, the common snail has a fixed home to which it returns after each feeding trip. Many years ago common snails were cooked and eaten by people in many parts of the country. Nowadays, the snail which is eaten is the Roman snail. To find this, you will have to look where the ground is chalky. Its shell is much larger than that of the common snail,

about four centimetres high. If you do find one, you will recognise it straight away because of its size.

Once you have started snail hunting, you will soon find the places where they hide when it is drier. You will begin to turn over large stones, always remembering to put them back exactly as they were. You will look in clumps of grass, in rotting tree stumps and around any ruins and walls. Sooner or later, in among the brambles, perhaps, you will come across the white-lipped and the brown-lipped snails. They have pretty shells, yellow or pinkish in colour, with brown bands on them. These shells are interesting because they do not all have the same number of brown bands. They may have one, two, three, four or five. The more bands they have, the darker the shell looks. These bands

Above When two slugs mate, they twine their bodies around each other while hanging by a slime string from a branch.

Above This tiny land snail has been accidentally spread from America to all other tropical countries. Compare its size with the match beside it.

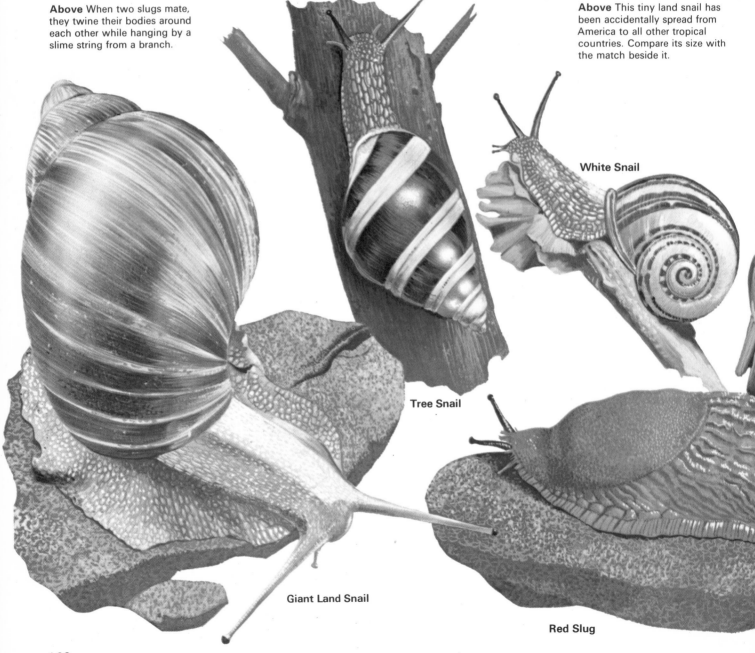

White Snail

Tree Snail

Giant Land Snail

Red Slug

are important in helping the snail to protect itself.

Thrushes like to eat these snails. They pick them up in their beaks and smash them against a stone to break the shells. The birds have a special stone for this. It is called an *anvil-stone* and you may find one if you look carefully. It will have plenty of broken snail shells around it. The colour pattern on the snail shell helps it to blend in with its surroundings. Those snails that live in the darker places under bushes need a darker shell than those that live out in the meadow where it is lighter. If you find an anvil-stone pick up some of the broken shells and count the bands on each. See if they are all the same type. If a thrush found them, they did not blend in very well with their surroundings, so try to find where they might have come from. It might be possible then to find some of the snails the thrush did not get and count the brown bands on those.

When you go out snail hunting, take your notebook and pencil with you. When you find snails, write down where it is. You might write, 'Common snail. Under old bricks in farm yard'. Or 'Brown-lipped snail. In brambles'. As time goes on, you will begin to find that certain kinds are found only in certain places. This is because each kind of snail is best adapted to living in a particular kind of place.

The snails of Britain may have quite pretty patterns on their shells, but their colours are rather dull. In Cuba and other hot countries, there are snails that have very bright shells red, black and vivid yellow. Mostly, however, land and fresh-water snails are dull coloured. The brightest shells are found on the sea snails, which is why they are collected so much. But a naturalist should be much more interested to find out as much as he can about the living animals, not just collect pretty shells.

The soil
A lump of soil picked up from the garden or from a farmer's ploughed field, looks very solid. But over half of the lump is empty space, with air and water between the soil particles. These three parts, the solid, the water and the air, make up most of the soil that we see. The solid part is made of pieces of rock. Of course they are very small pieces indeed. Because there are many different kinds of rock in the world, there are also many different soils. Some may be sandy and others made from clay. They vary in colour too; brown, black, red, dull yellow and all because they were made from different rocks. The tiny rock pieces have different shapes, and so as they lie against one another there are spaces left between them. The small spaces are usually filled with water because every particle has a thin layer, or *film*, of water around it. The bigger spaces have air in them.

It is in this dark world that the soil animals and plants live. Day after day, many of them never see daylight unless turned up by a spade or a burrowing animal. The largest animals that go underground, such as badgers or the aardvaarks of Africa, are easily seen, but the smallest are too small to see without a microscope.

Some of the most important living things in the soil are the very small *bacteria*. Bacteria are very tiny plants which are found in the air as well as in

Below Slugs and snails show a great variety of size and colour, but they all have eyes on stalks and a single foot.

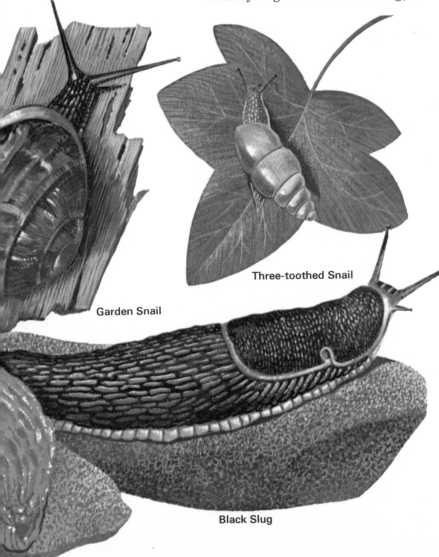

Three-toothed Snail

Garden Snail

Black Slug

the ground. In fact, they live almost everywhere and a few of them cause diseases. Luckily for us, most of them are harmless and some do a great deal of good. Many of those that live in the soil build up certain substances called *nitrates* which bigger plants need in order to grow. Under the microscope, bacteria look like dots and rods but they are so small that a quarter of a million of them could be covered by a full stop like the one at the end of this sentence.

Plants are everywhere. We think of those in the soil as being the large trees and flowers that can be seen all around. But only parts of them are actually in the soil. In damp weather it is sometimes possible to see green patches on the top of the soil. These are made up of masses of green plants, the mosses and algae. Algae grow under the soil as well as on top. If you remember, there are algae in pond water and some of those from the soil are very much like them.

Moving in the film of water around the soil particles are one-celled animals called *protozoa*. Sometimes they come to rest and make a hard wall around themselves. They will do this if the soil becomes too dry, or if there is not enough food. In this way, they can keep alive until rain comes. There are many kinds of protozoa in the soil, and new kinds are being discovered

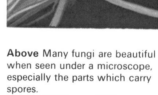

Below Earthworms have bodies made of many segments; roundworms do not. Some roundworms live inside animals.

Above Many fungi are beautiful when seen under a microscope, especially the parts which carry spores.

all the time. There are some that lash themselves along by one or two hairs on the end of their body. Another is called an amoeba. It has no fixed shape but as it moves, it pushes out what looks like a blunt finger. This gets longer and the rest of the animal 'flows' into it. These protozoa feed on the bacteria and algae that they meet on their travels. In turn, they will be eaten by other creatures. There are food chains in the world of the soil as there are in the pond and the sea.

Sometimes when weeding in the garden, among the grains of soil can be seen something that looks like a piece of very fine thread, about two and a half centimetres long. This is an animal called a roundworm and although not often noticed, roundworms live in the soil in enormous numbers. Somebody once found out that in the soil of a meadow there were so many that a square metre would have twenty million roundworms in it! Mainly because they are small, we

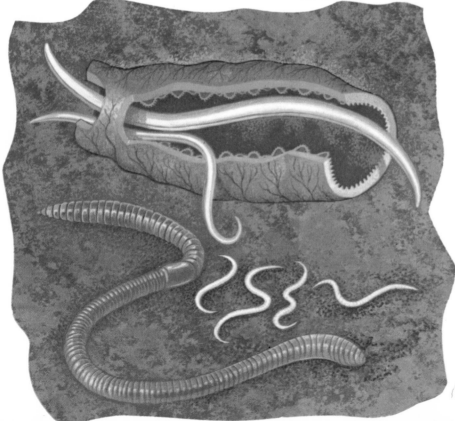

just do not see them. It would take about twenty-five small ones to make a centimetre and they are very thin, too. They live in the spaces and water films in the soil, feeding on bacteria, algae and protozoa. More important than the roundworms that live among the soil grains are the ones that live in plants and feed on them. These kinds cause all sorts of plant diseases in farm crops such as potatoes and sugar beet.

The eggs of those that harm potatoes are laid in the soil and may hatch each year, but most hatch only when the roots of potatoes get close to them. The young then force their way into the roots and live in the potato plant. The plants may still live, but the potatoes they form will be small.

Earthworms

Earthworms are very different from roundworms. They are larger and their bodies are made up of segments. With a magnifying glass it is possible to see that each segment has four pairs of bristles on it. If you run your finger gently along the underside of an earthworm, you can feel a slight roughness. This is caused by these bristles which stick out just a little way through the skin. The worm moves by being able to push against the soil with the bristles. A worm has a mouth but no

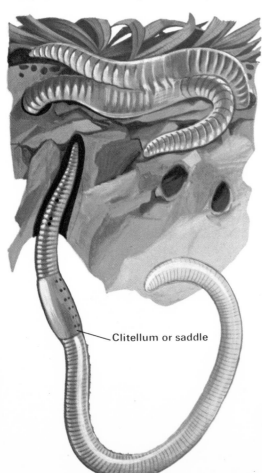

Clitellum or saddle

Above There are many kinds of earthworms living in the ground. It is easier to find them if the soil is dug when it is damp for then they are found nearer the surface. How many different ones can you find in your garden?

Left Worms mate on top of the ground but the eggs are laid in the soil. The thickened part of the worm's body is called the 'saddle' and is the part which makes the cocoon to contain the eggs.

teeth and it has no eyes. Because it is larger and stronger than the very tiny soil animals, it does not have only to stay in the water films and air spaces, but can burrow its way through the soil. As it forces its way forward, it eats some of the soil. Anything in it which is good for food is taken out inside the worm's body and the rest passes through. This is often left on the surface of the ground as a *worm cast*. In this way, the worms are always helping to turn over the soil and take air down into it. There are plenty of earthworms to do this. Although there are fewer earthworms than roundworms, a field will have many thousands in it and sometimes millions.

Over a hundred years ago, a very famous naturalist named Charles Darwin studied earthworms and wrote a book about them. He found out how many tons of soil the worms turn over each year. He also tried to find out what sorts of leaves worms like to eat when they come to the surface. You

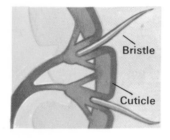

could try some of the experiments that Charles Darwin did. All you need are one or two fairly big flower-pots full of soil that is not too dry. Dig up a few earthworms and put some in each of the pots. They will soon burrow down. Each evening, place on top of the soil some small leaves of as many different plants as you wish. Pieces of cabbage, carrot, apple and grass leaves will do, but put some leaves that have a strong smell, such as lavender, if you can. During the night, the worms will come to the surface and take some of the leaves down, but they may leave others. Write down in your notebook which ones the worms take and which they leave.

If you would like to see how earth-worms turn the soil over, this is quite simple, too. A glass jar is needed. A jam jar will do, but if you can find something taller this will be better. Into the jar put a layer of soil, then a layer of sand, some more soil, some ashes if you have some, and then a last layer of soil. There is no special thick-ness for these layers, but you should be able to see them clearly. Next you must make a tube of dark paper or thin card to go around the jar. This

Above The top picture shows worm cocoons containing eggs. Beneath is a picture of a section of a worm's body to show the bristles which help it to get a grip on the ground when moving.

Below This beetle is a type of click beetle. The larvae of certain click beetles (bottom) live underground and are the 'wire-worms' that gardeners and farmers dislike so much because of the damage they do to the roots of plants.

need only be a piece wrapped around and kept in place with sticky tape. Make sure that the soil is damp and then put some worms on to it. They will burrow down and disappear from sight. After a few days, take off the paper tube. Some of the burrows may have been made close to the side of the glass so that you can see the size of them. If the worms have been burrow-ing well, you should be able to see that the different layers in the jar have been mixed up. You must not keep the worms too long. Let them go when you have seen what they can do.

Earthworms lay eggs. Near the head end of the worm is a thickened band called the *saddle*. Here the worm makes a slime tube around its body. It moves backwards slowly so that the slime tube is pushed towards the front end. On its way, the eggs are laid into it and as it is pushed over the end of the worm, the ends of the tube close up. The eggs are then in a bag, or *cocoon*. When the young worms come out, they are like their parents but much smal-ler. Not all worms are the same size, of course, but none in this country can match a certain kind that lives in Australia. These may be over three metres long!

Beetle larvae

There are many other animals living in the soil, eating rotting plants, dead animal remains and even, like some of the beetles, catching living things. Most of them play their part in keeping the soil a fit place for life to exist, but others are pests. Some pests cause great damage to crops and they only spend part of their lives in the soil.

One of these is called the wire-worm. It is not a worm at all, although its body is worm-shaped. At one end are three pairs of legs. It is an insect larva. This wire-worm, with the tough, yellowish-brown skin, is the larva of a beetle called a click beetle. During the summer, these beetles with their nar-row, brown body, are very common in fields and hedges. When they are caught and laid on their back, they can spring the right way up again with a sharp 'click'. This is how they get their name. Their eggs are laid close to the plant that the larvae will feed on. When they hatch, the larvae live under the soil among the plant roots. They may stay in the soil three, four, or even five years before they go a little deeper. There they change into

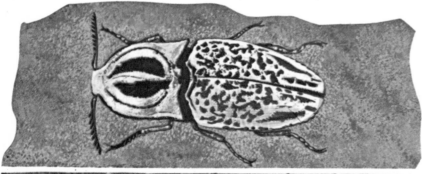

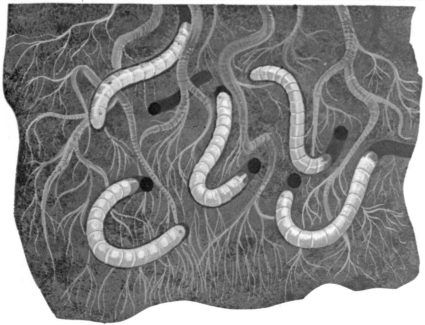

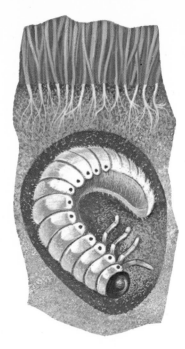

Above A cockchafer larva is large and white. The dark spots along the sides of its body are breathing holes.

pupae and in the spring, the beetles come out and struggle to the surface before flying away. Many of the wire-worms are eaten by birds, and farmers kill large numbers, but they still do a great deal of damage to root systems.

Another beetle larva that is some-times found among plant roots, is the big white grub of the cockchafer. These larvae stay in the soil for two or three years. When they are dug up by accident, they lie with their body curved round. They are fat when they are full-grown and about five centi-metres long. Some birds, such as rooks and starlings, eat them and even hedgehogs are said to dig for them, too.

Leather-jackets are also pests. They have brown, tough skins and are the larvae of crane flies. These are the large flies with long bodies and legs that are often seen in the autumn. Many people know them better by the name of Daddy-long-legs.

Above Cockchafers are also called 'May-bugs' because swarms of them fly about on May evenings. This picture shows two cockchafers mating.

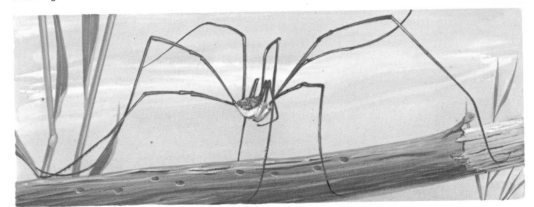

Left A harvestman. This is not an insect at all but belongs to the same group of animals as the spider.

Below left A crane fly. Because both the harvestman and the crane fly have long legs, they have the same nick-name 'Daddy-long-legs'.

Roots and fungi

You may see growing in the soil and among the rotting plants near the sur-face, some long, white threads. These are parts of plants called fungi. They are not often noticed as they feed on the dead animals and plants.

However, every now and again, part of these fungi grow up above the sur-face of the ground and then they are seen because this part is a toadstool.

If you look at a tree, you see only a piece of it. Under the ground, weaving their way among the soil grains are the roots. Miles and miles of them, spread-ing out sideways and pushing down deeper, the roots have work to do. They hold the tree firmly so that it will not blow over in the wind. The little hairs on the roots, lying in the mois-ture film, take water from the ground up to the trunk. There it goes upwards, right to the topmost leaf and is distri-buted throughout the tree.

167

Plants

There are plants growing in the dense steaming forests of South America and in the deserts of Africa. There are plants in English meadows and on mountains in New Zealand. They grow in hot lands and in cold. There are large ones and small ones; some that have flowers and some that do not. Without plants, there could be no animals. How do all these plants feed and grow and manage to live where they do?

If you carefully dig up a small flowering plant and gently knock any soil from it, you will see that it has several parts. Growing beneath the soil are the *roots*. These join the *stem* which grows above the ground. Attached to the stem are the *leaves* and perhaps some *flowers*. What work do these parts do?

The roots hold the plant firmly in the ground. They also take certain things from the soil and one of the most important is water. No plant can

live without water. It is part of the plant's food and it helps to keep the stem and leaves stiff. It is easy to see this when a flower is picked but not put into a jar of water. The flower goes very limp and wilts. Put it with the cut end of the stem in water and it may be able to draw up water and stiffen up again. The water goes through very narrow tubes which branch into every part of the plant. If you pick a small, pale-coloured flower and stand it in some red ink, you will be able to see where these tubes go. After a little while, the red ink is drawn up the stem and into the petals of the flower. The ink stains the little tubes pink and they show up very clearly.

Much of the water goes to the leaves because these are the plant's food factories. In the leaves, mostly on the underside, there are large numbers of holes. These are so small that they can only be seen with a microscope. Air can get into the leaves through these

Above The flowers in our gardens are often wild flowers from other parts of the world. Some have been collected from forests, many others from meadows and mountain sides.

Right Leaves are the food factories of plants. Using water taken up from the soil by the roots, carbon dioxide from the air and energy from the sun, plants are able to make sugar. Some is used at once, and the remainder is moved to storage places, perhaps the roots, and changed into starch.

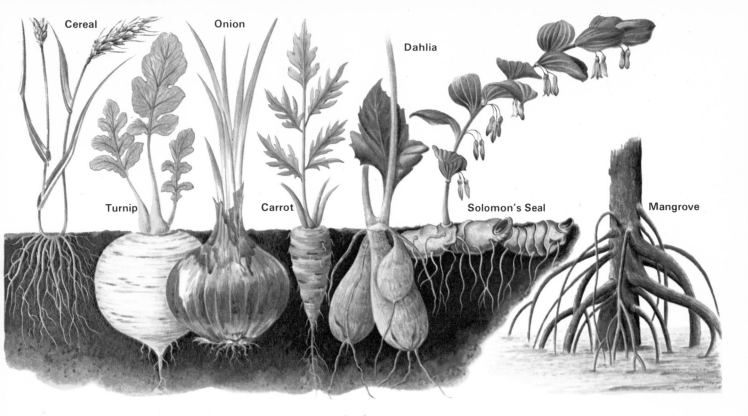

Cereal

Onion

Dahlia

Turnip

Carrot

Solomon's Seal

Mangrove

Above The parts of a plant that are underground are not always roots. Some plants have their stem and even leaves buried in the soil. These are often used as food stores. The mangrove (right) has roots that grow out above the water of the swamps where it lives.

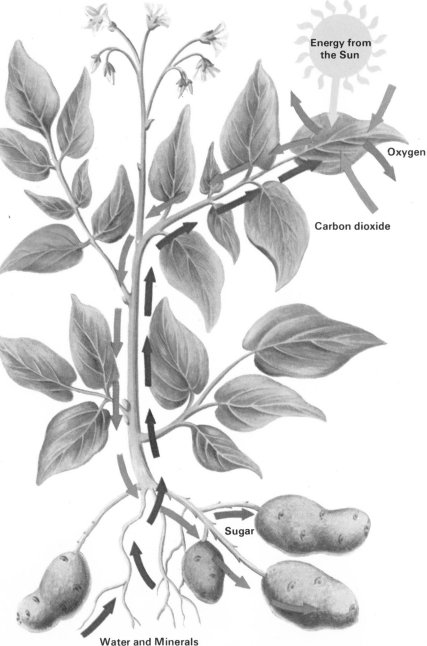

Energy from the Sun

Oxygen

Carbon dioxide

Sugar

Water and Minerals

holes. Air has several gases in it which cannot be seen. One is called *oxygen*. This is the gas that all living things, both animals and plants, must have. When we breathe, we are getting oxygen from the air. Plants breathe, too, but they do not have to make any movements like we do. The air simply flows in through those holes in the leaves. There is also a gas in the air called *carbon dioxide*. This is what the plant needs to help with food-making. So far it has some water and some carbon dioxide in its leaves. What else does it need? It needs some *energy*.

Our energy comes from the food we eat, but the plant is trying to make its own food so the energy it needs for this must come from somewhere else. It comes from the sun. Sunlight is a great store of energy and the leaves are able to trap some of it. The plant makes food in its leaves from water, carbon dioxide and energy from the sun. The food it makes is *sugar*. It may use some at once but most of the sugar is turned into *starch*. This can be stored more easily but can be changed quickly into sugar again when the plant needs it.

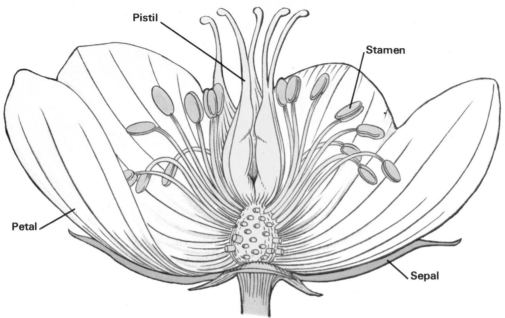

Pistil

Stamen

Petal

Sepal

Flowers

When we walk in the country, or go to a flower show, we see how different the flowers of plants can be. Some are very simple, but on the other hand, members of the daisy family are very complicated because what looks like a single flower is really many flowers growing tightly pressed together. There are flowers that open out flat and others that are long tubes. Some are red, some yellow, some white and others blue. But if you keep looking at several flowers you will soon notice that although they may seem so very different, they are much the same in many ways. For example, they most likely have a ring of coloured parts called the *petals*. There are some garden flowers that have many petals, but most wild flowers have fewer, sometimes only three, four or five. If the petals are joined together, then the flower becomes a tube.

Before the flower opens, the bud is often covered by *sepals*, which are like small, pointed, green leaves. When the flower opens, the sepals usually hang down beneath the petals. Inside the ring of petals are the parts which make the powdery *pollen*. There is also the small, green box with the little future seeds in it.

Why do plants have flowers?

There are many kinds of plants that do not have flowers at all. They seem to manage without them. So why do some plants have flowers with bright petals? The answer is that these flowering plants are going to make *seeds*. These plants will need the help of insects to make seeds and the bright petals are to attract them. Anyone watching flowers in the garden on a sunny day cannot help seeing the bees that visit one after the other. But bees are not their only visitor. Plenty of flies visit the flowers as well.

Often the flowers that flies visit are not the pretty ones we like in our gardens, but other kinds that grow in woods and forests. Butterflies visit flowers, too, and moths are attracted to those that are still open in the evening. The insects go to the flowers to feed on pollen or the sweet nectar. They may be attracted by the colour of the petals, or the shape, or the smell. So the insects get something from their visit, but what good is it to the plant? It is all connected with making seeds, but the insects do not know they are helping it!

171

From flower to seeds

As a flower grows on the plant, one part of it is like a small box. It is easy to see because it is usually a swelling at the top of the stem. In some flowers it is just below the petals; in others it is just above and may be hidden by them. Inside this box are some compartments. There may be only one, but more often there are two, three, or five of them. In each compartment are the future seeds, looking white and shiny. They are not proper seeds, yet, though. The top of the seed box may have a small piece, the *stigma*, sticking up from it to catch pollen.

The pollen is a fine powder which is made in ever smaller containers, *anthers*, on the ends of thin stalks called *stamens*. These pollen boxes show up either yellow or almost black inside the flower when they are ripe. If they are gently touched with the finger, pollen comes out of them.

Laburnum

Clematis

Dandelion

Poppy

Willow Herb

Milk Weed

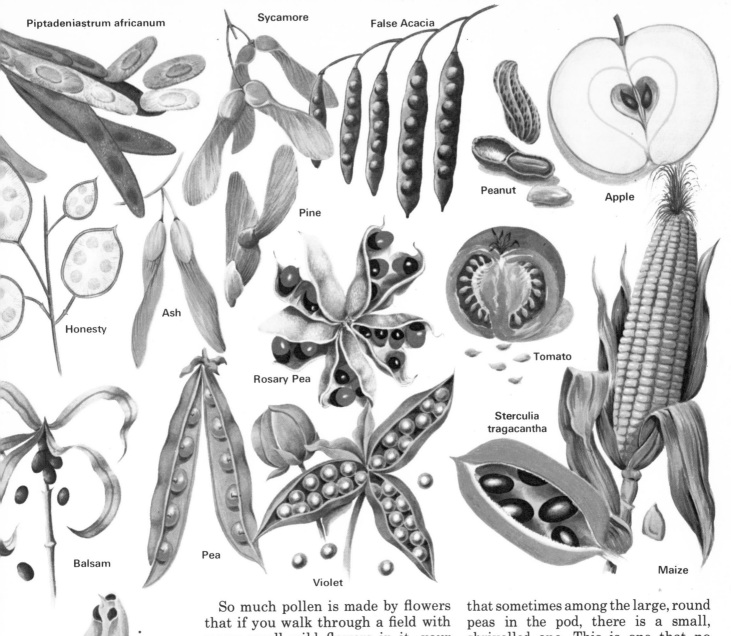

Piptadeniastrum africanum

Sycamore

False Acacia

Peanut

Apple

Pine

Honesty

Ash

Rosary Pea

Tomato

Sterculia tragacantha

Balsam

Pea

Violet

Maize

Snapdragon

Nigella or 'Love-in-a-mist'

So much pollen is made by flowers that if you walk through a field with many small wild flowers in it, your shoes will become quite yellow from the pollen that will be shaken on to them as you knock the flowers. Now, the pollen must get to the top of the seed box. It is better if the pollen from one flower goes to the seed box of another flower, as long as the second flower is of the same kind. This is where the insects come in. When they visit a flower they get pollen on their legs and body. Later they will visit another flower and some of this pollen will be brushed on to the top of the seed box of the new one.

Then a rather strange thing happens. A very, very thin tube grows from each pollen grain, down into the seed box. Each tube goes to one future seed and forces a way into it. The contents of the pollen grains go down the tubes and into the future seeds. Only if this happens will they grow into proper seeds. Perhaps you have helped to shell some garden peas. If you have, you may have noticed that sometimes among the large, round peas in the pod, there is a small, shrivelled one. This is one that no pollen reached and so it never grew.

The seeds will begin to grow when they are in the ground. This is one of the ways in which new plants are constantly being made. Like most living things, seeds vary in size. Seeds of some orchids are so small that they are a fine dust. A coconut is a seed, too, and that is thousands of times larger than the orchid seed. All seeds have a tough skin to protect them. They may have soft pulp around them, as plums and peaches do. They may even have wings so that when they fall from the plant, they glide a short distance away. Some, such as thistle seeds, have silky threads attached to them so that they drift a long way before coming to the ground.

Many seeds never manage to grow into plants. There may not be enough room for them among the other plants to seed themselves. They may not be able to get enough light, or air, or water.

Plants of deserts

Deserts are places where very little rain falls. Any plant that tries to grow in such dry places cannot usually live because it cannot get enough water. But there are some plants that can grow in deserts because they have become adapted to such dryness. When a plant grows in a moist country, there is always water being taken up by the roots. It moves up through the plant and at the end of the journey, any water left over from food-making goes out through the tiny holes in the leaves. Losing water like this does not matter if there is plenty left in the ground but if there is not, then a plant must not be so wasteful. Plants that live in deserts, or other dry places, are able to find some water in the ground. They may have long roots that can go deep into the ground where the water lies. When the roots have sucked it from the ground then the plants must store the water instead of losing it.

Above The stem of a cactus is able to swell and store water as soon as any rain falls. The places where the spines grow may really be shoots.

Left Desert plants flower regularly, although the very large cacti may not flower quite so often. Their flowers are sometimes brightly coloured.

Below Obtaining enough water is the main problem for plants growing in dry places. Many plants store water in their stems when it rains and others, like the plant below, store it in their fleshy leaves.

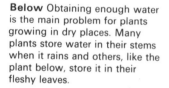

Below Gardeners who grow cacti and succulents as a hobby are likely to include the plants shown below in their collection. Some people like cacti so much that they grow nothing else.

Almost any desert scene, especially in America shows the strange plants called cacti. Cacti are able to store water in their stems. These stems are thick and have a very tough skin. Some of them are the size of young tree trunks, but inside they are soft and juicy, not hard and woody like trees. Because water is lost through the leaves, cacti do not have large, flat leaves like most of the plants you know. Instead, the leaves have become thin and shaped like needles. They are the prickles on the cactus plant and no water is lost through them.

Other plants of dry places have found a way to store water in their leaves. These become large and swollen and have a tough skin over them. These plants are called *succulents* and they may have prickles on them, too. Usually they are on the edges of the leaves and are strong and sharp.

Because of their strange shapes, many people grow cacti and succulents as a hobby. They may have very beautiful flowers on them as well. A very popular one is called the Christmas cactus because its bright red flowers bloom in December. There are cacti that only bloom once in their life. The flower does not last long either, but it will be long enough for the seeds to be formed. In a desert, the plants that bloom, usually do so after there has been rain. Even in very dry deserts, it rains a little.

Below The common name for this cactus is the prickly pear. Its real home is America but it has been brought to the warmer parts of Europe and is now quite common.

Above Very few deserts have no rain at all. As long as there is some now and again, there will be plants that are adapted to growing there.

175

Monkey Puzzle Tree

Blue Spruce

Poplar

Traveller's Tree

Beech

Horse Chestnut

Mangrove

Oak

A walk through a wood

In days gone by, many of the countries of Europe were covered by forests. Many of them have now gone, cut down to make room for farms and houses. But some woods are still left and what could be a better way to spend an afternoon than to walk among the trees and look at the life around?

The kind of tree depends on what the soil is like. If the soil is sandy, many of the trees will be pine or silver birch. The birch are easy to spot because of the white patches on the trunk. Where the ground has chalk in it, the trees may be beech with their smooth, grey bark. On clay soil, then almost certainly most of the trees will be oak. Oaks are the sort of trees that were grown for ship-building in the days when warships were made of timber. It is not often that a wood has only one type of tree in it, but always one kind is more common than the others, and so you can talk of an oak wood, a beech wood, or a pine wood.

It is interesting to collect leaves. They can be dried by pressing them for a few days between sheets of newspaper with books on top to weigh them down. Try to collect one or two leaves from every kind of tree you can find. There are plenty of books that will help you to name them and in this way you will learn to recognise the

Silver Birch

Maple

Coconut Palm

Cedar

Grass Tree

Californian Redwood

trees of your own country. In the winter, when the leaves have fallen, the bark is the part of the trees to look at. You cannot easily collect bark, but it is easy to make a collection of bark rubbings. First, hold a piece of white paper against the tree trunk so that it does not slip. Then rub hard with a thick wax crayon, backwards and forwards. The pattern of the bark will begin to show on the paper. With a little care, you can soon make a good set of rubbings and this will help you to recognise trees in winter.

Walk through an oak wood and you will see that there are plants that are taller than you are. They are not as tall as the trees and instead of having one thick trunk like the trees, they have several thinner ones. These are *shrubs*.

There are many small plants, too. There are small ones that you cannot help treading on and others that come up to your waist. Maybe some are even taller than that, but they all die back when they have finished seed-making. These sorts of plants are the *herbs* and there are many different kinds.

So in a wood the plants make several layers. There is the *tree layer*, the *shrub layer* and the *herb layer*. Some woods do not have them all. Beech woods do not, neither do many pine woods. They are too dark, for beech and pine trees make too much shade.

177

The changing wood

Suppose you walked through an oak wood once or twice every month, for a whole year. Do you think it would look the same each time? In the cold days of winter, it would seem an empty place. There would be very few plants in the herb layer. There might be some grass and perhaps some ivy on the ground. The shrubs and trees would look bare, none of them with any leaves except one or two dead ones that did not fall. But the buds are on the twigs, still folded up tightly. The plants of the wood are not dead. They are resting until the weather becomes warmer.

In February, the catkins appear on the hazel branches. They are often called 'lambs' tails' and they are really flowers which make clouds of pollen to be blown about by the wind. The future seeds are in separate flowers which are much smaller and harder to find. By March more and more plants are pushing their shoots up through the soil. Many trees flower now, but on the ground only the white anemones are in flower. In April, there are plenty of flowers. Golden yellow celandines make a carpet over some parts where the wood is more open. There are violets, too, and maybe primroses near the edge of the wood. By the end of the month, the bluebells are out. So many flowers bloom in the wood in early spring because this is when most light can get to them. Later on, the

Above Woods in the cooler countries, such as Britain, contain trees that lose their leaves in winter. On the right are some of the flowers and fruit of trees and shrubs which grow in woods from different parts of the world. Have you seen any of them?

Sloe

Cowberry

Pussywillow

Catkin

Yew

Horse Chestnut

Hazel Nut

Sweet Chestnut

California Nutmeg

Mountain Ash

Acorn

Rosehip

Planchonella

Strawberry Tree

Alder

Pernettya

Mistletoe

Privet

179

leaves of the trees make a roof over the wood and there is much less light. So most of the plants of the herb layer have bloomed and made their seeds before summer starts. In the summer months the wood is full of leaves. The trees have them, the shrubs have them and so do the herbs. Away from the paths, it may even be difficult to walk because the plants are so crowded. This is because every little bit of sunlight must be caught so that food can be made in the leaves. In summer, many of the plants are trying to store food while they can.

As the days grow shorter in autumn, the leaves begin to fall and the herbs die down. A walk in September and October shows the plants beginning to get ready for the winter. Many of the herbs will die, but their seeds are in the ground ready to grow again in the spring. And so the winter comes again and the wood rests.

If you live in a warmer country, the plants you see will be different and they will have their own time for flowering. Some countries have only a wet season and a dry one, while there are others where it is hot and wet all the time. A walk in a wood or forest in countries with a different climate will show a different order of flowering, perhaps, from that of a cool oak wood. Then you must use your eyes. Like any good naturalist, you must observe and record, which simply means look and write down what you see. Over a year, you can work out whether the plants of your country have special times for growing and flowering and when these times are.

High up in the mountains, the trees which will grow are mostly those with long, thin leaves, often called needles. Trees of this type also form their seeds in cones, so are called conifers. In the picture above you can see a selection of cones.

181

Rain forests

Plants need water and sunlight if they are to grow. They need space and some warmth. If there is not enough water, as in the hot deserts, then the plants that grow there are able to store it. In the cooler countries where the winter months are cold and the days short, many plants die down and rest until the warmer, longer days of spring. Some parts of the world are very hot and very wet all the time. Places like this are found in South America, Africa and some countries of the East. In these places that are so hot and wet, are found rain forests, or jungles as they are often called.

Many kinds of plants grow in the rain forests. Because of the heat and the rain, trees grow tall. Their branches are all high up and there are so many crossing over each other that they make a roof over the forest. This stops much of the sunlight getting down to the ground so that the forest is quite a dark place. Plants must have light and many of them are climbers that grow taller and taller. They use the trees as supports and so they are able to get their leaves nearer to the light. In all rain forests, there are many of these long vines, twining around the trees. Some plants get nearer the light by growing on the

Above and right In the hot, steamy rain forests, leaves are shaped so that the rain runs off them easily. Trees are tall, and long; hanging creepers are common. Some trees have orchids and ferns growing on their branches. The flowers that grow in these rain forests often have vivid colours and exotic shapes.

branches of the trees, or in hollows where the branches grow out from the trunks. There are plants without flowers, called ferns, which grow like this. There are also flowering plants, especially the very beautiful orchids, that find these high places just what they need.

The leaves of many of these plants are long and pointed so that the rain runs off them easily. Because of the poor light, there are not many plants in the lower layers. When a tree falls, however, it will leave a space among the branches where the sunlight can get through. In clearings like this the smaller plants can grow well. They can also grow along the banks of rivers that flow through the forest. A trip up the river in a boat is then like moving between high green walls, splashed here and there with the colours of bright flowers.

Only a person with plenty of time and a great deal of money can hope to see plants growing in every country of the world. But many of the plants can be seen without having to travel far. In most countries, there are large gardens, called Botanic Gardens, where plants from all over the world are grown. Those that have come from very hot places may have to be grown in heated glasshouses. Low growing plants from mountains are put into rock gardens. Everywhere can be seen the plants from cool countries. If you live near some of the big cities of the world, such as London, there are often very large gardens like those at Kew, where you can see banana trees, orchids, cacti and almost any plant that you can think of.

Insect-eating plants

There are a few plants that cannot get *nitrogen* from the ground. All plants must have it, but in some wet, boggy places there is not enough of it in the soil. Nitrogen is found in meat also, so there are a few plants that eat meat to get it! One that grows in some of the countries of Europe is the sundew. It lives in wet places and the leaves are round and flat, like little plates about the size of a finger-nail. They are green, and like all green plants, their leaves are able to make sugar. Over the leaf and around the edges, are red hairs. At the end of these hairs are tiny beads of a sticky fluid. When a small insect lands on a leaf or walks on to one, it gets stuck. The hairs on the edge of the leaf slowly bend over to hold the insect down. The plant is then able to dissolve the soft parts of the insect and take it into the leaf where it can be used. The hard skin and the wings are left on the leaf to be blown away by the wind.

Even stranger plants called pitcher plants are found in the tropics. A pitcher is like a vase or bottle, and these plants get their name because the leaves are folded to make a pitcher. The pitcher has part of the leaf growing as a lid over the open end. When the lid opens, insects come to the plant. They are attracted by the colour of the pitcher which is dull red and green. Once they go into the pitcher, they usually fall. The rim of it is very slippery so they cannot walk on it. There are some stiff, sharp-pointed

hairs on the rim, too. These point down into the pitcher so that an insect that tried to get out would be forced down again. There is some liquid in the bottom of the pitcher. The insects fall into this and their soft parts are dissolved away, or *digested*, by the plant.

There are many kinds of pitcher plant. In one kind, the pitcher hangs down on the end of a stalk. Another grows from the ground like a long ice-cream cone.

Above and left Sundews are found in wet places. Their short red hairs have a bead of sticky liquid on the end to trap small insects.

Below and below left Pitcher plants are found in tropical countries. Insects must fall straight into them before they can be digested as food. The pitchers of different species vary in shape and colour.

184

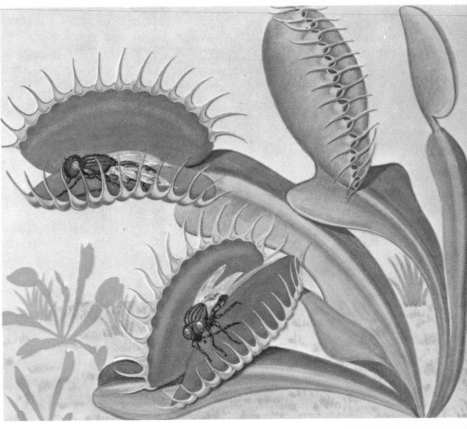

Above An enlarged picture of a Venus' fly-trap. Once an insect is trapped, there is no escape for it.

Left This is the type of pitcher plant that has the pitcher growing upwards from the ground. It is found in North America.

Below Another species of sundew. This one grows in Australia and has very narrow leaves.

The Venus' fly-trap grows in the boggy parts of Carolina, in America. This is an insect-eater, too. It has leaves with two lobes at the end. They have little spikes around the edge. These lobes lie open like the pages of a book when the plant is trying to catch something. On the lobes are three long hairs. When an insect lands on the leaf and touches the hairs, the two lobes close up quickly. The spikes around the edges fit between one another and the insect is trapped. Like the sundew and the pitcher plant, the Venus' fly-trap then digests the meaty parts of the insect. When only the skin is left, the lobes of the leaf open again. If anything touches the *trigger-hairs*, the leaf closes up. Anything meaty and the two halves keep tightly shut, but if it is only a twig or something that cannot be eaten, the lobes soon open out again. Some people grow these plants in a greenhouse for fun.

Insect-eating plants are an interesting example of how living things can change over millions of years.

Insect-eaters, like most other plants, make food in their leaves. However, they differ from other plants because they have changed the shape of their leaves to form insect traps. These strange plants have also *evolved* colours, and in some cases, smell as well, in order to entice insects to them.

185

Mosses

When there has been a fire that has burnt everything growing on a piece of ground, it is interesting to watch the burnt patch week after week. At first, the ground is black and there is no sign of life, but soon small plants appear. Most likely they will not be flowering plants at all, but some of the huge group of plants that do not have flowers. Over the burnt patch, tufts of moss will start to grow. There are many different mosses and most of them prefer damp places, but not all. Cushions of moss are common on stone walls. A moss plant has small stems and many tiny leaves. There may be some very fine rootlets to hold the moss plant in place, but they are not like the roots of a flowering plant.

In the spring and summer, the moss plant sends up a number of stalks that are very thin, almost like hairs. On the top of each stalk is a box, often egg-shaped. Some kinds of moss have a hairy cap over each box. These boxes are full of *spores*. Mosses do not make seeds as the flowering plants do. Instead they make spores which are very much smaller. When the spores are ready to grow, the top comes off the box and the spores are flung out.

Because they are so tiny, they are very light and they may be blown a long way by the wind. If they settle on a patch of empty ground, perhaps a burnt patch, the spores begin to grow and thin, green strands begin to cover the ground. These are the new moss plants.

Right Lichens are really two types of plants growing together. The main part is a fungus and within it grow tiny, single-celled algae. They are among the slowest growing of all plants. Some lichens are used for making dyes and others can be eaten.

Below Moss can be found growing around the bottom of trees and on the floor of woods. It can also grow where there have been bonfires. Bog mosses grow in very wet places and soak up water like a sponge.

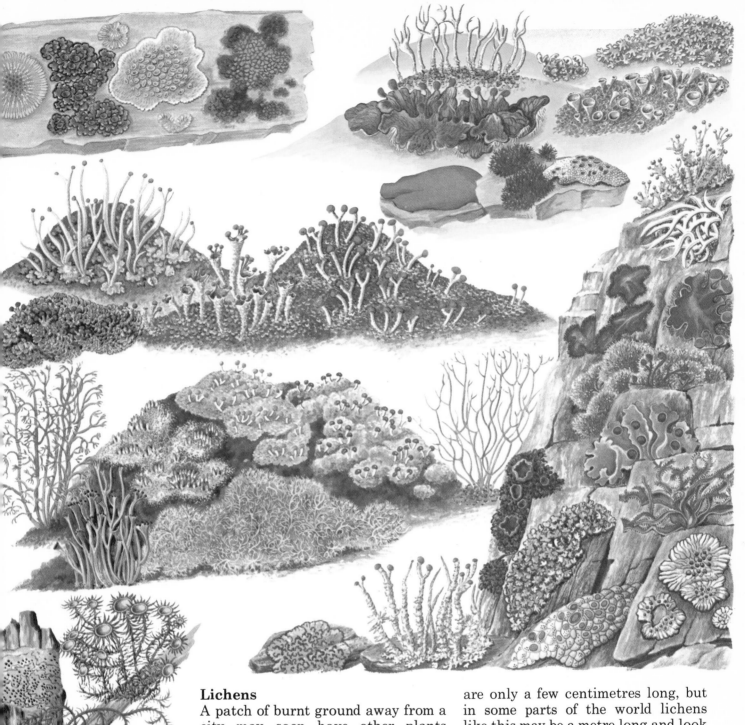

Lichens

A patch of burnt ground away from a city may soon have other plants growing on it besides mosses. There may be lichens as well. Lichens do not grow well where the air is not clean, so they do not grow very often in cities and it is best to go well away into the country to see them. Many houses and walls in the country have grey or yellow crusty patches on them. These are lichens that grow in flat patches. Not only are they on walls, but on tree trunks, broken-off branches and almost anything that has not been moved for a long time. The grave-stones in country churchyards are often almost covered by these plants. In the wetter parts of the country, many trees have lichens growing on them that look like tufts of grey whiskers hanging down. They are only a few centimetres long, but in some parts of the world lichens like this may be a metre long and look rather like long beards. Small, shrubby lichens grow on wet ground.

In the cold lands of the Arctic, where many plants find it hard to grow, lichens are common. In fact, they are important as food for many animals. Reindeer eat a great deal of the lichen often called reindeer moss, although it is not really a moss at all.

Some of the prettiest lichens are those that grow on the ground. They are only two and a half centimetres high and they remind one of tiny egg-cups on stalks. Another similar kind has bright red tips on the ends of stalks. In some parts of America, this lichen is called 'British soldiers' because of the bright red coats that soldiers used to wear many years ago.

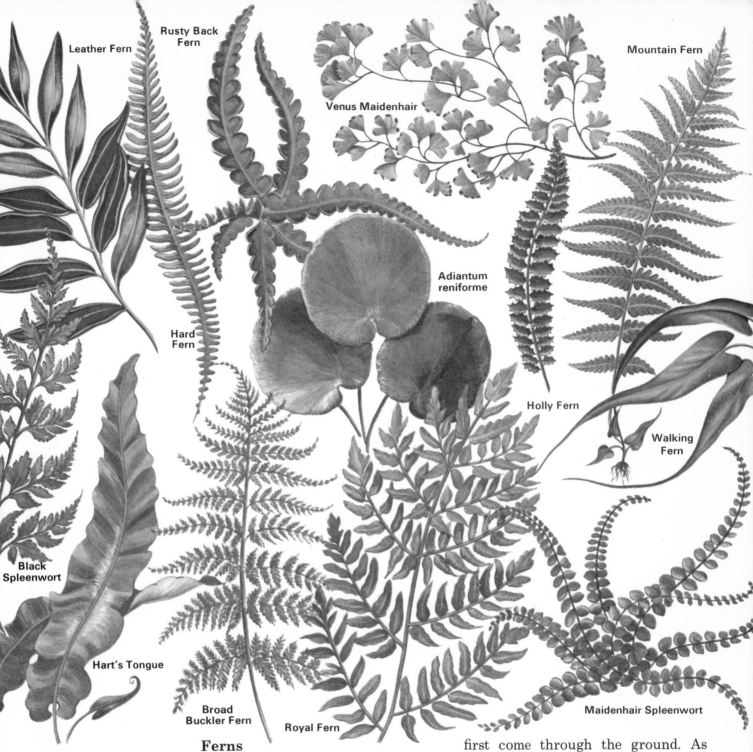

Leather Fern

Rusty Back Fern

Venus Maidenhair

Mountain Fern

Hard Fern

Adiantum reniforme

Holly Fern

Walking Fern

Black Spleenwort

Hart's Tongue

Broad Buckler Fern

Royal Fern

Maidenhair Spleenwort

Ferns

Above There are about 7000 different kinds of ferns in the world. Most of them grow in places that are warm and damp. Some even grow floating on water. However, a few kinds of ferns grow in dry places.

Left Most ferns are quite small but tree ferns can reach sixteen metres or more in height. They grow in hot, wet forests such as those of the West Indies and parts of Australia and New Zealand.

Go into almost any wood and you will see ferns growing. These are also plants that do not have flowers and make spores instead of seeds. Millions of years ago, the ferns were much more important than they are today. There are still many of them and about seven thousand different kinds are growing all over the world. Most of them like damp, shady places. A few even grow floating on water. Some have been given odd-sounding names, such as adder's-tongue fern and elkhorn fern. One very common one is bracken which grows about a metre tall in woods and on hill-sides. Another common one is male fern. Like all ferns, it has beautiful leaves which are neatly folded round when they

first come through the ground. As they grow, they uncurl slowly. In the late summer, brown spore-cases can be seen on the underside of the leaves. Each one is no bigger than a pin-head, but large numbers of spores drift away from them when they split. The spores do not grow right away into new fern plants. First they grow to form a flat, green piece, which is heart-shaped and smaller than your finger-nail. Only later do leaves begin to grow from this. The stems of some ferns grow under the ground and send up leaves every so often. In this way, the fern can cover large patches of ground.

In the tropical forests, there are many ferns that grow high in the trees, attached to the branches.

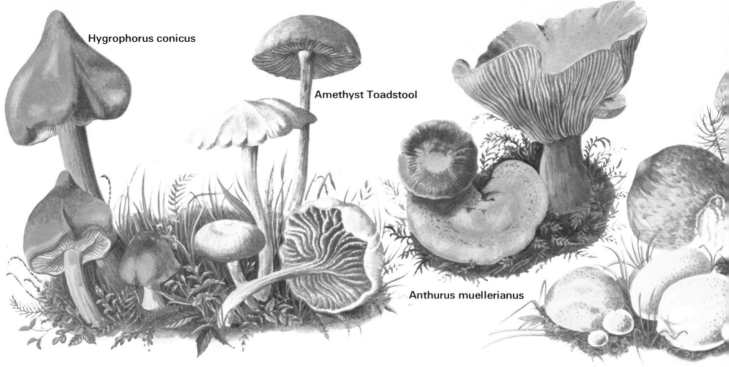

Hygrophorus conicus

Amethyst Toadstool

Anthurus muellerianus

Clavaria pallida

Fungi

Have you ever eaten mushrooms, or seen them for sale in a shop? And have you seen a piece of stale bread with a white or grey fluff on it? A piece of bread like this has 'gone mouldy'. The mushrooms and the mould on the bread are two plants that also belong to the flowerless group. This time, to the group called the *fungi*. Unlike other plants, fungi cannot make their food and so they live on rotting wood and leaves, or on stale food that we have not used. It is surprising where fungi can live. If some of the bark is pulled off a fallen tree that is rotting, there will be some white threads over the wood. This is the part of the fungus that does the feeding. It dissolves part of the wood

and takes it up into the threads. In this way fungi help to break down old dead plants; this is an important part of soil-making.

Sometimes the white threads bunch together and grow out into the air. This is the part of the fungus that we usually see and call a toadstool, if it is large. The work of the toadstool is to make spores, in the same way that mosses and ferns make them, too. The spores are blown away and grow into new threads. The spores are coloured black, or brown, or even pink. You can see them if you pick a toadstool which is shaped like an umbrella. A big mushroom will do well. Pull off the stalk and lay the top of the toadstool flat on to a piece of white paper. Be very careful not to touch it any

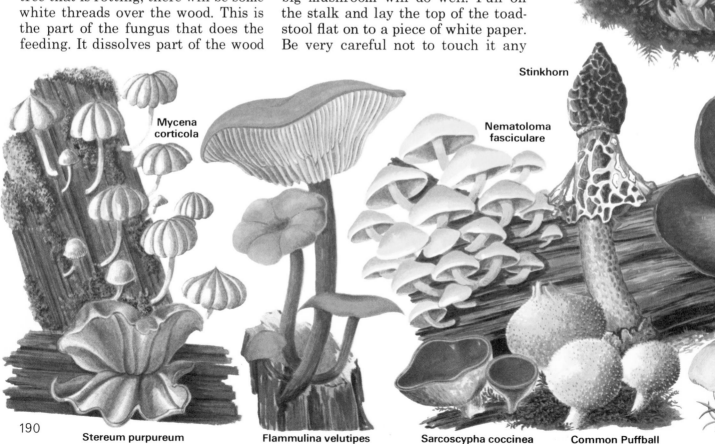

Mycena corticola

Stinkhorn

Nematoloma fasciculare

Stereum purpureum

Flammulina velutipes

Sarcoscypha coccinea

Common Puffball

Verdigris Agaric

Inocybe fastigiata

Russula emetica

Wood Agaric

Helvella crispa

more and leave it on the paper until the next day. If you then lift the toadstool carefully, you will see a pattern on the paper. It will look like the spokes of a wheel and probably be coloured brown. The side of the toadstool that was touching the paper has flat gills also coming from the centre like the spokes of a wheel. The spores are made on the gills and so when they dropped on to the paper, the pattern was made.

Toadstools can be found at most times of the year, but the best time is in the autumn. Then a walk through the woods and fields will show many different kinds. Some, like the mushroom, can be eaten but others are very poisonous. Most of them grow on the ground, but there are fungi that grow

from the trunks of trees. These are called *bracket fungi* and they often become very hard. If you become interested in fungi and start hunting for them, you will soon notice that each kind of fungus grows in a certain place. Under pine trees you can find the fungus with a bright red cap. This is a poisonous one and would make you very ill if you were to eat it by accident. In other kinds of woods grows the fungus with a bright yellow cap. If you run your finger-nail gently across the gills, it will make a rustling noise. The prettiest of the umbrella-shaped fungi is the one called the fly agaric. This is found quite often under birch trees. The cap is bright red and has small white patches on it. But it is very poisonous and best left alone.

Cup Fungus

Fairy Ring Mushroom

Shaggy Inkcap

Otidea onotica

Deathcap

Fly Agaric

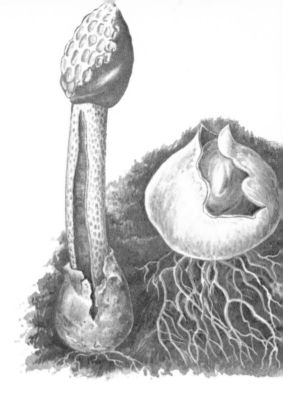

Earth-balls are very common in woods. They are ball-shaped and grow close to the soil. So do the puffballs which burst open when they are ripe and puff their spores into the air. The giant puffball may be over thirty centimetres across. There are several different kinds of fungi that grow on old tree stumps. Some are like small, orange, branching trees. One fungus that is always exciting to find is the stinkhorn. This grows about fifteen centimetres high and seems to be all stalk, but on top is a very dark brown, slimy mass of spores. As you can tell from its name, it has a horrid smell. It attracts flies which land on the spores. When they fly off, they carry spores with them on their feet. If you look among the dead leaves near the stinkhorn, you may find one that has not begun to grow upwards. It is like an egg made of jelly. If you carefully pull up the 'egg' you can take it home. It will grow if it is placed on wet cotton-wool and it is possible to watch the stinkhorn break from the 'egg' and grow taller and taller. It takes several hours and is best done at the end of the garden because of the smell.

There is no end to the fungi that can be found in the countryside. It is never easy to find the right name for each one, even with books to help, but this is not really very important. If you make small sketches with notes about the colour, this is just as good. And, of course, always write down where the fungi are growing when they are found.

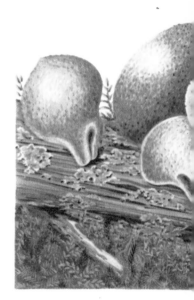

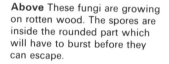

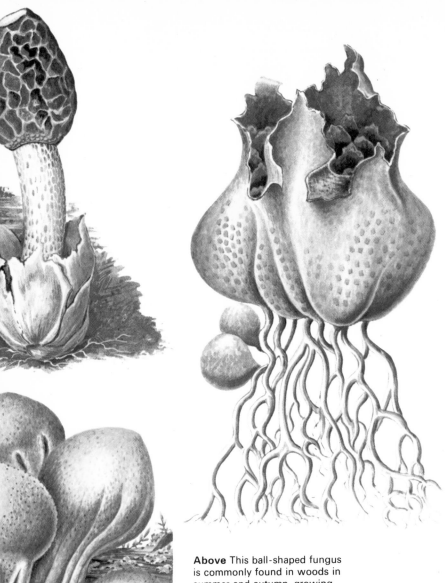

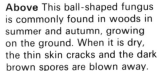

Above This ball-shaped fungus is commonly found in woods in summer and autumn, growing on the ground. When it is dry, the thin skin cracks and the dark brown spores are blown away.

What to do with plants

If you are interested in plants, you may want to collect some. Fungi soon rot and so they should be left alone. Lichens dry very well and can be kept in empty match boxes. Ferns and flowering plants can be dried and this will preserve them. If a flower is put into a box and covered with fine, dry sand, the flower will lose any water it has in its petals and they will become dry and papery. The shape of the flower stays and sometimes the colour. This is fun to try, but when the flower is dry, storing it is a problem. So most people who want to make a collection of plants, dry them in some kind of press which flattens them. Pressing plants is quite easy. You will need two pieces of plywood or hardboard, about forty centimetres long and twenty-five centimetres wide. Between the boards you will need plenty of sheets of newspaper about the same size. Last of all you will need six bricks. If the bricks are wrapped up in brown paper like a parcel, they will not make a mess. Any plants you collect are placed carefully between the sheets of paper.

Start with one board on the table. Place a few sheets of paper on the board and then a plant. Cover the plant with a few more sheets of paper and then put in another plant. So you can go on, making sandwiches of paper and plants, until all your plants are in the press. The second board is put on the top of the pile and then the six bricks. These make the weight that will flatten the plants. The paper removes the moisture in them.

After a few days, the plants should be dry. They will be quite stiff if they are finished. Then they can be stuck on to sheets of stiff paper, or into a drawing book. You can use glue for sticking or pieces of sticky tape. You should try to find out the name of each plant from books and then you should write this by the plant, and also where it was found and the date. Do not try to press too many plants at first. Try two or three and never, never, pick large bunches of wild flowers. When you find that you can press flowers well, then why not try to make a small collection of the plants that grow near your home, or even of the weeds that grow in your garden? You will certainly learn a great deal about plants this way.

Mammals

Mammals are animals with warm bodies. To help them keep warm, they have a coat of fur or hair. Their young are born alive and active, not inside a shell as birds are. When the babies are born, they are fed on milk made by their mother.

They are a very large group of animals, and mammals can be found in most countries of the world. There are those like the lion and the giraffe that live in hot countries. On the other hand, mammals such as the polar bear and the musk ox are better adapted for a life in the cold. You have already read about the mammals that live in water and those that fly. On the land, mammals can be found that live in trees and do not often come down. No animal can

move about among tall trees in the same way as it would on the ground, so the tree-living mammals may have special eyes and arms to help them get about without falling. There are mammals that live under the ground. This may mean that they will have to dig a great deal, so their legs may be extra strong to do that. On the ground there are large mammals and small ones, slow mammals and fast-moving ones. There are some with long coats, others with short. A few mammals have become friends of man, or work for him, but most are shy and keep away from people if they can. In fact, there are many, many different kinds of mammal, all of them fitted for a special way of life and all of them interesting.

Star-nosed Mole

East American Mole

UNDER THE GROUND

Some days when walking across a field, small heaps of earth can be seen here and there. These have been thrown up by burrowing animals, the moles.

A mole is about fifteen centimetres long with thick, soft black fur. The fur stands upright so that the mole can move forwards or backwards through its tunnels without getting the fur tangled up in any roots. It has a very short tail and a rather long nose that is very sensitive. Many people think that moles have no eyes but this is not true. Since they generally live under the ground, eyes are not very important to a mole, so they are small and hidden by the fur. Their ears are hard to see, too. The mole has wonderful front feet. They are

Above The star-nosed mole has a number of feelers on the end of its nose which gives its head a strange appearance. The Eastern American mole has webbed feet but it does not live in water.

Below The mole uses its front foot for digging. It is tough with strong claws to cut into the soil. With both front feet working hard, moles can burrow at an amazing speed.

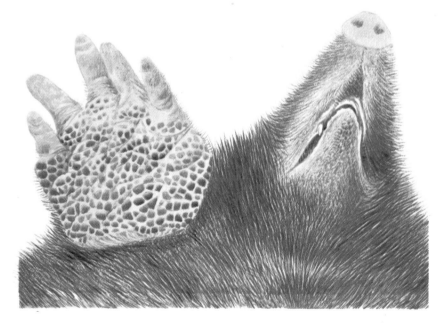

very strong with large claws and turned backwards so that the mole can scrape away at the soil more easily. In fact, moles can burrow very fast indeed. Most of the time they dig for their food which is mainly worms. Of course, they will eat anything else which they can find, if it can be eaten. Worms are not always easy to find, so if a mole is hunting one day and there are more worms than it needs, it will store them. It bites the worms with its sharp little teeth in such a way that the worms are not killed. They keep alive but cannot move. Then the mole digs a small store-room off one of its tunnels and puts the worms in that. In this way, it will always have some food put by for a bad day. Moles even make their nests underground and the young moles are born there.

Badgers

Badgers do not spend as much time under the ground as moles do. They dig burrows, where they live during the day. A number of burrows together is called a *sett*, and some setts are very old. Families of badgers have lived in them for many years. These mammals are much larger than moles. A male badger, called a *boar*, can weigh sixteen kilograms or more. Their greyish coat is rough and on their face are black and white stripes. It may be that badgers are able to see one another better by having these stripes. They do not come out of the sett until dusk and without the white patches, they would be hard to see. During the night, the badgers shuffle about, hunting for beetles, worms, snails and almost anything else. Often they eat grass if meat is hard to find. Badgers are very clean animals and the entrance to some of their tunnels may show heaps of grass and bracken. This shows that a badger is having a spring-clean. It is his old bedding which has been thrown out. The badger will have taken new bracken for a clean bed. Badgers burrow a great deal and their front legs and shoulders are very strong. The claws on their front feet are long, too, to help with the digging.

Above The old country name for the badger is 'Brock'. Badgers are quite common, but very shy, and because they stay in their sett during the day, they are not often seen.

Below The Ratel, or honey-badger, is found in Africa, the Middle East and India. Its long claws are useful for breaking open bees' nests so it can take the honey. A bird called the honeyguide leads the ratel to the bees' nest.

Jerboas

A burrowing mammal of the deserts is the jerboa. These small mammals with soft fur, dig burrows where they can go when it is too hot during the day. They find their food above the ground and have very large hind legs. With these, they are able to jump about and go quite a long way looking for insects and plants. This is necessary because food can be rather scarce in the desert.

ON THE GROUND
Food

All mammals must eat. Many are plant-eaters and these, in turn, will be food for the meat-eaters. The plant-eaters do not all eat in the same sort of places. There are the grass-eaters that take only the plants close to the ground. Certain mammals eat the leaves of small shrubs, while others go for the low branches of trees. Then there are those, such as elephants and giraffes, that can reach the leaves high up on the trees. In this way the food is divided up so that the animals are able to share it.

The meat-eaters are usually fast-running so that they can run down and kill their prey. But some are not hunters at all and feed on the animals that have already died, or on the left-overs from a hunter's meal. There are some meat-eating mammals that find their food in ant-hills. Ant-eaters have found a way to get meat without having to run very fast and although one ant would not be much of a meal, where the ant-eaters live there are huge numbers of them. It is often possible to tell what an animal eats by looking at its teeth. A plant-eater will need good grinding teeth because grass and leaves take plenty of chewing. Meat-eaters need some teeth for killing and ripping, and others for slicing up the tough, raw meat. Ant-eaters need no teeth at all really, just a sticky tongue for collecting the ants.

Right All living things need energy. Plants are able to store the sun's energy in the food they make. To get this energy for themselves, there are many animals that eat plants. There are plenty of plants in the world so plant-eating animals are common. A smaller number of animals obtain their energy by eating, not the plants, but the plant-eaters instead. Last of all, there are a few animals that eat mostly plant-eaters, but may once in a while tackle one of the smaller meat-eaters too. Animals of this kind can be called super meat-eaters.

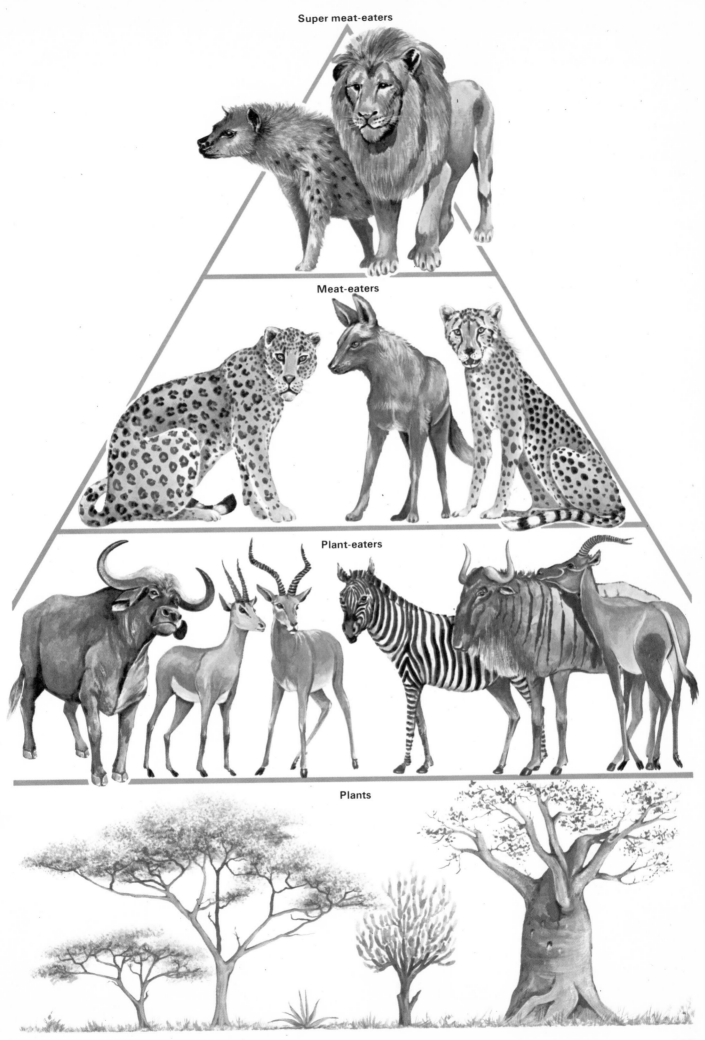

Super meat-eaters

Meat-eaters

Plant-eaters

Plants

ANIMALS THAT GNAW

If you have ever kept pet mice, you will know that they cannot be housed in a wooden cage because they will eat their way out. Mice, rats and other animals that gnaw have special front teeth for doing this. Gnawing wears away the animal's teeth, so the front ones always have to keep growing. In this way they never wear out. Rats and mice are found all over the world. House mice are able to live wherever there are people, but other kinds live in woods and fields. The little harvest mice climb around among the stalks of grasses and in fields of wheat. They make nests built around the stalks in summer, but in winter they go underground. There are huge numbers of mice, but because most of them are small and keep out of the way, there do not seem to be many. Most of their food is made up of seeds and parts of plants, but like many animals, they will often eat anything.

Bank Vole

Dormouse

European Harvest Mouse

House Mouse

Black Rat

Common Black-bellied Hamster

Wild Cavy

Collared Lemming

Red Squirrel

Eastern Grey Squirrel

Above left The wood mouse, or long-tailed field mouse as it is also called, is a little larger than a house mouse. The fur of its back is reddish-brown and its belly is greyish-white. It feeds on nuts, berries, grain and insects and is very common in woods and fields.

Above The nest that the tiny harvest mouse makes in summer is a hollow ball of grass or blades of corn, a little way above the ground. Harvest mice weigh so little that they can scramble about on the stalks, curling their tail around them as extra support.

Left The commonest kinds of mice in North America are the white-footed mice and the deer mice. They look very much alike. Deer mice are a little larger than house mice and in many ways are similar to the wood mice of Europe.

Voles and hamsters are relatives of mice. Golden hamsters are popular as pets and it is fascinating to watch them eat. Many mammals have pouches between their teeth and their cheeks where food can be stored to be carried back to the animal's home. Hamsters have very large cheek pouches and they will stuff so much food into them that their heads look huge.

High up in the Andes mountains of South America live the gnawing animals called chinchillas. They need to keep very warm because the winds in the mountains are very strong and cold. So these beautiful grey mammals have some of the thickest and softest fur of any mammals in the world.

Above Meadow voles are among the commonest mammals in Europe. They have much blunter noses than mice and a shorter tail. Although they breed fast and have many young each year, they are eaten in huge numbers by birds of prey, weasels and foxes.

Left The chinchillas of the Andes are about the size of rats. They have very soft, grey fur and at one time nearly became extinct because they were so over-hunted. Chinchillas cannot burrow because their claws are too small, but they can run about very well among the stones and rocks of the mountainside.

Above Tree porcupines move about slowly among the branches, feeding on leaves and bark. They sleep during the day and come out at night. The quills of the tree porcupines are much shorter than those of ground-living varieties.

Right Porcupines are found in parts of Europe, in Africa and Asia. If they are attacked, they raise their quills and charge backwards. The quills are very pointed and may injure the attacking animal very seriously.

Porcupines

Another gnawing animal with very strong teeth and jaws is the porcupine. These animals are well known because of their quills, those sharp, stiff bristles that they use for defending themselves. They wander about at night looking for roots, fruit and green-stuff to eat, making plenty of noise to warn other animals they are about.

Rabbits

Rabbits are gnawing animals also, although they are not very close relatives of the other gnawing animals you have read about. The rabbits of Europe and Australia are burrowing animals, but they do not do this as much now as they used to. There is a disease which kills rabbits and it spreads among them when they are together down their burrows. Many

thousands have died from this disease and now many naturalists believe that the ones that are left do not go underground as often. They still make small burrows when they are going to have their young. These burrows have a room at the end where the mother rabbit can make a nest, using some of her own fur.

The young rabbits must be kept warm for they are born without any fur of their own at first. They are blind, too, and so they have to be carefully looked after until they can see and until they are big enough to look after themselves.

Rabbits can run very quickly indeed. Their back legs are very strong so that if there is danger, they can run away with long leaps. Their ears are large so that they are able to hear the slightest sound.

Above Hares do not burrow as rabbits do. The young are born on the ground, and the mother does not even make a nest for them. Leverets, as the young hares are called, are born covered with fur and their eyes open.

Below The snowshoe hare of America has a white coat in winter. It also grows long hair under its feet so that it can walk about more easily on the snow.

GRAZING AND BROWSING ANIMALS (THE LEAF-EATERS)

In the great grasslands that stretch right across Africa, thousands of graceful animals called antelopes, are using grass for food. As there are hundreds of miles of grasslands, the herds of antelopes can be large. Many of them, however, move about in smaller family groups. Most of them are some shade of brown and are not easy to spot among the tall, dry grass. All the many different types of antelopes have horns and each type has its own special shape. The horns of the big sable antelope are great curved

Dik-Dik

Eland

Impala

Bushbuck

Sable Antelope

Kudu

Gerenuk

Saiga Antelope

Nyala

Waterbuck

ones that arch backwards over its neck. The little dik-diks that are only about thirty centimetres high themselves, have short, straight horns that are only a few centimetres long. The impalas have horns which spread apart and have a twisted appearance.

Although most of the antelopes eat grass and other low-growing plants, one kind eats leaves which are quite high up on the trees. The gerenuk has long legs and a long, thin neck. To get at the high leaves, the gerenuk stands up on its hind legs and so can reach much higher than any of the other antelopes.

Deer

There are no antelopes in Europe, but instead there are deer. There are some that can be seen in parks, partly tame. These are usually fallow deer with spotted backs and antlers that are wide at the top like a spade. Antlers are different from horns. They are solid and a new set has to be grown each year. This is one of the ways in which deer are different from antelopes. Among the mountains of Scotland and in some of the European forests live herds of the much larger red deer. Once there were plenty of them, but they are good to eat, so many were killed. Because they are plant-eaters they would also damage crops, so now they live where they cannot do much harm.

The smaller roe deer do not roam around in herds, but only in twos and threes.

Marsh Deer

Reindeer

Axis Deer

Roe Deer

Fallow deer

Red Deer

Wapiti

Moose

To the people of the Arctic, the reindeer is more than just a wild animal. For hundreds of years the Lapps of the far north of Norway have lived with reindeer. From them they have been able to get meat to eat and skins for clothing and blankets. The long hair can be woven into cloth. Reindeer milk is very good to drink and the live animals can be used for pulling sledges and for riding. The animals live mainly on mosses, lichens and a little grass. The herds roam many miles for food and the Lapps follow them. There are also reindeer in North America, but they are larger and the Americans call them caribous.

The largest kind of deer is the moose. Some moose live in North America, although there is a type of moose that lives in Europe and Asia. They munch leaves and bark, and are very fond of water plants. In summer, they can be seen standing in quite deep ponds, going underwater now and again to get more plants from the bottom.

Cattle

Cows have been kept by farmers for a very long time and we depend on them for milk and those foods such as butter and cheese that are made from it. There are wild cattle in some parts of the world. High up in the mountains of Tibet live yaks. Although there are still small herds of wild yaks, many of them are kept like our cows for milk and meat. They are used for riding and carrying goods, too.

In North America live bison, although the Americans call them buffaloes. Once there were enormous herds of these animals and they were hunted only by the Indians. When the settlers came and built the railways, so many bison were shot that they almost died out. Now hunting them is no longer allowed. There are bison in Europe, too, but they are smaller than the American ones.

Antelopes, deer, and cattle, as well as goats, chew the cud. This means that when they eat, they first bite the grass and leaves and swallow them without chewing them properly. Later on, the animals can bring the food back to their mouths and chew it.

African Buffalo

Bantin

Gaur

Indian Water Buffalo

Yak

Musk Ox

Zebu

Gayal

American Bison

Giraffes

Giraffes have the longest necks of any mammals and so they are able to eat the leaves above the heads of any other animals. All giraffes live in Africa, in the grasslands where there are trees as well as grass. A giraffe can eat the leaves four to six metres up. It pulls thin branches into its mouth with a tongue that is forty-five centimetres long. Then by pulling its head away, all the leaves are ripped off. Being tall is useful for eating, but is not so good for drinking. If a giraffe puts its head down to drink, its mouth does not reach the water. To get lower, it has to stand with its front feet a long way apart and this brings its neck closer to the ground. Giraffes chew the cud in the same way as cattle do.

Left and below left
Male giraffes may grow as much as six metres tall but the females are shorter. Although their neck is so very long, it has the same number of vertebrae as most other mammals. Not only does their height help them when feeding, but also enables them to spot any dangerous animals from afar.

The pattern on their body makes giraffes difficult to see among the trees. If they are attacked, they defend themselves by kicking at their foe. They have short horns which are generally used when the males fight each other. Giraffes used to be hunted for sport, but now they are protected animals, living in national parks where tourists like to watch them.

Right and below Kangaroos belong to the group of mammals known as *marsupials*. The babies are carried around in the mother's pouch. Wallabies are similar to kangaroos but smaller. The Red and the Great Grey are the largest kangaroos and may weigh up to one hundred kilograms. The back legs of kangaroos are very strong. Their small front legs are used for holding food. Their long tail helps them to balance when they jump, and supports them when they rest.

Kangaroos

When Captain Cook sailed to far off places in 1770, he explored along the coast of Australia. He saw many strange animals and plants and some of the strangest mammals that he saw were kangaroos. They are plant-eating animals that live only in Australia. They move around in herds, jumping on their long hind legs. So strong are these back legs, that the animals can travel at speeds of up to forty-eight kilometres an hour. The sheep farmers do not like kangaroos because they eat the grass and low-growing plants that are needed for the sheep.

When young kangaroos are born, they are only about three centimetres long. At once they struggle into the pouch in the front of the mother's body. There they are able to feed on milk and be safe while they grow. Even when they are big enough to run about and feed on their own, they still run back to the pouch if there is any danger, or if they are tired.

Elephants

Largest of the plant-eating mammals are the African elephants. These are larger than the Indian ones which are trained to work in the forests of the East, moving the trees that have been cut down.

The African elephants move into the woodlands sometimes, and at other times come into the grasslands. Because they need a great deal of food, a herd of elephants travels long distances. They eat leaves, branches and the bark of trees, using their trunks to pull off what they want. They also push trees over, sometimes quite large ones. This may be to get at the branches, but quite often they seem to do it for fun.

An elephant's trunk is really a very long nose and it is extremely useful. Not only is it used for getting food, but for drinking and bathing as well. The elephant can suck water into its trunk and then blow it out again. If it points its trunk over its back, then the water is used for a shower, but if the elephant wants a drink, the trunk is put into its mouth before the water is blown out. The trunk is also used to sniff the air to see if there are other animals about. It also helps to make the elephants' strange trumpeting noises.

Below These African elephants will probably roll in the mud after bathing. Although their skin is so thick, it can become sore from insect bites and the heat of the sun. A coating of mud helps protect it.

Tusks are elongated front teeth. Elephants have four other teeth to chew their food. They are very large and when they wear out, others grow to take their place.

The tusks of an elephant are two of its teeth that grow extra long. The other teeth inside its mouth are large, but there are only a few of them and they are grinders for chewing up the leaves.

Although they are so large, elephants can move extremely quietly when they wish. This is because they walk on the tips of their toes and the space behind them is filled with a cushion of tough flesh. This means that when each foot comes down, no hard parts thud on the ground.

There are so many kinds of plant-eating mammals that the list seems to have no end. Camels are plant-eaters of the dry places. The rhinoceros and hippopotamus are two that every traveller to Africa hopes to see. Horses are plant-eaters that have been of use to man for centuries. And everyone knows of the giant panda from the bamboo forests of China.

Some mammals are so large that they have no enemies except man. Others become food for the meat-eating mammals.

Above Rhinoceroses are thick-skinned, heavy animals. They are plant-eaters. Their horns are formed from tough hairs matted together, and the horns are very hard and strong.

Below The hippopotamus spends its day in rivers, often with only its eyes, ears and nostrils showing above the surface. When darkness falls, it comes out onto the bank to feed.

HUNTERS

If you have a cat or dog as a pet, you will be able to see that it has four long, pointed teeth near the front of its mouth. These are its *fangs* and all mammals that hunt and kill for food have them. Farther back, the teeth are made for cutting so that the raw meat can be eaten more easily. A pet cat may still hunt for mice and birds, even though its owner feeds it at home.

The big cats must hunt all the time. Two of the cat family that are found in Africa are the cheetah and the lion.

Cheetahs have long legs and can run very fast. It is said that they can run at 113 kilometres an hour for short distances. That is as fast as motor cars are supposed to go on British roads, so this gives you a good idea of the cheetah's top speed. With a speed like that, it can run after

Below All these flesh-eating animals belong to the cat family. They all have the sleek, strong body of the hunting animal and their deadly fangs for killing. Many of the big cats are still hunted for their beautifully marked skins. Because of this, some of them are becoming rare.

Lynx

Puma

Tiger

Cheetah

Male Lion

Above The male lion is a fighter whose job is to defend the area where the pride lives and to protect the females and cubs. The lioness is a hunter, killing zebras and larger antelope for food. Sometimes lions eat meat from animals that others have killed and so become scavengers as well as hunters.

and catch any kind of antelope. It brings down the animal it is chasing and grabs it by the throat. The other name for the cheetah is the hunting leopard. They used to be found in India as well as Africa and in that country they were tamed and used when hunting for sport.

Lions are much larger than cheetahs. They live in small groups called *prides*. The male lions have manes of long hair on their head, neck and chest; the females do not. When they hunt, it is the females that catch the prey which is usually an antelope. When the antelope is dead, the males of the pride eat first and then the females and cubs. Lions do not hunt very often, and spend much of their time sleeping. They live in the grasslands and although most of them are in Africa, there are still a few in India.

Jaguar

Leopard

Serval

Tigers are cats, too, but they all live in India and a few other parts of Asia. Those that live in the cold countries have a thick coat. In hotter countries they go into the water as much as they can to keep cool. Tigers have a pattern of black stripes on their orange coloured fur. Like most cats they hunt alone and although they kill large animals, they will also eat mice, fish and almost anything they can catch.

Other hunting mammals are more like dogs. Foxes are very common and in some places are beginning to live much nearer towns now than they did years ago. They dig a burrow in which to live, but they may sometimes take over old rabbit or badger burrows. The fox of Europe is a reddish-brown colour all the year round. The Arctic fox is brown in summer but turns white when the winter comes. In this way, it blends in with the colour of the snow when it is hunting.

Wolves are very much like dogs in their shape. Some people think that

Above Wolves are hunting animals that look very much like Alsatian dogs but they howl rather than bark. They are usually a brownish-grey colour but there are black ones and, in the far north, some may be almost white.

Left Foxes are very dog-like in shape. There are several different species and they are found in many countries. The silver fox is bred for its skin on fur farms in America and Scandinavia.

our pet dogs are descended from wolves and this may be true. Wolves used to be found in many countries, but now they live mostly in the forests of the northern countries. They may live in small family groups or in large packs. The animals they feed on, such as lemmings and deer, roam about, so wolves also have to travel long distances after them.

Not all the flesh-eating mammals are like cats and dogs. There is a group of them with long bodies and short legs that are great hunters. Stoats and weasels are in this group, and so are mink which are sometimes kept on farms for their fur. A stoat has reddish fur but its tail is black at the tip. Stoats that live in cold countries get a white coat in the winter and then they are called ermine. The black hairs on the tail do not change. Ermine fur is used for decoration on some ceremonial robes. The tails show up as black patches in the rest of the white fur.

Weasel

Pine Marten

Otter

American Badger

Mink

Ermine

Skunk

Wolverine

SCAVENGERS

Although most of the flesh-eating mammals hunt and kill for food, there are some that do not do so much of this. These animals feed on the meat that is left on the bones of a dead one, after a lion or tiger has had its fill. Animals that get their food like this are called scavengers. The best known are jackals and hyaenas. Hyaenas move around in groups, sometimes hunting, but more often looking for the remains of some dead animal. They are about the size of large dogs. Their neck and jaws are very strong and they have a short mane along their back that slopes down from their high shoulders.

There are several kinds of hyaena but they all have very large, strong teeth. Because of these teeth, they are able to crack bones which most other animals cannot do. When they prowl at night, hyaenas make rumbling noises, but when they find food then their cry sounds more like a person laughing.

Jackals are much smaller animals that look much more like dogs. They live in Africa, India and many hot countries. They scavenge but they may hunt in packs as well. During the heat of the day they sleep in holes, or lie in any water they can find. Night is the time when they come out to feed.

Above Hyaenas are strong animals. Although they are scavengers, they have been known to hunt as well. During the day, they rest in burrows or among rocks.

Below All these different animals belong to the group of mammals called the insect-eaters. While some of them eat an exclusive diet of insects, others eat other things as well.

INSECT-EATERS

The giant ant-eater lives in the forests and grasslands of South America. It is a fairly large animal, over two metres long, covered with shaggy grey hair. There is a dark stripe with white edges that runs from its throat to its shoulder. The tail is about a metre long and has long hair on it, so that it looks rather like a flag hanging out behind. On its front feet are two long claws. They are so long that the animal turns them inwards and walks on its knuckles. Perhaps the oddest-looking part of the ant-eater is its head. This is very long and thin, with a tiny mouth at the end. Ant-eaters can only eat small insects, usually ants or termites. They can break open the nests with their big claws, and then pick up the ants with their long, sticky tongue.

Above Armadillos are insect-eaters of South America. They are protected by hard, bony armour over their body. Certain kinds roll into a ball when they sense danger.

Left The giant ant-eater of South America must be one of the strangest looking mammals in the world. It is well adapted for getting its food of ants or termites from their nests.

Below The hedgehog is protected by sharp spines over its back. They can lie fairly flat but when the hedgehog is alarmed it can raise them. It can also roll itself into a ball.

Because their food is so small, it needs no chewing so ant-eaters have no teeth. When they sleep, they curl up and cover themselves with their bushy tail.

There are many animals that are insect-eaters. Except for the ant-eater, most of them are small. In fact, among the insect-eaters are the smallest mammals in the world. These are the pygmy shrews. Small mammals like the shrews need to eat almost all the time and soon die if they cannot get food. Hedgehogs are insect-eaters, too, but they will eat other things as well and they are even very fond of bread and milk. A saucerful of this put out in the garden each night, is a good way to tempt these likeable animals closer to your house.

MAMMALS IN TREES

Many mammals stay on the ground. Some, like the bats, are able to fly. But there are some mammals that live between the ground and the sky. These are the ones that have made the trees their living place. In most tropical countries, monkeys are a common sight. These and many of the apes and mammals related to them, live in trees and are able to move so quickly through them that they are fascinating to watch. There are many kinds, from small marmosets to large gorillas and orang-utans. The larger ones climb so that they can feed on leaves and fruit, but it is the smaller ones that are so expert at swinging from branch to branch. Gibbons are very good at this. They have long hands and arms and

Black-tailed Marmoset

Orang-utan

Lar Gibbon

Spider Monkey

Tree Kangaroo

Capuchin Monkey

they can swing and leap high up in the trees without falling. The monkeys of the American forests are able to use their tails as an extra hand. The spider monkeys can curl them round the branches and even hang by them. This is something that African and Asian monkeys cannot do.

Monkeys are able to move swiftly through trees because they have feet and hands that can grasp branches. Also because they can judge exactly how far away a branch is. They can judge distance because, like us, their eyes are in the front of their head. The apes are some of the most intelligent of the mammals. Chimpanzees certainly seem to be, and are always popular in zoos, because they are able to play rather as children do.

Gorilla

Bonnet Monkey

Chimpanzee

Proboscis Monkey

Douroucouli

223

Ruffed Lemur

Sifaka

Ring-tailed Lemur

Indris

Aye-Aye

Fat-tailed Dwarf Lemur

Lemurs and squirrels

Near the coast of south-east Africa is the island of Madagascar. There it is possible to find a group of mammals that live nowhere else in the world. These are the lemurs. Not all of them are tree-living, but most of them are because they are leaf or insect-eaters. Instead of claws at the end of their toes, they have nails rather like yours and mine.

In Europe, the tree-living mammals are the squirrels. There are two kinds, the red squirrel that likes to live in pine woods, and the grey. The grey type is found in Britain, often in parks. Grey ones were brought from America, which is their real home and released in Britain. Now they are more common than the red. The squirrels that we see have bushy tails and large eyes. They not only jump from tree to tree, but run up and down them with tremendous skill. When they come down, it is nearly always head first. They collect nuts and seeds on the

Above Lemurs are very interesting mammals. They belong to the group of animals scientists call *primates*. Monkeys and apes are primates, so are humans. Lemurs have large eyes and soft fur, and most of them live in trees. Ring-tailed lemurs are sometimes kept as pets in Madagascar in the same way that people in Europe keep cats in their homes.

South American Squirrel

Red Squirrel

American Ground Squirrel

Grey Squirrel

African Ground Squirrel

Grey Gentle Lemur

Mongoose Lemur

Fork-marked Lemur

Mouse Lemur

Greater Dwarf Lemur

ground to eat. They hold them between their front feet to nibble at them and often like to sit on a tree stump and use it as a 'dining-table'. It is common to find these in woods where there are squirrels. The young squirrels are born in nests, called *dreys*, which the parents make with twigs high among the branches.

Some mammals are known as flying squirrels. Most of them live in Asia but some types are found in Europe and North America. They have bodies very much like squirrels but they have flaps of skin between their front and back legs. They cannot really fly, but are able to make enormous leaps from tree to tree. As they jump from a branch they hold their four legs sideways so that the flaps of skin are stretched out to make a parachute. Their tail is held out straight behind them. Just as they are about to hit the tree trunk they are aiming for, they swoop upwards and land so that their feet can grasp the bark.

Below Squirrels are found in most countries. In Europe, it is the red squirrel that is seen most but in Britain the grey squirrel has been introduced from America.

Flying squirrels do not really fly but glide from one tree to another. Ground squirrels may dig large numbers of burrows and make a 'town'.

Giant Malabar Squirrel

American Flying Squirrel

Prevost's Squirrel

Chinese Flying Squirrel

European Flying Squirrel

225

Koalas and sloths

Australia is the home of several unusual animals and one of these is the koala. These mammals are like tubby, grey teddy-bears. They are mammals of the trees, eating the leaves of the eucalyptus, or gum trees, and no others. They have pouches for the young as kangaroos have, but the baby koala stays there only a short while. Then it is carried on its mother's back, clinging to her fur. When the young one is naughty, the mother koala is said to put it over her knee and spank it! Huge numbers of koalas were once killed for their fur, but that is no longer allowed.

Above The only country in the world where koalas live is Australia. Once hunted for their fur, they are now protected in national parks where they can be seen climbing among the branches of gum trees.

Another strange mammal of the trees, but this time of the South American forests, is the sloth. Sloths have long, shaggy hair which may have green algae growing on it. This makes the whole animal a greenish colour so that these sloths are very difficult to see among the branches. Quite often, moths hide in the long hair, too. The sloths hang upside down, holding on to the branches with their claws which are long and hook over them easily. So well made for moving in this way are the sloths' legs, that they are almost helpless on the ground. They can swim quite well, which is rather surprising.

Above and left The sloths of South American forests live in an upside-down world, for almost the whole of their life is spent hanging from branches. All their movements are slow, whether they are travelling, eating or fighting. Two sloths will fight if they find themselves on the same branch until one is killed or driven away.

HOW MAMMALS CAN PROTECT THEMSELVES

When there is danger about, many mammals stay very still. This is known as *freezing* and in some mammals it is a very good means of defence. Young deer are left on their own by their mothers for the first few days after they are born. They have a spotted coat and this looks like the patches of light and shade beneath the undergrowth where the fawns lie. At the slightest sound they 'freeze' and are very difficult to see. The Virginia opossum plays dead if it is in danger. It lies on its side with its body limp. Its tongue may hang out and its eyes are closed. If it is touched, it makes no movement at all. In fact, it looks so dead that any hunting animal will probably leave it completely alone. But when the danger is passed, the opossum becomes very much 'alive' again and runs off.

Above This American opossum is acting dead because danger is nearby. It is rather like a rat in shape and about the size of a cat.

Below The markings on a fawn's coat are like the pattern of sunlight and shadow on the ground. This helps the young animal to blend in with its surroundings.

Although many mammals may 'freeze' at the first hint of danger, if the danger comes too close then they may well run. For many mammals, fast running is the best way they can protect themselves. Deer and antelope show this well and their long, slim legs and light bodies make them able to run very fast. The rabbits and hares can also run quickly because they have such strong back legs to push them along. When you want to run fast, you run on your toes, not with your feet flat. Many of the fast running mammals also do this. Antelopes and deer walk and run on only two toes on each foot. These are the longer ones, so they are really running on tip-toe. Horses do even better than that. Their hooves are the tip of the longest toe on each foot and their other toes have almost completely disappeared.

Camouflage

Almost all animals are camouflaged by having the same colour as the places where they live. The polar bear that lives among the snow and ice of the far north has white fur. The kangaroo rats of the hot, sandy deserts, have sandy-coloured fur. The light coloured lion blends in with the pale, dried-up grass of Africa. In Britain, the hares that spend much of their time lying in the furrows of ploughed fields have a grey-brown colour that matches the soil. In the jungles of Burma and Malaysia, the

228

Above Running fast is a way to escape from enemies. For deer and antelope it is often the only way. They can move very quickly, sometimes making huge leaps as they go.

Left Tapirs are leaf and fruit-eaters and are about the size of small cows. The colour pattern of the Malay tapir makes it difficult to be seen in the forest. The young tapir has rows of white spots along its body which disappear as it gets older.

tapirs roam. They have a colour-pattern which seems of very little use. They are black on the front of their body and back legs, while the rest of them is white. We can see them very easily in a zoo, but in their proper home they feed at night when the moon is very bright and patches of moonlight and patches of dark shadow are everywhere. This is how the tapirs are protected. They, too, look just like patches of moonlight and shadow.

The pattern of sunlight and shadow is copied by a number of animals. You have already read about the young deer that has the coat with light spots over it to match the pattern in the undergrowth where it stays. The spotted coat of the leopard and the striped one of the tiger also help them to blend in with their surroundings.

You know, too, that some animals of cold countries change the colour of their coat in winter so that the new white one will match the snow. The Arctic fox does this and so do Arctic hares. Some of the lemmings and stoats change as well.

There is another way in which colour may protect the animal and that is by it having a coat with a *dazzle pattern* on it. You can tell if something is coming down the road whether it is a car or a horse, and you can do this because you look at the outline. If it were somehow possible to make the outline less easy to see, it would be much more difficult to tell what the object was. This is done in war-time by putting nets over big guns so that their outline is not clear to aeroplanes flying overhead. Warships are painted with zig-zag patterns so that an enemy sailor looking at one from some distance away, cannot see the outline properly. He can see

Left Tigers live in India and much of Asia. Because they have been hunted for so long, they are now rare. Tigers are the strongest of the big cats and their pattern of stripes helps them to hide when they are hunting.

Right Animals of the far north, such as this Arctic fox, change the colour of their coat to white in the winter. In this way they are not easily seen against the snow when they are hunting, or perhaps being hunted themselves.

Below Zebra drinking at dusk. The dazzle pattern of their markings makes them difficult to see in a poor light.

that it is a ship, perhaps, but he cannot see how large it is, or how many guns it has. This 'dazzle pattern' has been copied from nature. A zebra's black and white stripes will not make it blend in with its surroundings very much during the day. A hunting animal will not have very much trouble seeing them. But not much hunting is done in the heat of the day, and anyway zebras can protect themselves by running fast if they see the attacker coming. In the poor light of the early morning or late evening, they cannot be seen so well. It is at these times that their dazzle pattern works so well. Their outline is broken up and against the background of tall grass and trees, they are pretty well invisible.

Looking at pictures of animals, or those in a zoo or museum, have you ever noticed how many of them are a lighter colour underneath than they are on top? This is yet another way in which colour helps to protect. If the sun shines down on a car, it makes the top of it the brightest part, but underneath it is darker and in shadow. This makes the car look solid to our eyes. It would do the same for an animal's body. So by having a dark-coloured back and light colour beneath, the animal can alter this and look flat instead of solid. This makes it more difficult for a hunting animal to see it.

Below During the summer, the stoat has a reddish-brown fur on its back and is light underneath.

Below In the winter the stoat's fur changes to an all-white coat, with a black tip to the tail. It is now called ermine.

Teeth and claws

If an animal cannot escape by running then it will turn and fight with whatever weapons it has. Some animals will use their teeth and their claws. The meat-eaters are well equipped for this.

All the cat family, from the small pets to the largest lions, leopards and tigers have claws with sharp ends. Cats keep them sharp by rubbing them on trees. If you have a pet cat and you tease it, you will find that in order to use its claws to cause most damage, it will hold your arm with its front feet and rip with its back ones. If cats are only squabbling with one another, they may just hit out with a front paw and then the claws will not do so much damage. This often happens when lions are eating. The young cubs often get hit like this by the adults. The

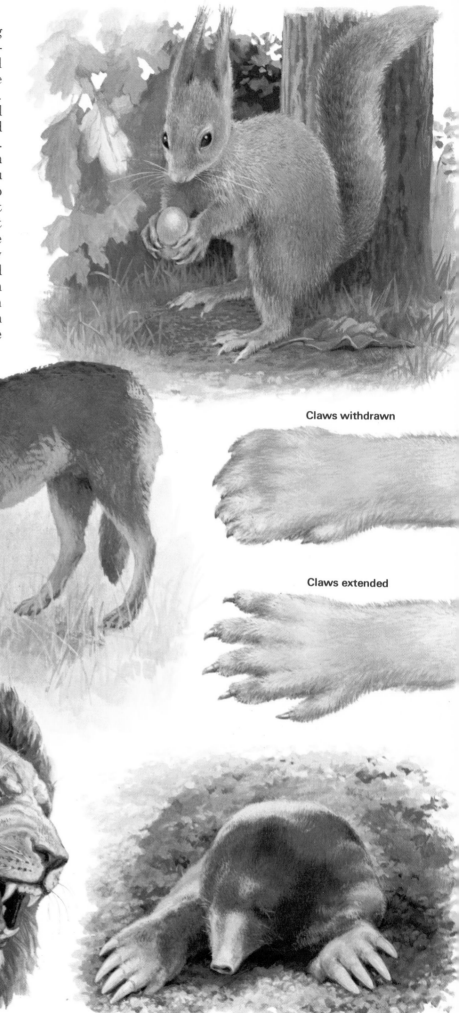

Claws withdrawn

Claws extended

flesh-eaters also have good teeth for fighting. Those four long fangs that kill prey, can wound also.

But not only meat-eaters can use their feet and teeth. Many animals, such as horses and giraffes, can kick and bite too. Kangaroos rear up with their front legs off the ground. They balance themselves on their long hind feet and their tail. They can then lash out with their back feet, sometimes even both at the same time by leaning on their tail. The long claws on the feet are sharp enough to rip open an attacking animal.

Even the gnawing animals can use their teeth for protection. They may not kick, but a bite from a rat can be very painful indeed.

Gazelle
Africa

Watusi Cow
Africa

Pronghorn
N. America

Reindeer
*N. America,
Norway*

Chamoix
Pyrenees, Al

Fallow Deer
U.K.

Moose (Elk)
N. America, Norway

Wild Goat
W. Asia, Crete

Musk Ox
Greenland, Alaska, Canada

Gemsbok (Oryx)
S.W. Africa

Anoa
Celebes

Horns and antlers

Other animals have horns and antlers that can be used as weapons. The difference between horns and antlers is that horns are hollow. They fit over bony parts which grow from the animal's skull. Antlers, on the other hand, are solid. They grow from the animal's head and last a year. When they fall off, the animal may eat them and a new set begins to grow for the next year. Antelopes and cattle have horns; deer have antlers. Much of the time, both horns and antlers are used for showing off. It is usually the males that have them and they fight each other when they are looking for mates in the breeding season. They do not often hurt each other with them. It is more like a wrestling match and when one feels it is being beaten, it breaks away and runs off. Stags, which are male red deer, have been known to die because their antlers became so locked together that the animals could not pull them apart. Then the stags have died because they could not eat.

Musk oxen that live in Greenland and Canada, defend themselves with their horns. Their chief enemies are wolves and when there is danger, the male oxen of the herd make a ring, their heads and horns facing outwards. The females and young are protected inside the circle. Any wolf that attacks can be flung away by the antlers.

Gnu
Africa

Big Horn Sheep
USA

Markhor
Afghanistan

Red Deer
Europe

American Bison

Impala
Africa

235

Spines

A few mammals protect themselves by having sharp spines over part of their body. Hedgehogs have many short ones. They cover the top of the head, the back and down the sides, but there are none underneath. If they are in any danger, they are able to roll themselves into a ball so that it is hard for any attacking animal to be able to get at them.

Porcupines have longer spines and use them in a different way. When the Indian crested porcupine is defending itself, it makes its quills stand up.

Right The porcupine will rattle its long quills if it is alarmed. If this is not enough warning, any attacking animal is likely to be badly hurt when it comes up against its rigid quills.

Above and right Hedgehogs and some armadillos roll into a ball when attacked. They are then very well protected.

Then it grunts and rattles its quills as a warning. If the attacker does not go away, the porcupine runs backwards towards it. The spines stab the animal and may sometimes even kill it.

Armadillos that live in South America are covered by a hard armour. One kind is able to roll itself up so that every part of it is protected. The small fairy armadillo, which is about the size of a large mouse, has armour over its back and rear. It is able to make a burrow quickly, and the hard shield at the rear blocks up the entrance.

236

Scent

There is a group of mammals that can protect themselves by producing a very unpleasant scent. They have glands near their tail from which the animals can squirt an evil-smelling liquid. The polecat uses this way of defending itself, and so do its relatives the mink and the badger, although they will use teeth as well. The mammal that makes the greatest use of scent is the skunk. Skunks have a very clear pattern of black and white stripes or spots on their body. This is a warning pattern to let other animals know that they can protect them-selves well. However, if they are attacked, they first make certain warning movements. Each type of skunk has its own special warning movement. Some stamp on the ground with their feet. The striped skunk lowers its head and pushes its tail into the air. The spotted skunk has the strangest movement of all. It walks on its front feet for several seconds with its back legs up in the air. If the attacker is still not put off, the skunks shoot out their liquid from the stink glands. They can shoot as far as three metres and the smell is so bad that the attacking animal will run off.

Above The striped skunk of America is well-known for being able to defend itself by squirting a horrible-smelling liquid at any attacker. It is only a small animal but even much larger ones have learnt to be careful of skunks and leave them alone.

Right Polecats are also able to produce an unpleasant smell, but it is not as bad as that of the skunk. In some countries, domesticated polecats, called ferrets, are kept by some people who use them to catch rabbits.

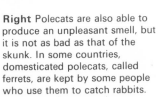

Left Fairy armadillos look rather strange, but their shape is their best protection. When danger threatens, they dig an escape burrow, and use their rear armour to block the entrance.

Common Iguana
S. America

Milk Snake
USA and Canada

Plica Lizard
S. America

Spotted Turtle
USA

Reptiles

What is a reptile?

Many, many millions of years ago, amphibians were the most important animals on the earth. But they could only live where it was damp and where there was water in which to lay their eggs. When the earth became a much drier place, there were not many places where the amphibians could live. They began to be less important and instead, there evolved animals that could live where it was drier. These animals were the reptiles. They had dry, scaly skins and although they still had to lay eggs, they did not have to lay them in the water. This was because the

eggs had a tough shell so that they would not dry up. The baby reptile inside the egg had its own food and water supply, too, so that it could live and grow inside until it was large enough to hatch out. When that happened, the baby reptile could begin to look after itself. This is still true of modern reptiles. They have dry, scaly skins and they lay eggs. At least, most of them do. They are cold-blooded animals which really means that their body is as hot or warm as the air around them. They cannot keep themselves warm all the time as mammals and birds can. If they lie in the sun

Tokay Gecko
S.E. Asia

Giant Cuban Anole

Crocodile
Africa, Asia and America

Common European Viper

Giant Skink
Australia

Lace Monitor
Australia

they get warm and active, but if they keep in the shade for too long, or on a cold day, they get cold and sluggish. In some of the cooler countries, reptiles may sleep right through some of the coldest winter months.

At first sight, a grass snake, a crocodile and a pet tortoise do not seem to be very much alike. They are, though, because they are all reptiles. Each one of them is cold-blooded, has a dry, scaly skin and lays eggs. They look different because they live in different places and in different ways. A grass snake belongs to the snakes and lizards group of reptiles. Snakes are very similar to lizards but they just do not have any legs. They are fast movers and can catch other living creatures for food. Crocodiles and alligators are adapted for living in rivers. They are flesh-eaters and lie in wait to catch animals coming to drink or else catch fish and frogs when they are swimming. Tortoises are plant-eaters. They do not need to move very fast for this and so they have grown a heavy shell for protection. Turtles, which are close relatives of tortoises, live in the sea. In the water, they are able to move very much faster.

Some small reptiles

There are a few countries that have almost no reptiles in them at all, but most countries have some, even though they may not be very big ones. In the cooler countries of Europe, the reptiles most likely to be found are a few snakes and lizards. The smooth snake is found in certain places, especially dry sandy heaths where it eats the lizards that live there. More common are the grass snake and the adder. Although there are plenty of these reptiles, they are very shy creatures and they usually disappear if anyone gets too close to them. The grass snake is a dark green or a greyish-brown colour, with some black marks on its sides. The best way of recognising it is by the yellow or orange patch on its neck. Grass snakes are very good swimmers and can catch frogs and small fish. They do not chew their food, for snakes have no chewing teeth. Whatever a snake catches is swallowed whole. Because their jaws work in a different way from a mammal's, they are able to open their mouth very wide. In this way they can swallow animals which would seem to be too large for them.

If a grass snake is caught, it may hiss but it is not likely to bite. Although they have teeth, they do not seem to use them to defend themselves. They lay eggs, sometimes as many as forty, in heaps of leaves. The young snakes when they hatch are about twenty centimetres long so they have plenty of growing to do to reach the metre or more that adult grass snakes can reach.

Above A grass snake eating a frog. Grass snakes are commonly found near water and can sometimes be seen in ponds and rivers, for they are excellent swimmers.

Above and right Rattlesnakes produce living young. Spring is usually the mating season and sometimes two males will go through a combat dance, rearing up and pushing each other to decide which one will mate with a female.

240

Above Snakes cannot chew their food so they swallow their prey whole. They can do this because they are able to open their mouth very wide indeed. The two sides of the lower jaw can be pushed apart, too.

Below Young Indian cobras hatching from their eggs are already able to spread their hoods and strike just as well as the adult cobra. Cobras are very venomous snakes and many people die from their bite every year.

Above This snake laying its eggs is a bull snake from North America. Although many species of snakes lay eggs, there are some that give birth to living, active young instead by keeping the eggs inside their body until they hatch.

Above The scarlet snake is found in the south-east of the United States. This one shows the typical forked tongue of the snake. Unlike the shell of a bird's egg, that of a snake is softer and more leathery.

Adders, or vipers as they are sometimes called, are poisonous snakes. They are shorter than grass snakes and are a grey or brown colour. They have a darker zig-zag pattern down the back so that it is fairly easy to tell them apart from grass snakes. They feed on small mammals and lizards which they kill with poison when they bite. Adders do not lay eggs. Their young are born in the late summer and are very active right away.

A lizard that looks like a snake because it has no legs is the slow worm. This is a bad name for it. It is not a worm and it is certainly not slow. Its jaws are different from those of a snake. Snakes' jaws can open so wide that they can swallow animals several times larger than their own head, but lizards cannot. Slow worms, like other lizards, can only eat much smaller animals such as slugs.

Left Slow worms are sometimes called blind worms, but they are neither slow, blind, nor worms. They are lizards without legs that can be found along the edges of woods, at the bottom of hedges, and in churchyards, too.

Right Worm lizards live in Florida. They live underground and feed on worms and insects. Their eyes are hidden under their skin and they look so much like worms that many people would not recognise them as reptiles.

Right The two-legged worm lizard, or ajolote, has no back legs and only small front ones. It is a strange looking reptile that is found in Mexico and California. Worm lizards stay underground for most of their life.

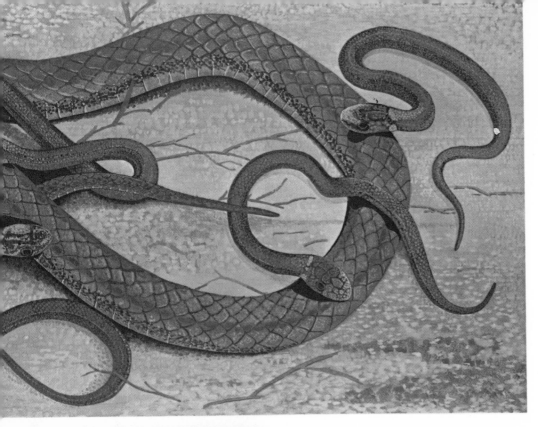

In sandy places, it is sometimes possible to see the sand lizard. The female is brown with black spots on it, but the male is a lovely green colour, especially in the late spring.

Common lizards are often seen sunning themselves. They are normally a brownish colour and are often difficult to spot when they keep very still. They have long tails and any enemy of the lizards that grabbed one by the tail would be in for a shock. A lizard can let part of its tail break off and when this happens, the lizard can escape quickly while the attacker is startled by holding a wriggling tail with no lizard on the end!

Snakes of warmer countries

Among the snakes that are not venomous (a better word to use than poisonous when talking about snakes), are the boas and pythons. Some of them are three metres long and they kill their prey by squeezing. When a python catches food, it bites the small mammal or bird that it is after. At the same time, the snake coils its body around it and squeezes so that the creature cannot breathe. When it is dead, the snake uncoils itself and swallows its prey. The pythons and boas have lovely patterns on their skin and they also have the remains of back legs. A pair of claws show on the outside of the body, right back near where the tail starts. Inside the snake, beneath the skin, are some small bones that are all that are left of the back legs the snakes' ancestors had.

Snakes eat all manner of living animals, but a few have turned to egg-eating for their food. A good many snakes will eat an egg if they find one,

Below and below right
Venom is injected down a channel in the fang of a venomous snake. When the snake's mouth is open, the fangs point forward and the glands are ready to send the venom down to them. When the mouth is closed, the fangs fold back.

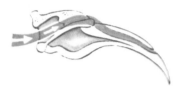

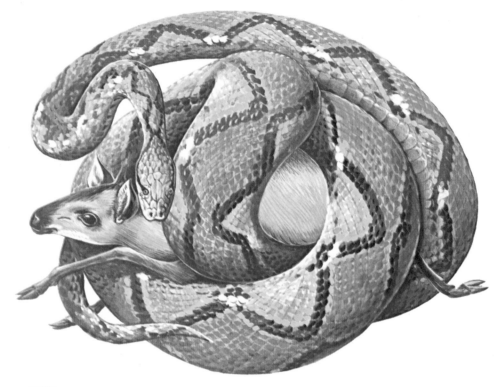

Left Snakes that kill by squeezing are called *constrictors*. Pythons, boa constrictors and anacondas belong to this group. They are all very strong and many, but not all, are very long. When the prey is dead, the snake must swallow it whole. In this picture, a python is killing a duiker.

Green Tree Python

Copperhead

King Cobra

244

Right An egg-eating snake works its jaws over and round an egg larger than its own head. Once in its mouth, a hole is made in the shell. The snake can then swallow the contents of the egg and get rid of the shell.

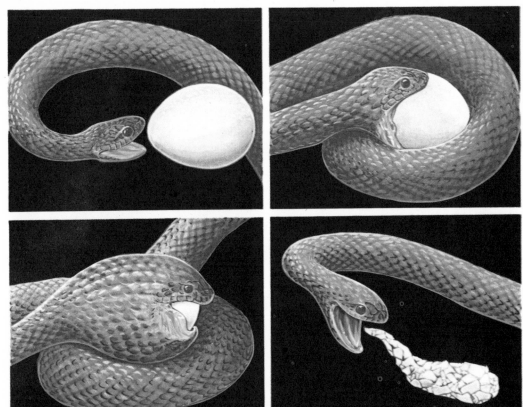

Below Here are seven different snakes from all over the world. Although they are similar in shape, their colours vary enormously. Usually the colour pattern helps the snake to blend in with its surroundings.

but there is a group of African snakes that eat very little else. They have mouths and necks which stretch well so that they can swallow quite large eggs. At the back of the throat is a set of bony points that act like a saw and cut a hole in the egg shell. The inside of the egg is pushed out into the snake's stomach and they get rid of the empty shell.

The snakes that have a venomous bite, have two long teeth in their top jaw called the fangs. These are hollow in some snakes, but others have a groove down the side of them. Above the teeth, under the skin, are the *venom glands*. These are special parts that make the venom and store it until it is needed. When the snake strikes at its prey, it stabs with its fangs and the venom runs from the glands, down the fangs and into the body of the animal it has caught. The venom works quickly and the victim cannot move far before dying. The snake quickly finds it and eats it.

Adder

Black Mamba

Coral Snake

Bushmaster

Books about India usually show pictures of the snake charmers. These men carry snakes in a basket and when the lid is taken off, they rear up. The snake charmer plays a tune on a flute and sways from side to side as he plays. The snakes follow his movement and sway also. The snakes that are used are often cobras which are able to spread out the skin of their neck to make the *hood*. On the back of the hood are dark markings shaped like a pair of spectacles. The cobra is a very venomous snake and many people die each year in India from cobra bites.

Some kinds of African cobras can spit their venom quite a long way. They shoot it at the eyes and face of the animal they are attacking. When these snakes are kept in zoos, they may spit at the people looking at them. The venom hits the glass front of the cage and does not hurt the visitors.

Some of the venomous snakes have beautiful patterns on their skin. The Gaboon viper and the rhinoceros viper have very vivid ones. They help to break up the outline and make the snakes very difficult to see among the dead leaves and plants on the forest floor.

America has some deadly snakes. The rattlesnakes are some of the most venomous. They get their name because at the end of the tail are some extra-large, thick scales, which have a special shape so that when the snake moves its tail, the scales make a rattling, almost a buzzing, noise. The snake uses its rattle as a warning so that people and animals will leave it alone.

Above The cobra belonging to this snake charmer has spread its hood and the spectacle-like markings on the back of it can be clearly seen. Snake charmers give their shows in the streets and market-places.

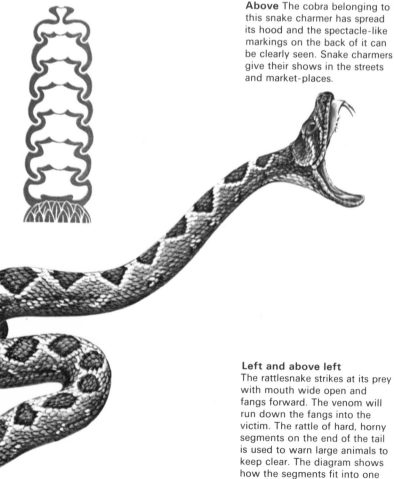

Left and above left
The rattlesnake strikes at its prey with mouth wide open and fangs forward. The venom will run down the fangs into the victim. The rattle of hard, horny segments on the end of the tail is used to warn large animals to keep clear. The diagram shows how the segments fit into one another.

Long-nosed Tree Snake
Malaya

Cooke's Tree Boa
S. America

African Rock Python

Gaboon Viper
S. Africa

Black-necked Spitting Cobra
Africa

Corn Snake
USA

Lizards

There are only two kinds of venomous lizards, the Gila monster and the beaded lizard that is related to it. Both kinds live in dry places and are only found in parts of America, mainly in Mexico. Although they have a venomous bite, they do not have fangs like the snakes. Instead, they must bite and hang on because the venom comes from the glands in a different way and goes to a number of teeth, not just two.

The largest kind of lizard is the Komodo dragon. It certainly is a large reptile, with a heavy body and strong claws and a long tail, but it cannot breathe fire like the dragons of the story books! Komodo dragons may grow to be three metres long and they live only on a few small islands in the East Indies. Most of them are on the island of Komodo which is only thirty-two kilometres long.

Thailand Water Lizard

Frilled Lizard
Australia

Flap-necked Chameleon
Africa

Bosc's Monitor
Australia

Collared Lizard
USA

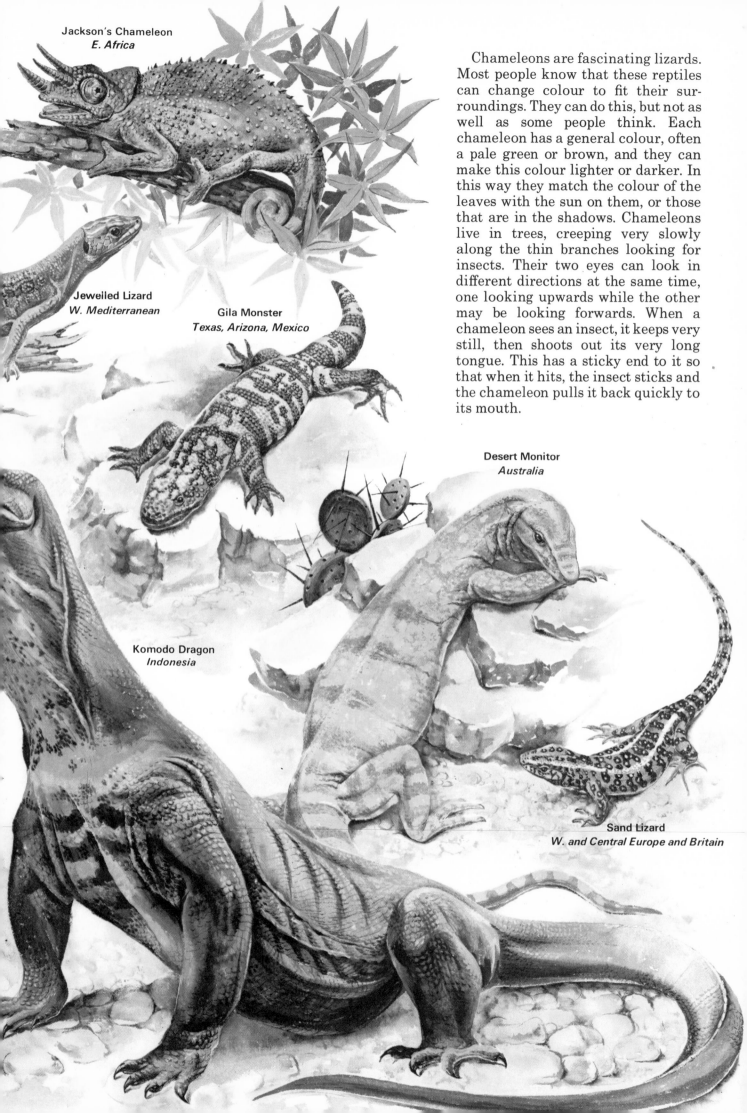

Jackson's Chameleon
E. Africa

Jewelled Lizard
W. Mediterranean

Gila Monster
Texas, Arizona, Mexico

Komodo Dragon
Indonesia

Desert Monitor
Australia

Sand Lizard
W. and Central Europe and Britain

Chameleons are fascinating lizards. Most people know that these reptiles can change colour to fit their surroundings. They can do this, but not as well as some people think. Each chameleon has a general colour, often a pale green or brown, and they can make this colour lighter or darker. In this way they match the colour of the leaves with the sun on them, or those that are in the shadows. Chameleons live in trees, creeping very slowly along the thin branches looking for insects. Their two eyes can look in different directions at the same time, one looking upwards while the other may be looking forwards. When a chameleon sees an insect, it keeps very still, then shoots out its very long tongue. This has a sticky end to it so that when it hits, the insect sticks and the chameleon pulls it back quickly to its mouth.

Giant tortoises

Have you heard of the Galapagos Islands? They are small islands near South America that are very hot, but naturalists are interested in them because of their animal life. Giant tortoises still lumber about. There are not as many now as there used to be because they were often caught for food by sailors in the days of the sailing ships. The tortoises could be taken on board the ships and kept alive during long trips until fresh meat was needed. Then they could be killed and eaten. However, they did not kill them all and those that were left, laid eggs so that a few still survive.

European Tortoise

Diamond Back Turtle
USA

Loggerhead Turtle
Warm Seas

Soft-shelled Turtle
Asia, Africa, America

Giant Tortoise
Galapagos Islands

250

Star Tortoise
India and Ceylon

Eastern Box Turtle
Carolina USA

Serrated Terrapin
N. America

Painted Terrapin
N. America

Red-eared Terrapin
N. America

Hawksbill Turtle
Warm Seas

Green Turtle
Australia

Index

Figures in bold type refer to illustrations